TEXT BOOK OF PATHOPHYSIOLC

[According to latest syllabus of B. Pharm - II Semester of Pharmacy Council of India]

Dr. Praveen Kumar

Associate Professor,

Department of Pharmaceutical Chemistry,

Faculty of Pharmacy,

Uttar Pradesh University of Medical Sciences,

Saifai, Etawah

Mr. Gyanendra Kumar Saxena

Associate Professor

Maharana Pratap College of Pharmacy,

Kanpur (U. P.)

Dr. Nandhakumar Jothivel

Principal & Professor

Indira Gandhi Institute of Pharmaceutical

Sciences, Ernakulam (Kerala)

Kuldip Kumar Savita

Associate Professor

Smt. Vidyawati College of

Pharmacy

Gora Machhiya Kanpur Road Jhansi

(U.P.)

Dr. Vikash Gupta

Professor & Principal

KNP College of Pharmacy,

Bhopal (M. P.)

NOTION PRESS

1

TEXT BOOK OF PATHOPHYSIOLOGY

NOTION PRESS

PREFACE

The authors feel great pleasure in presenting the first edition of the book **"Text Book of Pathophysiology"** for graduate and post graduate students. The present book on **Text Book of Pathophysiology** has been written according to the latest syllabus of B. Pharm – II Semester of Pharmacy Council of India and covers full course of the subject.

THE SALIENT FEATURES OF THE BOOK ARE: -

- *Easy to understand style of writing* which makes the book a self-study material.
- *Each new concept has been introduced through day-today problem of interest* to the students which makes the subject matter interesting.
- *The language of the book, on the whole, is lucid and easy to understand.*
- Wherever needed *neatly labeled figures have been drawn?*

The authors hope that the students, teachers and other readers will find the book interesting and to the point covering the course. We hope that the students will receive the book warmly.

I express a sincere thank you to the Management of Department of Pharmaceutical Chemistry, Uttar Pradesh University of Medical Sciences, Faculty of Pharmacy, Maharana Pratap College of Pharmacy, Indira Gandhi Institute of Pharmaceutical Sciences, Indira Gandhi Institute of Pharmaceutical Sciences, SRM Modinagar College of pharmacy and KNP College of Pharmacy, for their support during the writing of this book.

Every effort is made to keep the book error free. The author will gratefully acknowledge the suggestions to improve the book to make it more useful.

Wishing our readers success in examination and life ahead. The authors feel that their efforts will be fully rewarded if the book serves the purpose for which it is written.

TEXT BOOK OF PATHOPHYSIOLOGY
CONTENTS

Introduction, Pathophysiology, Epidemiology, Symptoms and Complication, Diagnosis, Treatment, Complications, Prevention:

- **Infectious diseases:**
  - Meningitis
  - Typhoid
  - Leprosy
  - Tuberculosis,
  - Urinary tract infections
- **Sexually transmitted diseases**
  - AIDS
  - Syphilis
  - Gonorrhea

CHAPTER - 1

BASIC PRINCIPLES OF CELL INJURY AND ADAPTATION

INTRODUCTION

Cell injury and adaptation are fundamental concepts in pathology, the study of diseases and their effects on the body's tissues and organs. Let's delve into each of these concepts in detail:

CELL INJURY:

Cell injury refers to the harmful effects that various insults or stressors can exert on cells, leading to structural or functional abnormalities. These insults can be physical, chemical, infectious, immunologic, or genetic in nature. When cells are exposed to injurious stimuli beyond their adaptive capacity, they undergo various changes that can range from reversible alterations to irreversible damage, ultimately leading to cell death.

1. **Causes of Cell Injury:**
   a. **Physical Agents**: Trauma, temperature extremes (heat or cold), radiation.
   b. **Chemical Agents**: Toxic substances such as drugs, pollutants, alcohol, and heavy metals.
   c. **Biological Agents**: Microorganisms such as bacteria, viruses, fungi, and parasites.
   d. **Immunologic Reactions**: Autoimmune diseases where the immune system attacks the body's own cells.
   e. **Genetic Abnormalities**: Inherited disorders that affect cellular functions.

2. **Types of Cell Injury:**
   a. **Reversible Cell Injury**: Cell damage that can be recovered if the injurious stimulus is removed promptly. Examples include cellular swelling, fatty change (accumulation of fat droplets), and hydropic degeneration.

b. **Irreversible Cell Injury**: Severe and prolonged injury that leads to cell death. This can manifest as necrosis (uncontrolled cell death) or apoptosis (programmed cell death).

CELLULAR ADAPTATION:

Cellular adaptation is the response of cells to stress or changes in their environment in an attempt to maintain homeostasis and ensure survival. When faced with adverse conditions, cells can adapt by altering their structure, function, or metabolism. These adaptive changes help cells cope with the stressor and maintain normal function. However, if the stressor persists or exceeds the cell's adaptive capacity, it may lead to cell injury or death.

1. **Types of Cellular Adaptation:**
   a. **Hypertrophy**: Increase in the size of cells due to increased workload or hormonal stimulation. For example, cardiac hypertrophy in response to hypertension.
   b. **Hyperplasia**: Increase in the number of cells due to cell division, often in response to hormonal stimulation or tissue damage. Examples include the proliferation of breast tissue during pregnancy and the regeneration of liver cells after injury.
   c. **Atrophy**: Decrease in the size of cells due to decreased workload, disuse, or loss of trophic signals. Skeletal muscle atrophy due to immobilization is a common example.
   d. **Metaplasia**: Reversible change in which one differentiated cell type is replaced by another cell type better suited to withstand the stressor. For instance, in response to chronic irritation, the normal columnar epithelium of the respiratory tract may undergo metaplastic change to squamous epithelium

DEFINITIONS OF CELL INJURY AND ADAPTATION

Certainly, here are detailed definitions of both cell injury and adaptation:

Cell Injury:

Cell injury refers to the deleterious effects caused by various stressors or insults on cells, resulting in structural and/or functional abnormalities. These stressors can include physical, chemical, biological, immunological, or genetic factors. When cells are exposed to these stressors beyond their adaptive capacity, they undergo alterations ranging from reversible changes to irreversible damage, potentially leading to cell death.

Detailed Explanation:

Cell injury occurs when cells are subjected to conditions or stimuli that disrupt their normal homeostasis. These insults can disrupt cellular structures, impair metabolic processes, or interfere with essential cellular functions. Cell injury can manifest in various ways, including cellular swelling, accumulation of intracellular substances (such as lipids or proteins), disruption of membrane integrity, and ultimately, cell death. The severity and type of cell injury depend on factors such as the nature, duration, and intensity of the insult, as well as the cell type and its adaptive capacity.

Adaptation:

Cellular adaptation refers to the ability of cells to respond and adjust to changes in their environment or to stressors, with the goal of maintaining cellular homeostasis and ensuring survival. When confronted with adverse conditions or stimuli, cells can undergo adaptive changes in their structure, function, or metabolism to better withstand the stressor and maintain normal cellular function. These adaptations are reversible and aim to restore or preserve cellular integrity and function under challenging circumstances.

Detailed Explanation:

Cellular adaptation represents the dynamic response of cells to changes in their microenvironment or physiological demands. Cells can adapt through various mechanisms, including alterations in cell size (hypertrophy or atrophy), changes in cell number (hyperplasia or metaplasia), modifications in cell phenotype or function, and adjustments in metabolic pathways. These adaptive changes enable cells to better cope with stressors or physiological demands, thus promoting their survival and maintaining tissue homeostasis. However, if the stressor persists or exceeds the cell's adaptive capacity, it may lead to cell injury or death.

HOMEOSTASIS

Homeostasis is the physiological process by which cells, tissues, organs, and organisms maintain a stable internal environment despite external fluctuations or changes. It involves the regulation of various parameters such as temperature, pH, osmolarity, nutrient levels, and metabolic waste products within narrow ranges compatible with cellular function. Homeostasis is essential for the optimal functioning of cells and the overall health of an organism.

1. **Detailed Explanation:**

   In the context of cell injury and adaptation, homeostasis plays a crucial role in ensuring that cells can function optimally and maintain their structural and functional integrity under changing conditions or stressors. Cells rely on intricate molecular mechanisms and feedback loops to sense and respond to alterations in their environment, thereby preserving homeostasis and promoting survival.

2. **Homeostasis in Cell Injury:**

   Cell injury disrupts homeostasis by interfering with normal cellular functions and processes. When cells are exposed to injurious stimuli beyond their adaptive capacity, homeostatic mechanisms may become overwhelmed, leading to cellular dysfunction, structural damage, or even cell death. For example, oxidative stress caused by an imbalance between reactive oxygen species (ROS) production and antioxidant defenses can disrupt cellular homeostasis, leading to oxidative damage to lipids, proteins, and DNA.

3. **Homeostasis in Adaptation:**

Cellular adaptation represents the response of cells to maintain homeostasis in the face of changing environmental conditions or stressors. Cells adapt through various mechanisms to restore or preserve cellular homeostasis and ensure survival. For instance, in response to increased workload or hormonal stimulation, cardiac myocytes may undergo hypertrophy to maintain cardiac output and meet increased demands. This adaptive response helps restore homeostasis by enhancing contractile function and structural integrity.

4. **Balance between Cell Injury and Adaptation:**

The balance between cell injury and adaptation determines the fate of cells and tissues in response to stressors. While cellular adaptation aims to restore homeostasis and promote cell survival, excessive or prolonged stress can lead to maladaptive responses and cell injury. Understanding the interplay between cell injury and adaptation is essential for deciphering the pathophysiology of diseases and developing therapeutic interventions aimed at restoring homeostasis and preserving cellular function.

COMPONENTS AND TYPES OF FEEDBACK SYSTEMS

the components and types of feedback systems in the context of cell injury and adaptation:

1. **Components of Feedback Systems:**

Feedback systems involve a series of components that work together to regulate physiological processes in response to internal or external stimuli. The main components of a feedback system include:

2. **Sensor or Receptor**: This component detects changes in the internal or external environment and generates signals in response to these changes. In the context of cell injury and adaptation, sensors may include membrane receptors, intracellular signaling molecules, or specialized proteins that sense alterations in cellular homeostasis.

3. **Integrator or Control Center**: The integrator receives input from the sensors and compares it to a set point or desired range. Based on this comparison, the integrator initiates appropriate responses to restore or maintain homeostasis. In multicellular organisms, control centers may include regulatory centers in the brain, such as the hypothalamus, or local regulatory mechanisms within tissues or organs.

4. **Effector**: Effectors are the components that carry out the responses initiated by the control center. These responses aim to counteract deviations from the set point and restore homeostasis. Effectors may include cells, tissues, organs, or molecules that mediate physiological changes to achieve the desired outcome.

5. **Types of Feedback Systems:**

   Feedback systems can be classified into two main types based on the direction of the feedback loop and its effect on the initial stimulus:

6. **Negative Feedback System:**
   a. In a negative feedback system, the response generated by the effector opposes the initial stimulus, thereby dampening or reversing the deviation from the set point.
   b. Negative feedback systems are essential for maintaining stability and homeostasis in biological systems.
   c. Examples of negative feedback systems in cell injury and adaptation include:

i. **Regulation of body temperature**: When body temperature rises above the set point, thermoreceptors in the skin and hypothalamus detect the change and trigger responses such as vasodilation and sweating to lower temperature.

ii. **Regulation of blood glucose levels**: High blood glucose levels stimulate the release of insulin, which promotes glucose uptake by cells, leading to decreased blood glucose levels.

7. **Positive Feedback System:**

a. In a positive feedback system, the response generated by the effector amplifies the initial stimulus, leading to an increase in the deviation from the set point.

b. Positive feedback systems are less common in biological systems and are often associated with processes that require rapid amplification or completion.

c. Examples of positive feedback systems in cell injury and adaptation include:

i. **Blood clotting**: When a blood vessel is injured, platelets release chemicals that attract more platelets to the site of injury, leading to the formation of a blood clot.

ii. **Uterine contractions during childbirth**: The stretching of the cervix during childbirth stimulates the release of oxytocin, which causes uterine contractions, further stretching the cervix and promoting the release of more oxytocin.

CAUSES OF CELLULAR INJURY

Cellular injury can occur due to a variety of factors, ranging from physical trauma to chemical exposure to biological agents. Understanding these causes is crucial for identifying potential threats to cellular integrity and developing strategies for prevention and treatment. Here are the main causes of cellular injury in detail:

1. Physical Agents:

Physical agents exert mechanical forces or energy on cells, leading to structural damage or functional impairment. Common physical agents include:

a. **Trauma:** Mechanical injury resulting from accidents, falls, or blunt force trauma can cause tissue damage, disrupt cellular membranes, and induce inflammation.

b. **Temperature Extremes**: Exposure to extreme heat (burns) or cold can damage cellular membranes, denature proteins, and disrupt metabolic processes.

c. **Radiation**: Ionizing radiation (such as X-rays, gamma rays) and ultraviolet (UV) radiation can cause DNA damage, oxidative stress, and cellular dysfunction, increasing the risk of mutations and cancer.

2. Chemical Agents:

Chemical agents include toxic substances that can disrupt cellular structure and function. Examples include:

a. **Drugs and Medications**: Certain medications, especially at high doses or with prolonged use, can exert toxic effects on cells and organs, leading to cellular injury or dysfunction.

b. **Environmental Toxins**: Exposure to pollutants, heavy metals (such as lead, mercury), pesticides, and industrial chemicals can damage cellular membranes, impair cellular metabolism, and cause oxidative stress.

c. **Toxic Metabolites**: Accumulation of endogenous metabolites (e.g., ammonia, bilirubin) due to metabolic disorders or impaired excretion can lead to cellular injury, particularly in organs like the liver and kidneys.

3. Biological Agents:

Biological agents include pathogens such as bacteria, viruses, fungi, and parasites, which can directly infect cells or produce toxins that damage cellular structures. Examples include:

a. **Infections**: Pathogens invade host cells, disrupt cellular functions, replicate within cells, and induce inflammatory responses, leading to tissue damage and organ dysfunction.

b. **Toxins**: Bacterial toxins (e.g., exotoxins, endotoxins) and viral proteins can directly damage cellular membranes, alter intracellular signaling pathways, and induce cell death.

4. Immunologic Reactions:

Immunologic reactions involve the immune system's response to foreign antigens or self-antigens, leading to tissue damage. Examples include:

a. **Autoimmune Diseases**: Autoimmune disorders occur when the immune system mistakenly targets and attacks the body's own cells and tissues, leading to chronic inflammation and tissue damage.

b. **Hypersensitivity Reactions**: Allergic reactions and hypersensitivity disorders involve exaggerated immune responses to harmless substances, resulting in tissue injury and inflammation.

5. Genetic Abnormalities:

Genetic abnormalities can predispose cells to injury or dysfunction due to inherited mutations or genetic disorders. Examples include:

a. **Genetic Disorders**: Inherited disorders such as cystic fibrosis, sickle cell anemia, and lysosomal storage diseases can impair cellular functions, disrupt metabolic pathways, and lead to tissue damage.

b. **Mutations**: Mutations in oncogenes, tumor suppressor genes, or DNA repair genes can increase the risk of cancer and predispose cells to malignant transformation.

PATHOGENESIS (CELL MEMBRANE DAMAGE, MITOCHONDRIAL DAMAGE, RIBOSOME DAMAGE, NUCLEAR DAMAGE)

The pathogenesis of cell injury in terms of damage to key cellular components, including the cell membrane, mitochondria, ribosomes, and nucleus:

1. Cell Membrane Damage:

The cell membrane, also known as the plasma membrane, serves as a barrier between the cell's internal environment and the extracellular space. Damage to the cell membrane can disrupt cellular homeostasis and lead to various pathological consequences:

a. **Mechanism of Damage**: Cell membrane damage can occur due to physical trauma, chemical toxins, or immune-mediated reactions. For example, mechanical trauma can cause rupture or lysis of the membrane, while toxins may disrupt membrane integrity by altering lipid composition or inducing pore formation.

b. **Consequences**: Damage to the cell membrane results in increased permeability, allowing ions, molecules, and cellular contents to leak out of the cell. This disrupts ion gradients, impairs cellular function, and may lead to cell swelling, osmotic imbalance, and ultimately cell death if severe or prolonged.

2. Mitochondrial Damage:

Mitochondria are the powerhouse of the cell, responsible for generating adenosine triphosphate (ATP) through oxidative phosphorylation. Damage to mitochondria can impair ATP production and trigger cell death pathways:

a. **Mechanism of Damage**: Mitochondrial damage can occur due to oxidative stress, calcium overload, or mitochondrial toxins. For example, reactive oxygen species (ROS) generated during oxidative stress can damage mitochondrial DNA (mtDNA) and proteins, leading to dysfunction.

b. **Consequences**: Impaired mitochondrial function results in decreased ATP production, disruption of cellular metabolism, and release of pro-apoptotic factors such as cytochrome c. This initiates apoptotic pathways, leading to programmed cell death (apoptosis) if the damage is severe or irreversible.

3. Ribosome Damage:

Ribosomes are cellular organelles responsible for protein synthesis. Damage to ribosomes can disrupt protein synthesis and impair cellular function:

a. **Mechanism of Damage**: Ribosome damage can occur due to exposure to toxins, oxidative stress, or disruptions in ribosomal RNA (rRNA) synthesis or processing. For example, certain drugs or toxins may bind to ribosomal subunits, inhibiting protein synthesis.

b. **Consequences**: Impaired protein synthesis results in decreased production of essential proteins needed for cellular functions such as enzyme activity, structural integrity, and signaling pathways. This can lead to cellular dysfunction, altered gene expression, and ultimately cell death if protein synthesis is severely compromised.

4. Nuclear Damage:

The nucleus contains the cell's genetic material (DNA) and is essential for controlling gene expression and cellular functions. Damage to the nucleus can disrupt DNA integrity and gene regulation:

a. **Mechanism of Damage**: Nuclear damage can occur due to DNA mutations, radiation exposure, or chemical toxins that interfere with DNA replication or repair mechanisms. For example, ionizing radiation can cause double-strand breaks in DNA, leading to chromosomal aberrations.

b. **Consequences**: Nuclear damage results in genomic instability, alterations in gene expression, and impaired DNA replication and repair. This can lead to cell cycle arrest, apoptosis, or cellular senescence, depending on the extent of DNA damage and the cell's ability to repair it.

MORPHOLOGY OF CELL INJURY – ADAPTIVE CHANGES (ATROPHY, HYPERTROPHY, HYPERPLASIA, METAPLASIA, DYSPLASIA)

The morphology of cell injury with a focus on adaptive changes, including atrophy, hypertrophy, hyperplasia, metaplasia, and dysplasia:

1. Atrophy:

Atrophy refers to the decrease in cell size or tissue mass due to a reduction in cell number, cell size, or both. It is a common adaptive response to decreased workload, loss of trophic signals, or aging:

a. **Mechanism**: Atrophy can occur through various mechanisms, including decreased protein synthesis, increased protein degradation (via autophagy or the ubiquitin-proteasome pathway), and apoptosis of cells.

b. **Examples**: Skeletal muscle atrophy due to disuse (e.g., immobilization, bed rest), brain atrophy in neurodegenerative diseases (e.g., Alzheimer's disease), and organ atrophy following loss of hormonal stimulation (e.g., thymic atrophy after puberty).

2. Hypertrophy:

Hypertrophy refers to the increase in cell size or tissue mass due to an increase in cell size without an increase in cell number. It is often seen in response to increased functional demand or hormonal stimulation:

a. **Mechanism**: Hypertrophy occurs through an increase in cellular protein synthesis, leading to an enlargement of organelles (e.g., hypertrophy of cardiomyocytes results in enlarged mitochondria and myofibrils).

b. **Examples**: Cardiac hypertrophy in response to hypertension or valvular heart disease, skeletal muscle hypertrophy in response to exercise or weightlifting.

3. Hyperplasia:

Hyperplasia refers to the increase in the number of cells in a tissue or organ due to cell proliferation. It is often a response to increased hormonal stimulation or tissue damage:

a. **Mechanism:** Hyperplasia involves an increase in the rate of cell division and replication, leading to an expansion of the cell population within the affected tissue.

b. **Examples:** Benign prostatic hyperplasia in response to hormonal changes in aging men, compensatory liver hyperplasia after partial hepatectomy, and endometrial hyperplasia in response to estrogen stimulation.

4. Metaplasia:

Metaplasia refers to the reversible change in which one differentiated cell type is replaced by another cell type better suited to withstand the new environmental conditions or stressors:

a. **Mechanism:** Metaplasia involves reprogramming of stem cells or undifferentiated cells to differentiate into a different cell type in response to chronic irritation or injury.

b. **Examples:** Squamous metaplasia of bronchial epithelium in response to cigarette smoke, Barrett's esophagus (intestinal metaplasia) in response to chronic gastroesophageal reflux disease.

5. Dysplasia:

Dysplasia refers to the abnormal growth or development of cells within a tissue or organ, characterized by disordered cellular architecture, increased nuclear size, and altered nuclear-to-cytoplasmic ratio:

a. **Mechanism:** Dysplasia often arises from genetic mutations or chronic inflammation, leading to abnormal cell proliferation, differentiation, and maturation.

b. **Examples:** Cervical dysplasia detected on Pap smear, oral epithelial dysplasia in response to chronic tobacco use, and colorectal epithelial dysplasia in patients with inflammatory bowel disease.

CELL SWELLING

Cell swelling, also known as cellular edema, is a common manifestation of cell injury characterized by an increase in the intracellular volume of cells due to the influx of water and electrolytes. This process is often reversible and represents an early stage of cellular injury. Let's explore cell swelling in detail:

1. **Mechanisms of Cell Swelling:**

   Cell swelling can occur due to various physiological and pathological processes, including:

   a. **Increased Permeability of Cell Membrane**: Disruption of the cell membrane, either through direct damage or activation of membrane channels, can lead to the influx of extracellular fluid and ions into the cell.

   b. **Disturbance in Ion Homeostasis**: Alterations in ion gradients, particularly an influx of sodium ions (Na^+) and chloride ions (Cl^-), can lead to osmotic imbalance and water movement into the cell.

   c. **Energy Depletion**: Decreased ATP production or ATP depletion impairs ion pumps (such as the sodium-potassium pump), leading to intracellular sodium accumulation and subsequent water influx.

   d. **Increased Intracellular Osmolarity**: Accumulation of osmotically active substances, such as proteins, carbohydrates, or metabolic byproducts, within the cell can draw water into the cytoplasm.

2. **Consequences of Cell Swelling:**

   Cell swelling can have several consequences, including:

   a. **Disruption of Cellular Functions**: Increased cell volume can impair cellular organelles and structures, leading to functional disturbances. For example, swelling of mitochondria can disrupt oxidative phosphorylation and ATP production.

   b. **Compromised Membrane Integrity**: Severe cell swelling can lead to stretching and rupture of the cell membrane, resulting in leakage of cellular contents and inflammation.

c. **Impaired Cellular Communication**: Swollen cells may exhibit altered membrane receptors and signaling pathways, affecting intercellular communication and tissue homeostasis.

d. **Compression of Capillaries**: In tissues with limited space, such as the brain, cell swelling can increase intracranial pressure and compress adjacent blood vessels, leading to ischemia and further tissue damage.

3. **Causes of Cell Swelling:**

Cell swelling can be triggered by various factors, including:

a. **Hypoxia and Ischemia**: Reduced oxygen supply impairs cellular metabolism and ion transport, leading to cell swelling.

b. **Toxic Injury**: Exposure to toxins, drugs, or metabolic byproducts can disrupt ion homeostasis and cellular integrity, resulting in swelling.

c. **Inflammatory Mediators**: Inflammatory processes can lead to increased vascular permeability and the release of cytokines that promote cell swelling.

d. **Electrolyte Imbalance**: Disturbances in electrolyte concentrations, such as hyponatremia or hypokalemia, can affect osmotic gradients and induce cell swelling.

4. **Relevance in Disease and Adaptation:**

Cell swelling is a hallmark feature of various pathological conditions, including ischemic injury, toxic insults, and inflammation. However, it can also represent an adaptive response aimed at protecting cells from more severe forms of injury. For example, mild cell swelling may help cells resist osmotic stress or maintain homeostasis in response to physiological challenges.

INTRA CELLULAR ACCUMULATION

Intracellular accumulation refers to the abnormal accumulation of various substances within cells, leading to their accumulation beyond normal physiological levels. These substances can include normal cellular constituents, such as proteins and lipids, as well as abnormal substances like pigments, glycogen, and crystals. Intracellular accumulation can occur due to various factors and may represent an adaptive response, a consequence of cellular injury, or a manifestation of underlying disease processes. Let's explore intracellular accumulation in detail:

Types of Intracellular Accumulation:

1. **Protein Accumulation (Proteinosis):**
   a. **Mechanism**: Protein accumulation can occur due to increased synthesis, decreased degradation, or impaired clearance of proteins. This can result from cellular stress, dysfunction of protein folding mechanisms, or defects in protein degradation pathways.
   b. **Examples**: Accumulation of misfolded proteins in neurodegenerative diseases (e.g., Alzheimer's disease, Parkinson's disease), proteinuria in renal diseases (e.g., nephrotic syndrome), and accumulation of abnormal proteins in liver diseases (e.g., alpha-1 antitrypsin deficiency).

2. **Lipid Accumulation (Steatosis):**
   a. **Mechanism:** Lipid accumulation occurs when the synthesis, uptake, or storage of lipids exceeds their utilization or export from the cell. This can result from conditions such as obesity, diabetes, alcohol abuse, or metabolic disorders.
   b. **Examples**: Fatty liver disease (hepatic steatosis), atherosclerosis in blood vessels, and lipid accumulation in foam cells in atherosclerotic plaques.

3. **Glycogen Accumulation (Glycogenosis):**
   a. **Mechanism**: Glycogen accumulation occurs due to increased synthesis or decreased breakdown of glycogen within cells. This can

result from metabolic disorders affecting glycogen metabolism or hormonal imbalances.

   b. **Examples**: Glycogen storage diseases (e.g., Pompe disease, McArdle disease), glycogen accumulation in hepatocytes in diabetes mellitus.

4. **Pigment Accumulation:**

   a. **Mechanism:** Pigment accumulation can occur due to the deposition of endogenous or exogenous pigmented substances within cells. This can result from metabolic disturbances, environmental exposures, or genetic disorders affecting pigment metabolism.

   b. **Examples:** Lipofuscin accumulation in aging cells, melanin accumulation in melanocytes (e.g., freckles), hemosiderin accumulation in macrophages (e.g., hemosiderosis).

5. **Calcium Accumulation:**

   a. **Mechanism**: Calcium accumulation occurs when intracellular calcium levels exceed the capacity of calcium-binding proteins and storage organelles. This can result from cellular injury, metabolic disturbances, or dysregulation of calcium homeostasis.

   b. **Examples**: Dystrophic calcification in injured or dying tissues, calcification of atherosclerotic plaques, and calcium accumulation in mitochondria during cell death.

Consequences and Clinical Relevance:

Intracellular accumulation can have various consequences depending on the nature, extent, and duration of accumulation. It can disrupt cellular functions, impair organelle structure, induce cellular stress responses, and contribute to tissue damage and dysfunction. Intracellular accumulation is often associated with the pathogenesis of numerous diseases, including metabolic disorders, inflammatory conditions, genetic disorders, and toxic exposures. Understanding the mechanisms and consequences of intracellular accumulation is essential for elucidating the pathophysiology of diseases and developing therapeutic strategies to mitigate cellular damage and promote tissue recovery.

CALCIFICATION

Calcification refers to the abnormal deposition of calcium salts, primarily hydroxyapatite (calcium phosphate crystals), within tissues. This process can occur in various organs and tissues throughout the body and can have significant implications for tissue structure and function. Calcification can be classified into two main types: dystrophic calcification and metastatic calcification.

1. Dystrophic Calcification:

Dystrophic calcification occurs in areas of damaged or necrotic tissue and is characterized by the deposition of calcium salts in the presence of normal serum calcium levels. It is often associated with chronic inflammation, tissue injury, or ischemic necrosis:

a. **Mechanism**: Dystrophic calcification occurs when calcium salts precipitate within dying or degenerating tissues as a result of cell death, release of intracellular calcium, and exposure to calcium-binding proteins and phosphates.

b. **Examples**: Dystrophic calcification can occur in atherosclerotic plaques in blood vessels, damaged heart valves, necrotic areas in organs such as the kidneys (as seen in renal infarcts), and areas of chronic inflammation (e.g., tuberculosis granulomas).

2. Metastatic Calcification:

Metastatic calcification occurs in normal tissues and organs as a result of systemic factors leading to hypercalcemia (elevated serum calcium levels). It is often associated with disorders of calcium metabolism, renal failure, or hormonal imbalances:

a. **Mechanism**: Metastatic calcification occurs when there is an imbalance between calcium influx and excretion, leading to elevated serum calcium levels. The excess calcium is deposited in various tissues and organs throughout the body.

b. **Examples**: Metastatic calcification can occur in the kidneys, lungs, gastric mucosa, blood **ves**sels, and soft tissues. It is commonly seen in patients with hyperparathyroidism, chronic renal failure, vitamin D intoxication, or disorders of phosphate metabolism.

3. Consequences and Clinical Relevance:

Calcification can have significant consequences depending on the location and extent of deposition. In tissues such as blood vessels, heart valves, and kidneys, calcification can impair function, leading to cardiovascular diseases, renal failure, and other complications. In soft tissues, calcification can cause pain, inflammation, and tissue damage.

4. Diagnosis and Treatment:

Diagnosis of calcification often involves imaging modalities such as X-rays, computed tomography (CT) scans, or ultrasound. Treatment depends on the underlying cause and may involve addressing the underlying disorder (e.g., treating hyperparathyroidism), managing complications (e.g., cardiovascular disease), and in some cases, surgical intervention to remove calcified tissues or replace damaged organs (e.g., heart valve replacement).

ENZYME LEAKAGE AND CELL DEATH

Enzyme leakage and cell death are key events in the process of cell injury, representing critical aspects of cellular pathology. Let's explore these phenomena in detail:

Enzyme Leakage:

1. **Mechanism:** Enzyme leakage occurs when cellular membranes, particularly the plasma membrane and organelle membranes, are damaged or disrupted, leading to the release of intracellular enzymes into the extracellular space or into other cellular compartments. Enzyme leakage can occur due to various insults, including physical trauma, chemical toxins, inflammatory mediators, and ischemic injury.

2. **Consequences**: Enzyme leakage has several significant consequences:
   a. It serves as a marker of cellular injury, as elevated levels of specific enzymes in the blood or other body fluids can indicate tissue damage or dysfunction.
   b. The leaked enzymes can catalyze biochemical reactions outside the cell, contributing to tissue injury and inflammation.
   c. Enzyme leakage can lead to the loss of cellular integrity and function, disrupting normal physiological processes and cellular homeostasis.

3. **Clinical Relevance**: Measurement of enzyme levels in the blood or other body fluids, such as serum creatine kinase (CK) for muscle injury, serum alanine aminotransferase (ALT) and aspartate aminotransferase (AST) for liver injury, and serum lactate dehydrogenase (LDH) for general cellular injury, is commonly used in clinical practice to diagnose and monitor various diseases and conditions associated with tissue damage.

Cell death:

1. **Types of Cell Death**:
   a. **Necrosis**: Necrosis is characterized by uncontrolled cell death, often associated with swelling, rupture of the cell membrane, and release of cellular contents into the extracellular space. It is typically a response to severe and acute injury, such as ischemia, trauma, or toxic insults.
   b. **Apoptosis**: Apoptosis, or programmed cell death, is a highly regulated process characterized by cell shrinkage, chromatin condensation, fragmentation of the nucleus, and formation of apoptotic bodies. It

plays essential roles in tissue homeostasis, development, and immune regulation.

2. **Mechanisms of Cell Death:**
    a. **Necrosis:** Necrosis can occur through various mechanisms, including mitochondrial dysfunction, calcium overload, oxidative stress, and membrane damage. It is often associated with inflammation and can lead to tissue damage and loss of function.
    b. **Apoptosis**: Apoptosis is regulated by a complex network of signaling pathways involving caspases, Bcl-2 family proteins, death receptors, and mitochondrial factors. It can be triggered by extrinsic (death receptor-mediated) or intrinsic (mitochondria-mediated) pathways and is characterized by orderly and controlled dismantling of the cell.

3. **Adaptation and Response to Cell Death:**
    a. Cells can adapt to stress and injury by activating various survival pathways, such as autophagy, DNA repair mechanisms, and antioxidant defenses.
    b. In some cases, cells may undergo reversible injury and recover normal function if the stressor is removed or attenuated.
    c. However, if the injury is severe or prolonged, cells may progress to irreversible injury and undergo cell death.

4. **Clinical Relevance**: Dysregulated cell death processes contribute to the pathogenesis of numerous diseases, including ischemic heart disease, stroke, neurodegenerative disorders, cancer, and autoimmune diseases. Understanding the mechanisms and regulation of cell death is essential for developing therapeutic strategies to target and modulate these processes for disease intervention.

ACIDOSIS & ALKALOSIS

Acidosis and alkalosis refer to disturbances in the body's acid-base balance, which can have profound effects on cellular function and homeostasis. Let's explore acidosis and alkalosis in the context of cell injury and adaptation:

Acidosis:

1. **Definition**: Acidosis is a condition characterized by an excess of acid in the body, leading to a decrease in blood pH below the normal range (pH < 7.35). It can result from either an increase in acid production or a decrease in acid elimination or buffering capacity.

2. **Mechanisms of Cellular Injury**:

    a. Acidosis disrupts cellular function by altering enzyme activity, protein structure, and ion gradients across cell membranes.

    b. Intracellular acidosis can impair cellular metabolism, mitochondrial function, and ATP production, leading to cellular dysfunction and injury.

    c. Acidosis can also lead to the accumulation of toxic acidic metabolites within cells, further exacerbating cellular damage.

3. **Consequences and Clinical Relevance:**

    a. Acidosis can have systemic effects on various organs and tissues, including the brain, heart, kidneys, and muscles.

    b. Severe or prolonged acidosis can lead to tissue hypoxia, impaired organ function, and ultimately, cell death.

    c. Acidosis is commonly observed in conditions such as diabetic ketoacidosis, lactic acidosis, renal failure, and respiratory failure.

Alkalosis:

1. **Definition**: Alkalosis is a condition characterized by an excess of alkali (base) in the body, leading to an increase in blood pH above the normal range (pH > 7.45). It can result from either a decrease in acid production, an increase in alkali intake or retention, or a loss of hydrogen ions.

2. **Mechanisms of Cellular Injury:**

a. Alkalosis can alter ion gradients across cell membranes, leading to changes in membrane potential and impairing cellular excitability.

b. Intracellular alkalosis can affect enzyme function, protein structure, and cellular metabolism, disrupting normal cellular processes.

c. Alkalosis can also lead to electrolyte imbalances, such as hypokalemia, which can further exacerbate cellular dysfunction.

3. **Consequences and Clinical Relevance:**

a. Alkalosis can affect various organ systems, including the nervous system, cardiovascular system, and kidneys.

b. Symptoms of alkalosis may include muscle weakness, irritability, tetany, and cardiac arrhythmias.

c. Alkalosis can occur in conditions such as vomiting, hyperventilation, excessive bicarbonate intake, and certain metabolic disorders.

4. **Adaptation to Acid-Base Imbalance:**

5. **Compensatory Mechanisms**: The body has various compensatory mechanisms to maintain acid-base balance and minimize the effects of acidosis or alkalosis.

a. **Respiratory compensation**: Hypoventilation in response to acidosis or hyperventilation in response to alkalosis can help restore normal blood pH by altering carbon dioxide levels.

b. **Renal compensation**: The kidneys can regulate acid-base balance by adjusting hydrogen ion secretion and bicarbonate reabsorption or excretion.

6. **Cellular Adaptations**: Cells may also adapt to acid-base imbalances by altering ion transport, enzyme activity, and metabolic pathways to maintain cellular homeostasis.

a. For example, in acidosis, cells may increase the activity of buffering systems and ion pumps to minimize intracellular acid accumulation.

b. In alkalosis, cells may decrease the activity of ion transporters and enzymes sensitive to pH changes to prevent further intracellular alkalinization.

ELECTROLYTE IMBALANCE

Electrolyte imbalance refers to disturbances in the concentrations of ions, including sodium (Na^+), potassium (K^+), calcium (Ca^{2+}), chloride (Cl^-), bicarbonate (HCO_3^-), and magnesium (Mg^{2+}), within the body's extracellular and intracellular compartments. These imbalances can disrupt cellular function, impair physiological processes, and contribute to cell injury and adaptation. Let's explore electrolyte imbalance in detail:

1. **Mechanisms of Electrolyte Imbalance:**
   a. **Alterations in Ion Transport**: Dysregulation of ion transport mechanisms, such as ion channels, pumps, and exchangers, can lead to changes in ion concentrations across cell membranes.
   b. **Renal Dysfunction**: Impaired renal function can disrupt electrolyte balance by altering ion reabsorption, secretion, and excretion in the kidneys.
   c. **Gastrointestinal Losses**: Excessive loss of electrolytes through vomiting, diarrhea, or gastrointestinal disorders can lead to electrolyte depletion.
   d. **Endocrine Disorders**: Hormonal imbalances, such as hyperaldosteronism or hypoaldosteronism, can affect electrolyte balance by altering renal handling of ions.
   e. **Fluid Shifts**: Changes in fluid distribution between intracellular and extracellular compartments, such as dehydration or volume overload, can affect electrolyte concentrations.

2. **Effects of Electrolyte Imbalance on Cells:**
   a. **Cellular Swelling/Shrinkage**: Imbalances in ion concentrations can disrupt osmotic balance, leading to cellular swelling (hyponatremia, hypotonicity) or shrinkage (hypernatremia, hypertonicity).

b. **Membrane Potential Disturbances**: Alterations in ion gradients across cell membranes can affect membrane potential, leading to changes in cellular excitability and signaling.

c. **Metabolic Dysfunction**: Electrolyte imbalances can disrupt cellular metabolism, enzyme activity, and ATP production, impairing cellular function and energy balance.

d. **Calcium Homeostasis**: Dysregulation of calcium levels can affect intracellular signaling pathways, mitochondrial function, and cell death processes.

3. **Adaptation to Electrolyte Imbalance:**

a. **Intracellular Ion Regulation**: Cells may adapt to electrolyte imbalances by altering ion transport mechanisms, expression of ion channels and pumps, and intracellular buffering systems.

b. **Renal Compensation**: The kidneys play a crucial role in maintaining electrolyte balance through renal reabsorption, secretion, and excretion mechanisms. Renal compensation can help restore electrolyte balance in response to acute or chronic imbalances.

c. **Hormonal Regulation**: Endocrine hormones such as aldosterone, antidiuretic hormone (ADH), and parathyroid hormone (PTH) regulate electrolyte balance by modulating renal function and ion transport.

4. **Clinical Manifestations and Treatment:**

a. **Symptom**s: Electrolyte imbalances can manifest with a wide range of symptoms, including weakness, fatigue, muscle cramps, cardiac arrhythmias, seizures, confusion, and coma.

b. **Diagnostic Tests**: Electrolyte imbalances are typically diagnosed through blood tests, including serum electrolyte panels and arterial blood gas analysis.

c. **Treatment**: Treatment of electrolyte imbalances involves correcting the underlying cause and restoring electrolyte balance through oral or intravenous electrolyte replacement, fluid therapy, and management of associated conditions.

CHAPTER - 2

BASIC MECHANISM INVOLVED IN THE PROCESS OF INFLAMMATION AND REPAIR

INTRODUCTION

Inflammation and repair are fundamental processes orchestrated by the body's immune system in response to tissue injury, infection, or other harmful stimuli. Let's delve into the basic mechanisms involved in these processes in detail:

Recognition of Injury or Infection:

Inflammation typically begins with the recognition of tissue damage or the presence of pathogens by the immune system. This recognition can occur through various mechanisms, including the detection of foreign molecules called pathogen-associated molecular patterns (PAMPs) by pattern recognition receptors (PRRs) such as Toll-like receptors (TLRs) and NOD-like receptors (NLRs). Additionally, damage-associated molecular patterns (DAMPs) released from injured cells can trigger an inflammatory response.

Vasodilation and Increased Vascular Permeability:

Once the threat is recognized, the immune system triggers a cascade of events leading to vasodilation and increased vascular permeability in the affected tissue. This allows more blood to flow to the area and facilitates the migration of immune cells from the bloodstream to the site of injury or infection. Vasodilation is mediated by various inflammatory mediators, including histamine, prostaglandins, and leukotrienes.

Migration of Immune Cells:

Immune cells, particularly neutrophils and macrophages, are recruited to the site of inflammation in response to chemotactic signals released by injured tissues and activated immune cells. Chemokines, such as interleukin-8 (IL-8), play a crucial role in guiding immune cell migration to the inflamed tissue.

Phagocytosis and Destruction of Pathogens:

Neutrophils and macrophages are phagocytic cells capable of engulfing and destroying pathogens, cellular debris, and other foreign particles present at the site of inflammation. This process, known as phagocytosis, helps to clear the infection and promote tissue repair. Phagocytic cells also release various antimicrobial molecules and enzymes to aid in pathogen clearance.

Release of Inflammatory Mediators:

During inflammation, various inflammatory mediators, including cytokines, chemokines, and lipid mediators, are released by immune cells and injured tissues. These mediators help to amplify the inflammatory response, recruit additional immune cells, and regulate the activities of surrounding cells. Examples of inflammatory mediators include tumor necrosis factor-alpha (TNF-α), interleukins (ILs), prostaglandins, and leukotrienes.

Resolution of Inflammation and Tissue Repair:

Once the threat has been neutralized and the inflammatory process has served its purpose, the immune system initiates mechanisms to resolve inflammation and promote tissue repair. This involves the clearance of inflammatory cells and mediators from the affected tissue, as well as the activation of repair processes such as angiogenesis (formation of new blood vessels), fibroblast activation, and deposition of extracellular matrix components.

Resolution of Inflammatory Response:

Specialized pro-resolving lipid mediators, such as lipoxins, resolvins, and protectins, play a crucial role in resolving inflammation and promoting tissue repair. These molecules act to dampen the inflammatory response, stimulate the clearance of inflammatory cells, and promote the restoration of tissue homeostasis.

CLINICAL SIGNS OF INFLAMMATION

Clinical signs of inflammation are observable manifestations that indicate the presence of an inflammatory response in the body. These signs can vary depending on the severity and location of the inflammation but typically include:

Redness (Rubor):

1. Redness is one of the classic signs of inflammation, often noticeable due to increased blood flow to the affected area. This increased blood flow is a result of vasodilation, which occurs due to the release of various mediators such as histamine, prostaglandins, and bradykinin. These mediators cause the blood vessels in the affected area to widen, allowing more blood to flow through them. As a result, the area appears red or flushed.

   Mechanism:
   a. **Histamine:** Released from mast cells, histamine acts on blood vessels to dilate them, allowing increased blood flow to the affected area.
   b. **Prostaglandins**: These lipid compounds are synthesized in response to tissue injury and contribute to vasodilation and increased vascular permeability.
   c. **Bradykinin:** This peptide hormone causes vasodilation and increases vascular permeability, leading to redness and swelling.

Swelling (Tumor):

1. Swelling is another hallmark of inflammation, characterized by an accumulation of fluid (edema) in the tissues. Like redness, swelling is also a result of increased vascular permeability and vasodilation. As blood vessels become more permeable, fluid, proteins, and immune cells such as neutrophils and macrophages can leak into the surrounding tissues, causing swelling.

   Mechanism:
   a. **Increased vascular permeability**: Inflammatory mediators such as histamine, prostaglandins, and bradykinin cause the endothelial cells lining the blood vessels to contract, increasing their permeability to fluids and proteins.

b. **Fluid extravasation**: The increased permeability allows fluid to leak out of the blood vessels and into the surrounding tissues, leading to swelling.

c. **Leukocyte migration**: In addition to fluid, immune cells like neutrophils and macrophages also migrate to the site of inflammation, contributing to swelling as they accumulate in the tissues.

Heat (Calor):

1. Heat is a characteristic sign of inflammation, often perceptible as increased warmth in the affected area. This heat results from the increased blood flow to the site of inflammation, a process known as vasodilation. Vasodilation occurs in response to the release of various inflammatory mediators such as histamine, prostaglandins, and bradykinin. These mediators cause the blood vessels in the affected area to widen, allowing more blood to flow through them. As a result, the affected area feels warmer to the touch compared to surrounding   tissues.

Mechanism:

a. **Vasodilation:** Inflammatory mediators act on blood vessels, causing them to dilate. This dilation increases blood flow to the affected area, which contributes to the sensation of warmth.

b. **Increased metabolic activity**: The influx of immune cells, such as neutrophils and macrophages, to the site of inflammation leads to increased metabolic activity, which generates heat as a byproduct.

Pain (Dolor):

1. Pain is another hallmark sign of inflammation, often described as a sensation of discomfort, tenderness, or soreness in the affected area. Pain serves as a protective mechanism, alerting the individual to tissue damage or injury and prompting behaviors that help protect the injured area from further harm.

Mechanism:

a. **Inflammatory mediators**: Various mediators released during the inflammatory process, including prostaglandins, bradykinin, and cytokines, sensitize pain receptors (nociceptors) in the affected tissues, increasing their responsiveness to stimuli and amplifying the sensation of pain.

b. **Tissue injury:** Inflammation often occurs in response to tissue injury or damage. Injured tissues release chemical signals that activate pain receptors, signaling the presence of damage and triggering pain sensations.

c. **Pressure:** Swelling associated with inflammation can exert pressure on surrounding tissues and nerves, leading to discomfort and pain.

Loss of Function (Functio Laesa):

Loss of function refers to impairment or restriction of normal tissue function in the affected area. It is a less commonly recognized but important sign of inflammation. The extent of loss of function can vary depending on the severity and location of the inflammation.

Mechanisms of Loss of Function in Inflammation:

1. **Tissue Swelling:** Swelling associated with inflammation can physically impede the normal movement or function of affected tissues. For example, swelling in a joint can restrict its range of motion, leading to functional impairment.

2. **Pain-Induced Limitations**: Pain associated with inflammation can cause individuals to limit movement or use of the affected area to avoid exacerbating discomfort. This self-imposed restriction can result in temporary loss of function.

3. **Tissue Damage**: In severe cases of inflammation, tissue damage or destruction can occur, leading to permanent loss of function. For example, chronic inflammation in organs such as the lungs or liver can impair their function over time.

These clinical signs are collectively known as the cardinal signs of inflammation and are often used by healthcare professionals to assess and diagnose inflammatory conditions. It's important to note that not all signs may be present in every case of inflammation, and the severity of symptoms can vary depending on the underlying cause and individual factors. Additionally, chronic inflammation may exhibit subtler or more prolonged manifestations compared to acute inflammation.

DIFFERENT TYPES OF INFLAMMATION

Inflammation can manifest in various forms, each with distinct characteristics, underlying mechanisms, and clinical implications. Here are some different types of inflammation:

Acute Inflammation:

1. **Nature:**
    a. Acute inflammation is a rapid and short-lived response to tissue injury, infection, or other insults.
    b. It is typically characterized by a rapid onset and resolves within a few days to weeks once the underlying cause of inflammation is eliminated.
2. **Cause:**
    a. Acute inflammation is triggered by various stimuli, including physical trauma, pathogens (such as bacteria or viruses), chemical irritants, or tissue necrosis (cell death).
3. **Histological Features:**
    a. Histologically, acute inflammation is characterized by the presence of neutrophils (a type of white blood cell) at the site of inflammation.
    b. Other features include vasodilation, increased vascular permeability, edema (fluid accumulation), and exudation of plasma proteins and inflammatory mediators into the affected tissues.

4. **Clinical Manifestations:**
   a. Common signs and symptoms of acute inflammation include redness (rubor), warmth (calor), swelling (tumor), pain (dolor), and loss of function (functio laesa).

5. **Resolution:**
   a. Acute inflammation typically resolves once the triggering stimulus is removed or neutralized and the damaged tissues undergo repair.
   b. Resolution is facilitated by the clearance of inflammatory cells and mediators, as well as the activation of anti-inflammatory pathways.

Chronic Inflammation:

1. **Nature:**
   a. Chronic inflammation is a prolonged and sustained inflammatory response that persists for weeks, months, or even years.
   b. Unlike acute inflammation, chronic inflammation can persist even after the initial trigger has been removed.

2. **Cause:**
   a. Chronic inflammation can result from persistent or recurrent exposure to low-grade irritants, persistent infections (e.g., certain bacteria or viruses), autoimmune reactions, or dysregulated immune responses.

3. **Histological Features:**
   a. Histologically, chronic inflammation is characterized by the presence of lymphocytes, macrophages, plasma cells, and fibroblasts in the affected tissues.
   b. Tissue destruction and repair processes may also be evident, leading to tissue remodeling and fibrosis.

4. **Clinical Manifestations:**
   a. Clinical manifestations of chronic inflammation may include persistent low-grade fever, fatigue, malaise, and other systemic symptoms.

b. Localized signs may include tissue destruction, scarring, and organ dysfunction, depending on the affected tissues and organs.

5. **Consequences:**

a. Chronic inflammation can contribute to the pathogenesis of various diseases, including autoimmune diseases (e.g., rheumatoid arthritis, inflammatory bowel disease), chronic infections (e.g., tuberculosis, hepatitis), and conditions such as atherosclerosis and cancer.

b. Prolonged activation of the immune system in chronic inflammation can lead to tissue damage, impaired organ function, and systemic complications.

Granulomatous Inflammation:

1. **Nature:**

a. Granulomatous inflammation is a specialized form of chronic inflammation characterized by the formation of granulomas, which are organized collections of immune cells.

b. Granulomas are typically composed of macrophages, epithelioid cells (activated macrophages), multinucleated giant cells, lymphocytes, and occasionally fibroblasts.

2. **Cause:**

a. Granulomatous inflammation can result from various stimuli, including persistent infections (e.g., tuberculosis, leprosy), foreign bodies (e.g., silica, sutures), autoimmune diseases (e.g., sarcoidosis), and certain granulomatous vasculitides.

3. **Histological Features:**

a. Histologically, granulomas are characterized by the presence of a central core of immune cells surrounded by a rim of fibroblasts and collagen fibers.

b. Within the granuloma, macrophages fuse to form multinucleated giant cells, which help contain and isolate the inciting agent.

4. **Clinical Manifestations:**

   a. Clinical manifestations of granulomatous inflammation vary depending on the underlying cause and affected organs.

   b. Common features may include the formation of nodules or masses, organ dysfunction, and systemic symptoms such as fever, fatigue, and weight loss.

5. **Consequences:**

   a. Granulomatous inflammation can lead to tissue damage, scarring, and impaired organ function, particularly if the granulomas persist or become extensive.

   b. In some cases, granulomatous inflammation may resolve spontaneously, while in others, it can progress and cause chronic complications.

Allergic Inflammation:

1. **Nature:**

   a. Allergic inflammation, also known as hypersensitivity reaction type I, is an exaggerated immune response to harmless environmental substances known as allergens.

   b. It is characterized by the release of inflammatory mediators such as histamine, leukotrienes, and cytokines in response to allergen exposure.

2. **Cause:**

   a. Allergic inflammation is triggered by exposure to allergens, which can include pollen, dust mites, animal dander, certain foods, and insect venom.

   b. Sensitization to allergens occurs upon initial exposure, leading to the production of allergen-specific IgE antibodies by B cells.

3. **Histological Features:**

a. Histologically, allergic inflammation is characterized by the infiltration of eosinophils, mast cells, and lymphocytes into affected tissues.

b. Mast cells play a central role in allergic inflammation, as they release histamine and other inflammatory mediators in response to allergen binding to IgE antibodies on their surface.

4. Clinical Manifestations:

a. Clinical manifestations of allergic inflammation vary depending on the route of allergen exposure and the affected tissues.

b. Common allergic conditions include allergic rhinitis (hay fever), asthma, atopic dermatitis (eczema), allergic conjunctivitis, and anaphylaxis.

5. Consequences:

a. Allergic inflammation can lead to symptoms such as sneezing, nasal congestion, itching, wheezing, coughing, skin rashes, and in severe cases, life-threatening systemic reactions.

b. Long-term exposure to allergens and chronic allergic inflammation can contribute to tissue damage, remodeling, and the development of chronic inflammatory conditions.

Autoimmune Inflammation:

1. Nature:

a. Autoimmune inflammation occurs when the immune system mistakenly identifies self-antigens as foreign and mounts an immune response against them, leading to tissue damage and inflammation.

b. In autoimmune diseases, immune cells, particularly lymphocytes (such as T cells and B cells), target and attack healthy tissues, resulting in chronic inflammation and tissue destruction.

2. Cause:

a. Autoimmune inflammation arises from dysregulation of the immune system, leading to loss of self-tolerance and the production of autoantibodies against self-antigens.

b. The exact causes of autoimmune diseases are complex and multifactorial, involving genetic predisposition, environmental factors, and dysregulation of immune pathways.

3. **Histological Features:**

a. Histologically, autoimmune inflammation is characterized by infiltration of immune cells, such as lymphocytes, plasma cells, and macrophages, into affected tissues.

b. Depending on the specific autoimmune disease, histological features may include tissue destruction, immune cell infiltration, and formation of autoantibodies and immune complexes.

4. **Clinical Manifestations:**

a. Clinical manifestations of autoimmune inflammation vary widely depending on the affected organs and tissues.

b. Common autoimmune diseases include rheumatoid arthritis, systemic lupus erythematosus (SLE), multiple sclerosis, type 1 diabetes, Hashimoto's thyroiditis, and inflammatory bowel disease (e.g., Crohn's disease, ulcerative colitis).

c. Symptoms may include joint pain and swelling, skin rash, fatigue, fever, neurological symptoms, gastrointestinal disturbances, and endocrine dysfunction.

5. **Consequences:**

a. Autoimmune inflammation can lead to chronic tissue damage, organ dysfunction, and systemic complications if left untreated.

b. Treatment typically involves immunosuppressive medications to modulate the immune response and reduce inflammation, as well as symptomatic management to alleviate symptoms and improve quality of life.

Sterile Inflammation:

1. **Nature:**
   a. Sterile inflammation occurs in the absence of microbial infection and is triggered by endogenous molecules released from damaged or stressed cells, known as damage-associated molecular patterns (DAMPs).
   b. DAMPs activate innate immune responses, leading to inflammation and tissue repair processes similar to those observed in response to infection.

2. **Cause:**
   a. Sterile inflammation can be triggered by various insults, including trauma, ischemia-reperfusion injury, environmental toxins, metabolic stress, and autoimmune reactions.

3. **Histological Features:**
   a. Histologically, sterile inflammation shares many features with inflammation triggered by microbial infection, including infiltration of immune cells, vasodilation, increased vascular permeability, and tissue damage.

4. **Clinical Manifestations:**
   a. Clinical manifestations of sterile inflammation depend on the underlying cause and affected organs or tissues.
   b. Examples of conditions associated with sterile inflammation include myocardial infarction (heart attack), stroke, acute pancreatitis, gout, rheumatoid arthritis, and sterile surgical wounds.

5. **Consequences:**
   a. Sterile inflammation can lead to tissue damage, fibrosis, impaired organ function, and chronic inflammatory diseases if left unchecked.

b. Treatment strategies for sterile inflammation may include anti-inflammatory medications, analgesics, and interventions aimed at addressing the underlying cause of tissue injury or stress.

These are just a few examples of the different types of inflammation that can occur in the body, each with its own unique features, triggers, and consequences. Understanding the specific type of inflammation involved is crucial for accurate diagnosis and targeted therapeutic interventions.

MECHANISM OF INFLAMMATION – ALTERATION IN VASCULAR PERMEABILITY AND BLOOD FLOW

The alteration in vascular permeability and blood flow is a crucial aspect of the mechanism of inflammation. This process involves complex interactions between endothelial cells lining blood vessels, circulating immune cells, and various inflammatory mediators. Here's a detailed explanation of how vascular permeability and blood flow are altered during inflammation:

Vasodilation:

1. **Definition:**
   a. Vasodilation refers to the widening or dilation of blood vessels, particularly arterioles and pre-capillary sphincters, resulting in increased blood flow to the affected area.

2. **Mechanism:**
   a. Inflammation triggers the release of various mediators, including histamine, prostaglandins, bradykinin, and nitric oxide.
   b. Histamine, released from mast cells and basophils, acts on endothelial cells to induce vasodilation by binding to H1 receptors.
   c. Prostaglandins, particularly prostacyclin (PGI2) and prostaglandin E2 (PGE2), are synthesized from arachidonic acid in response to tissue

injury or immune activation. They act on vascular smooth muscle cells to cause relaxation and vasodilation.

d. Bradykinin, generated from plasma proteins (kininogen) by the action of enzymes (e.g., kallikrein), induces vasodilation and increases vascular permeability.

e. Nitric oxide (NO), produced by endothelial cells in response to various stimuli, including inflammatory mediators, diffuses into nearby vascular smooth muscle cells, causing relaxation and vasodilation.

3. **Consequences:**

a. Vasodilation leads to an increase in blood flow to the affected tissues, facilitating the delivery of oxygen, nutrients, and immune cells necessary for tissue repair and defense against pathogens.

b. The dilation of blood vessels also contributes to the clinical signs of inflammation, such as redness (rubor) and warmth (calor), due to the increased blood flow to the affected area.

Increased Vascular Permeability:

1. **Definition:**

a. Increased vascular permeability refers to the loosening or widening of endothelial cell junctions in blood vessels, allowing fluid, proteins, and immune cells to leak out of the bloodstream and into the surrounding tissues.

2. **Mechanism:**

a. Inflammation triggers the release of inflammatory mediators, including histamine, bradykinin, leukotrienes, and certain cytokines (e.g., tumor necrosis factor-alpha, interleukin-1).

b. These mediators act on endothelial cells to disrupt intercellular junctions and increase endothelial cell contractility, leading to the formation of gaps between adjacent endothelial cells.

c. As a result, fluid, plasma proteins (e.g., fibrinogen, albumin), and immune cells (e.g., neutrophils, macrophages) can extravasate from the bloodstream into the surrounding tissues, leading to edema (fluid accumulation) and the formation of inflammatory exudates.

3. Consequences:

a. Increased vascular permeability allows immune cells and plasma proteins to access the site of inflammation, facilitating the removal of pathogens and damaged tissue components.

b. However, excessive or prolonged vascular permeability can contribute to tissue damage, edema formation, and impaired tissue function.

c. The leakage of plasma proteins into the surrounding tissues can also lead to the formation of fibrin-rich exudates, which may contribute to the repair process by providing a scaffold for tissue regeneration.

Chemotaxis:

1. Definition:

a. Chemotaxis is the directed movement of immune cells, particularly leukocytes such as neutrophils, monocytes, and macrophages, towards a chemical gradient of inflammatory mediators, known as chemoattractants, at the site of inflammation.

2. Mechanism:

a. In response to tissue injury or infection, damaged cells, activated immune cells, and resident cells release various chemoattractants, including chemokines, complement components (e.g., C5a), and lipid mediators (e.g., leukotriene B4).

b. These chemoattractants bind to specific receptors on the surface of leukocytes, triggering signaling pathways that induce cytoskeletal rearrangements and the formation of protrusions, facilitating cell movement.

c. Leukocytes migrate along the chemical gradient towards the source of the chemoattractants, guided by directional cues provided by the gradient.

3. Consequences:

a. Chemotaxis plays a crucial role in recruiting immune cells to the site of inflammation, allowing for the timely response to tissue injury or infection.

b. By enhancing the accumulation of leukocytes at the site of inflammation, chemotaxis promotes the removal of pathogens, cellular debris, and foreign substances, facilitating tissue repair and resolution of inflammation.

Adhesion:

1. Definition:

a. Adhesion refers to the process by which circulating leukocytes adhere to the endothelium of blood vessels, enabling their extravasation from the bloodstream into the tissues at the site of inflammation.

2. Mechanism:

a. Adhesion molecules expressed on the surface of both leukocytes and endothelial cells mediate the adhesion process.

b. Leukocyte adhesion molecules, such as selectins, integrins, and immunoglobulin superfamily members (e.g., ICAM-1, VCAM-1), are upregulated in response to inflammatory stimuli.

c. Endothelial cell adhesion molecules, including selectins and cell adhesion molecules, are also upregulated in response to inflammatory mediators.

d. Sequential interactions between these adhesion molecules enable leukocytes to tether, roll, firmly adhere to, and transmigrate across the endothelial barrier.

3. Consequences:

a. Adhesion facilitates the recruitment and extravasation of leukocytes from the bloodstream into the inflamed tissues, a process known as diapedesis or transendothelial migration.

b. Once extravasated, leukocytes can migrate towards the source of chemoattractants, phagocytose pathogens and debris, and contribute to the inflammatory response by releasing cytokines, chemokines, and reactive oxygen species.

Diapedesis (Transendothelial Migration):

1. **Definition:**

   a. Diapedesis, also known as transendothelial migration, is the process by which leukocytes (such as neutrophils, monocytes, and lymphocytes) migrate from the bloodstream across the endothelial barrier and into the surrounding tissues at the site of inflammation.

2. **Mechanism:**

   a. Diapedesis is a multi-step process involving interactions between leukocytes and endothelial cells.

   b. Initial leukocyte tethering and rolling along the endothelial surface are mediated by selectins (e.g., P-selectin, E-selectin) on endothelial cells and their ligands (e.g., sialyl-Lewis X) on leukocytes.

   c. Firm adhesion of leukocytes to endothelial cells is facilitated by integrins (e.g., LFA-1, Mac-1) on leukocytes binding to endothelial cell adhesion molecules (e.g., ICAM-1, VCAM-1).

   d. Following firm adhesion, leukocytes undergo flattening and crawling along the endothelial surface, eventually transmigrating across the endothelial barrier through intercellular junctions or directly through endothelial cells.

   e. Once in the extravascular space, leukocytes continue to migrate towards the source of chemoattractants, guided by chemotactic gradients.

3. **Consequences:**

   a. Diapedesis allows leukocytes to leave the bloodstream and enter the inflamed tissues, where they can perform their immune functions, including phagocytosis of pathogens, release of inflammatory mediators, and interaction with other immune cells.

   b. By infiltrating the site of inflammation, leukocytes contribute to the amplification and regulation of the inflammatory response, promoting tissue repair and resolution of inflammation.

Resolution of Vascular Changes:

1. **Definition:**

   a. The resolution of vascular changes refers to the restoration of vascular homeostasis and the return of blood vessel function to baseline following the resolution of inflammation.

2. **Mechanism:**

   a. Resolution of vascular changes involves the termination of inflammatory signaling and the clearance of inflammatory mediators and cells from the inflamed tissues.

   b. Anti-inflammatory mediators, such as lipoxins, resolvins, and protectins, are produced during the later stages of inflammation and act to dampen the inflammatory response.

   c. Endothelial cells actively participate in the resolution process by downregulating adhesion molecule expression, restoring vascular integrity, and promoting the clearance of leukocytes from the bloodstream.

   d. Macrophages play a central role in resolving inflammation by phagocytosing apoptotic neutrophils and debris, secreting anti-inflammatory cytokines, and promoting tissue repair and regeneration.

3. **Consequences:**

a. Resolution of vascular changes is essential for restoring tissue homeostasis and preventing chronic inflammation and tissue damage.

b. Successful resolution of inflammation allows for the repair and regeneration of injured tissues, restoring normal tissue function and preventing long-term complications.

Alterations in vascular permeability and blood flow are critical for the initiation, progression, and resolution of inflammation. Dysregulation of these processes can contribute to the pathogenesis of inflammatory diseases and may impair tissue healing and repair. Understanding the mechanisms underlying vascular changes during inflammation is essential for developing therapeutic strategies to modulate the inflammatory response and treat inflammatory conditions.

MIGRATION OF WBC'S

The migration of white blood cells (WBCs), particularly neutrophils and macrophages, is a fundamental aspect of the inflammatory response. This process, known as leukocyte extravasation or diapedesis, allows immune cells to leave the bloodstream and migrate to the site of inflammation to combat pathogens, clear debris, and promote tissue repair. Here's a detailed explanation of the migration of WBCs in the process of inflammation and repair:

Chemotaxis:

1. **Definition:**

    a. Chemotaxis is the directed movement of white blood cells (WBCs), particularly neutrophils, monocytes, and lymphocytes, in response to chemical gradients of chemoattractants at the site of inflammation or infection.

2. **Mechanism:**

    a. Chemotaxis is initiated by the release of chemoattractants, such as chemokines, complement components (e.g., C5a), and lipid mediators (e.g., leukotriene B4), from damaged tissues, activated immune cells, or invading pathogens.

b. Chemoattractants bind to specific receptors, known as chemokine receptors, expressed on the surface of WBCs, triggering intracellular signaling pathways that induce cytoskeletal rearrangements and cell polarization.

c. This results in the formation of protrusions, such as pseudopodia, at the leading edge of the cell, which extend in the direction of the chemoattractant gradient.

d. WBCs then migrate towards higher concentrations of chemoattractants, guided by the chemical gradient, until they reach the source of the inflammatory stimulus.

3. **Consequences:**

a. Chemotaxis plays a crucial role in recruiting WBCs to the site of inflammation or infection, facilitating their timely response to tissue injury or invading pathogens.

b. By enhancing the accumulation of WBCs at the site of inflammation, chemotaxis promotes the removal of pathogens, cellular debris, and foreign substances, contributing to tissue repair and resolution of inflammation.

Rolling Adhesion:

1. **Definition:**

a. Rolling adhesion, also known as tethering and rolling, is the initial interaction between circulating WBCs and the endothelium of blood vessels, allowing WBCs to decelerate and roll along the vessel wall.

2. **Mechanism:**

a. Rolling adhesion is mediated by interactions between selectins and their ligands expressed on the surface of WBCs and endothelial cells, respectively.

b. Endothelial selectins (P-selectin and E-selectin) are rapidly upregulated in response to inflammatory stimuli, such as cytokines (e.g., TNF-alpha, IL-1) or histamine, on the endothelial cell surface.

c. WBCs express selectin ligands, such as sialyl-Lewis X and PSGL-1 (P-selectin glycoprotein ligand-1), which bind to endothelial selectins with low affinity, allowing for transient interactions.

d. These selectin-mediated interactions result in the tethering and rolling of WBCs along the endothelial surface, facilitating their capture and subsequent firm adhesion.

3. Consequences:

a. Rolling adhesion enables circulating WBCs to interact with the endothelium and survey the vessel wall for sites of inflammation or injury.

b. This initial interaction slows down the movement of WBCs within the bloodstream, allowing sufficient time for subsequent interactions with adhesion molecules and eventual transmigration into the extravascular space.

Tight Adhesion:

1. Definition:

a. Tight adhesion, also known as firm adhesion, refers to the process by which circulating white blood cells (WBCs) firmly attach to the endothelium of blood vessels, enabling their subsequent transmigration into the surrounding tissues.

2. Mechanism:

a. Following initial rolling adhesion along the vessel wall, WBCs undergo activation in response to chemotactic signals and inflammatory mediators.

b. This activation leads to the upregulation of integrins, particularly members of the β2 integrin family (e.g., LFA-1, Mac-1), on the surface of WBCs.

c. Endothelial cells, in response to inflammatory stimuli, upregulate adhesion molecules such as ICAM-1 (intercellular adhesion molecule-1) and VCAM-1 (vascular cell adhesion molecule-1).

d. Activated integrins on WBCs bind with high affinity to their endothelial ligands, forming strong adhesive interactions.

e. This firm adhesion allows WBCs to resist the shear forces exerted by blood flow and become firmly attached to the endothelial surface, ready for transmigration.

3. **Consequences:**

a. Tight adhesion enables WBCs to anchor themselves to the endothelium, preparing them for the next step in the extravasation process.

b. Firm adhesion facilitates the localization of WBCs to sites of inflammation or tissue injury, ensuring their effective recruitment to the site of infection or damage.

Transmigration (Diapedesis):

1. **Definition:**

a. Transmigration, also known as diapedesis, is the process by which WBCs migrate across the endothelial barrier and into the surrounding tissues at the site of inflammation or infection.

2. **Mechanism:**

a. Transmigration involves several steps, including the recognition and binding of endothelial junctional proteins by WBCs, cytoskeletal rearrangements, and passage through the endothelial barrier.

b. WBCs interact with endothelial junctional proteins, such as PECAM-1 (platelet endothelial cell adhesion molecule-1) and CD99, which act as transmigratory receptors.

c. These interactions trigger signaling pathways within both WBCs and endothelial cells, leading to the reorganization of the actin cytoskeleton and the formation of transmigratory structures, such as pseudopodia and invadopodia.

d. WBCs then migrate between adjacent endothelial cells, either through paracellular routes (between cell junctions) or transcellular routes (directly through endothelial cells), guided by chemotactic gradients and adhesive interactions.

e. Once in the extravascular space, WBCs continue to migrate towards the source of chemoattractants, guided by chemotactic gradients.

3. Consequences:

a. Transmigration allows WBCs to exit the bloodstream and infiltrate the inflamed tissues, where they can perform their immune functions, including phagocytosis of pathogens, release of inflammatory mediators, and interaction with other immune cells.

b. By infiltrating the site of inflammation, WBCs contribute to the amplification and regulation of the inflammatory response, promoting tissue repair and resolution of inflammation.

Migration Within Tissue:

1. Definition:

a. Migration within tissues refers to the movement of white blood cells (WBCs), such as neutrophils, monocytes, and lymphocytes, within the extravascular space towards specific sites of inflammation or infection within tissues.

2. Mechanism:

a. Once WBCs have extravasated from the bloodstream and entered the tissues, they migrate towards the source of chemotactic signals or inflammatory mediators.

b. Migration within tissues involves interactions between WBCs and extracellular matrix components, as well as cell-cell interactions with other immune cells, stromal cells, and resident tissue cells.

c. WBCs utilize various mechanisms to navigate through the tissue microenvironment, including amoeboid movement, chemotaxis towards chemoattractant gradients, and haptotaxis along gradients of extracellular matrix proteins.

d. Chemokines, growth factors, and other signaling molecules guide WBCs towards specific tissue compartments or cellular targets within the inflamed tissues.

e. Directed migration within tissues allows WBCs to localize to areas of infection or tissue damage, where they can perform their effector functions.

3. Consequences:

a. Migration within tissues enables WBCs to survey the local microenvironment and interact with other immune cells, stromal cells, and tissue-resident cells.

b. WBCs can migrate towards areas of infection or tissue injury, where they can recognize and eliminate pathogens, clear cellular debris, and contribute to tissue repair and remodeling.

c. Directed migration within tissues ensures the effective recruitment and localization of WBCs to sites of inflammation or infection, optimizing the immune response and tissue repair processes.

Effector Functions:

1. Definition:

a. Effector functions of WBCs refer to the diverse range of immune responses and cellular activities performed by white blood cells to eliminate pathogens, clear cellular debris, and modulate the inflammatory response.

2. **Mechanism:**
   a. WBCs possess various effector mechanisms to combat pathogens and promote tissue repair, including phagocytosis, secretion of antimicrobial proteins and cytokines, cytotoxicity, and modulation of immune responses.
   b. Neutrophils are highly phagocytic cells capable of engulfing and destroying pathogens through the release of antimicrobial proteins, reactive oxygen species (ROS), and neutrophil extracellular traps (NETs).
   c. Monocytes differentiate into macrophages upon entering tissues, where they engulf pathogens and cellular debris through phagocytosis and secrete cytokines and growth factors to regulate inflammation and tissue repair.
   d. Lymphocytes, including T cells and B cells, play key roles in adaptive immunity, recognizing and responding to specific antigens, producing antibodies, and orchestrating immune responses to pathogens.
   e. Effector functions of WBCs also include the secretion of cytokines, chemokines, and other signaling molecules to modulate the activity of other immune cells and coordinate the immune response.

3. **Consequences:**
   a. Effector functions of WBCs contribute to the clearance of pathogens, resolution of inflammation, and promotion of tissue repair and regeneration.

b. By performing their effector functions, WBCs help to eliminate infectious agents, limit tissue damage, and restore tissue homeostasis following inflammation or injury.

c. Dysregulation of WBC effector functions can lead to chronic inflammation, tissue damage, and autoimmune diseases, highlighting the importance of proper immune regulation and function.

The migration of WBCs is a highly regulated and coordinated process essential for the initiation and resolution of inflammation. Dysregulation of leukocyte migration can contribute to the pathogenesis of inflammatory diseases and impair tissue healing. Therefore, understanding the mechanisms underlying WBC migration is crucial for the development of therapeutic strategies to modulate the inflammatory response and treat inflammatory conditions.

MEDIATORS OF INFLAMMATION

Inflammation involves a complex interplay of various mediators that orchestrate the immune response and tissue repair processes. These mediators include cytokines, chemokines, lipid mediators, complement proteins, and other signaling molecules. Here's an overview of the key mediators of inflammation:

Cytokines:

1. **Definition:**

   a. Cytokines are a diverse group of small proteins secreted by immune cells, stromal cells, and tissue-resident cells that regulate immune responses and mediate communication between cells.

2. **Types and Functions:**

   a. **Pro-inflammatory Cytokines**: Promote inflammation and immune activation. Examples include interleukin-1 (IL-1), interleukin-6 (IL-6), tumor necrosis factor-alpha (TNF-alpha), and interferons (IFNs). They stimulate the recruitment and activation of immune cells, induce the expression of adhesion molecules, and enhance the production of acute-phase proteins.

b. **Anti-inflammatory Cytokines**: Inhibit inflammation and promote resolution of the immune response. Examples include interleukin-10 (IL-10) and transforming growth factor-beta (TGF-beta). They suppress pro-inflammatory cytokine production, modulate immune cell function, and promote tissue repair and regeneration.

c. **Chemotactic Cytokines (Chemokines)**: Induce chemotaxis and guide the migration of immune cells to sites of inflammation. Chemokines are classified into subfamilies based on the arrangement of conserved cysteine residues (e.g., CXC, CC, CX3C). They regulate leukocyte trafficking, activation, and effector functions.

d. **Hematopoietic Growth Factors**: Stimulate the proliferation, differentiation, and maturation of hematopoietic cells. Examples include granulocyte-macrophage colony-stimulating factor (GM-CSF), granulocyte colony-stimulating factor (G-CSF), and erythropoietin (EPO). They promote the production and mobilization of immune cells from the bone marrow into the bloodstream.

3. **Functions in Inflammation:**
   a. Cytokines play critical roles in initiating, amplifying, and regulating inflammatory responses.
   b. Pro-inflammatory cytokines promote vasodilation, increased vascular permeability, leukocyte recruitment, and activation of immune cells at the site of inflammation.
   c. Anti-inflammatory cytokines counterbalance pro-inflammatory responses, dampening immune activation, and promoting resolution of inflammation.

d. Dysregulation of cytokine production or signaling pathways can lead to chronic inflammation, autoimmune diseases, or immune deficiency disorders.

Chemokines:

1. Definition:

a. Chemokines are a subgroup of cytokines that specifically regulate the migration and positioning of immune cells in response to inflammation or injury.

2. Types and Functions:

a. **Chemotactic Chemokines**: Induce directional migration (chemotaxis) of immune cells towards sites of inflammation. Examples include interleukin-8 (IL-8/CXCL8), monocyte chemoattractant protein-1 (MCP-1/CCL2), and macrophage inflammatory protein-1 alpha (MIP-1 alpha/CCL3).

b. **Homeostatic Chemokines**: Maintain basal leukocyte trafficking and positioning in non-inflamed tissues. They regulate immune surveillance and tissue homeostasis. Examples include CCL19 (MIP-3 beta) and CCL21 (SLC).

c. **Inflammatory Chemokines**: Induce the recruitment and activation of immune cells during inflammation. They are rapidly produced in response to inflammatory stimuli and contribute to the amplification and resolution of the inflammatory response.

3. Functions in Inflammation:

a. Chemokines guide the migration of leukocytes from the bloodstream into inflamed tissues through interactions with specific chemokine receptors expressed on the surface of immune cells.

b. They promote the sequential recruitment of leukocytes to sites of inflammation, coordinating the infiltration of neutrophils, monocytes, macrophages, and lymphocytes.

c. Chemokines regulate leukocyte adhesion, transendothelial migration, and tissue homing, contributing to the spatial organization and dynamics of the immune response.

d. Dysregulation of chemokine signaling can lead to aberrant leukocyte trafficking, chronic inflammation, and inflammatory diseases.

Lipid Mediators:

1. **Definition:**

   a. Lipid mediators are bioactive lipid molecules synthesized from membrane phospholipids in response to inflammatory stimuli. They include prostaglandins, leukotrienes, lipoxins, and platelet-activating factor (PAF).

2. **Types and Functions:**

   a. **Prostaglandins:** Produced from arachidonic acid by cyclooxygenase enzymes (COX-1 and COX-2). Prostaglandins, such as prostaglandin E2 (PGE2) and prostacyclin (PGI2), promote vasodilation, increased vascular permeability, and pain sensation. They also modulate immune cell activation, cytokine production, and fever response.

   b. **Leukotrienes**: Synthesized from arachidonic acid by 5-lipoxygenase (5-LOX). Leukotrienes, such as leukotriene B4 (LTB4) and leukotriene C4 (LTC4), induce chemotaxis, activation, and adhesion of leukocytes, particularly neutrophils and eosinophils, to sites of inflammation. They also promote bronchoconstriction and mucus secretion in the respiratory tract.

   c. **Lipoxins:** Derived from arachidonic acid by lipoxygenase enzymes. Lipoxins, such as lipoxin A4 (LXA4), have anti-inflammatory properties and promote the resolution of inflammation by inhibiting leukocyte recruitment, promoting phagocytosis of apoptotic cells, and suppressing pro-inflammatory cytokine production.

d. **Platelet-Activating Factor (PAF):** Produced by various cell types, including leukocytes, platelets, and endothelial cells. PAF induces platelet aggregation, leukocyte activation, and vascular permeability. It also stimulates the release of inflammatory mediators and promotes the adhesion of leukocytes to endothelial cells.

3. **Functions in Inflammation:**

   a. Lipid mediators regulate various aspects of the inflammatory response, including vascular changes, leukocyte recruitment, and immune cell activation.

   b. Prostaglandins and leukotrienes mediate vascular responses, such as vasodilation, increased vascular permeability, and leukocyte adhesion, contributing to the initiation and amplification of inflammation.

   c. Lipoxins and other specialized pro-resolving mediators (SPMs) promote the resolution of inflammation by counteracting pro-inflammatory signals, inhibiting leukocyte infiltration, and enhancing the clearance of apoptotic cells and debris.

   d. Dysregulation of lipid mediator pathways can contribute to chronic inflammation, autoimmune diseases, and inflammatory disorders, highlighting the importance of maintaining a balanced lipid mediator profile in the immune response.

Complement Proteins:

1. **Definition:**

   a. The complement system is a group of plasma proteins and membrane-bound receptors that play essential roles in innate and adaptive immunity. Complement proteins are involved in opsonization, inflammation, immune cell activation, and clearance of pathogens and immune complexes.

2. **Types and Functions:**

a. **Activation Pathways:** The complement system can be activated through three main pathways: the classical pathway (initiated by antibody-antigen complexes), the lectin pathway (initiated by recognition of carbohydrate patterns on pathogens), and the alternative pathway (initiated by spontaneous hydrolysis of C3).

b. **Complement Proteins**: Key complement proteins include C1q, C3, C4, C5, C6, C7, C8, and C9. These proteins undergo proteolytic cleavage to generate biologically active fragments, including C3a, C5a, and C5b-9 (membrane attack complex, MAC).

c. **Functions:** Complement proteins have diverse functions in inflammation, including opsonization of pathogens for phagocytosis (C3b), recruitment and activation of immune cells (C3a, C5a), induction of pro-inflammatory cytokine production (C5a), and direct lysis of pathogens through the formation of the MAC.

d. **Regulation:** The complement system is tightly regulated by various inhibitors, including soluble regulators (e.g., factor H, factor I) and membrane-bound regulators (e.g., CD55, CD59), to prevent excessive complement activation and tissue damage.

3. **Functions in Inflammation:**

   a. Complement proteins play essential roles in initiating and amplifying inflammatory responses, promoting the recruitment and activation of immune cells, and enhancing pathogen clearance.

   b. Activation products such as C3a and C5a act as potent chemoattractants, recruiting neutrophils, monocytes, and other immune cells to sites of inflammation.

   c. Complement activation facilitates opsonization of pathogens, enhancing their recognition and phagocytosis by immune cells.

   d. Excessive or dysregulated complement activation can contribute to tissue damage, autoimmune diseases, and inflammatory disorders, underscoring the importance of tight regulation of the complement system.

Histamine:

1. Source and Release:

    a. Histamine is a biogenic amine produced primarily by mast cells, basophils, and platelets. It is stored in cytoplasmic granules and released in response to various stimuli, including allergens, physical injury, and immune activation.

2. Functions:

    a. **Vasodilation:** Histamine induces vasodilation by acting on endothelial cells and smooth muscle cells in blood vessels. This leads to increased blood flow to the site of inflammation, resulting in erythema (redness) and warmth.

    b. **Increased Vascular Permeability**: Histamine increases vascular permeability by disrupting endothelial cell junctions, allowing plasma proteins and immune cells to extravasate from the bloodstream into the surrounding tissues. This results in edema (swelling) and facilitates the recruitment of immune cells to the site of inflammation.

    c. **Smooth Muscle Contraction:** Histamine acts on smooth muscle cells in the bronchi, gastrointestinal tract, and blood vessels, leading to bronchoconstriction, increased intestinal peristalsis, and contraction of small blood vessels (arterioles and venules).

    d. **Pruritus and Pain Sensation**: Histamine can stimulate sensory nerve endings, leading to itching (pruritus) and pain sensation.

3. Receptors:

    a. Histamine exerts its effects through four G-protein coupled receptors: H1, H2, H3, and H4.

    b. H1 receptors mediate vasodilation, increased vascular permeability, smooth muscle contraction, and pruritus.

c. H2 receptors are primarily found in gastric parietal cells and mediate gastric acid secretion.

d. H3 receptors are mainly found in the central nervous system and regulate neurotransmitter release.

e. H4 receptors are expressed on immune cells and play a role in chemotaxis and immune cell activation.

Bradykinin:

1. **Source and Formation:**

   a. Bradykinin is a peptide mediator generated from kininogen through the action of enzymes, primarily kallikreins, during inflammation, tissue injury, or plasma contact with foreign surfaces.

2. **Functions:**

   a. **Vasodilation**: Bradykinin induces potent vasodilation by acting on endothelial cells, leading to relaxation of vascular smooth muscle cells. This results in increased blood flow to the site of inflammation and contributes to erythema and warmth.

   b. **Increased Vascular Permeability**: Bradykinin increases vascular permeability by promoting the contraction of endothelial cells and opening intercellular junctions. This allows plasma proteins and immune cells to extravasate into the surrounding tissues, causing edema and facilitating the recruitment of immune cells.

   c. **Pain Sensation**: Bradykinin stimulates sensory nerve endings, leading to the sensation of pain (hyperalgesia) and increased sensitivity to pain (allodynia).

   d. **Inflammatory Response**: Bradykinin can stimulate the production and release of pro-inflammatory cytokines, chemokines, and other mediators, amplifying the inflammatory response.

3. **Receptors:**

a. Bradykinin exerts its effects through two G-protein coupled receptors: B1 and B2.

b. B2 receptors are constitutively expressed and mediate the vasodilatory, permeability-increasing, and pro-inflammatory effects of bradykinin.

c. B1 receptors are inducible and upregulated during inflammation. They contribute to the sustained inflammatory response and pain sensation.

These mediators interact in a highly coordinated manner to regulate the initiation, progression, and resolution of inflammation. Dysregulation of inflammatory mediators can lead to chronic inflammation and contribute to the pathogenesis of various inflammatory diseases. Therefore, targeting specific mediators of inflammation is a common therapeutic approach for treating inflammatory conditions.

BASIC PRINCIPLES OF WOUND HEALING IN THE SKIN

Wound healing in the skin is a complex and highly coordinated process involving several overlapping phases. These phases include inflammation, proliferation, and tissue remodeling. Here's a detailed overview of the basic principles of wound healing in the skin:

Inflammation Phase:

1. The process of wound healing begins immediately following injury with the inflammatory phase, which serves to control bleeding, remove debris, and prevent infection. Key events during this phase include:

   a. **Vasoconstriction**: Initially, blood vessels constrict to reduce blood loss.

   b. **Vasodilation and Increased Vascular Permeability**: Following vasoconstriction, blood vessels dilate, allowing increased blood flow to the wound site. This is accompanied by increased vascular permeability, allowing immune cells and plasma proteins to extravasate into the tissue.

   c. **Migration of Immune Cells**: Neutrophils are the first immune cells to migrate to the wound site, followed by macrophages. These cells phagocytose debris, dead cells, and pathogens, promoting tissue cleaning and preparing the wound bed for repair.

Proliferation Phase:

1. The proliferation phase is characterized by the formation of new tissue and the restoration of tissue integrity. Key events during this phase include:

   a. **Angiogenesis:** New blood vessels form from existing ones to supply oxygen and nutrients to the wound bed.

   b. **Fibroplasia**: Fibroblasts migrate to the wound site and proliferate, synthesizing collagen, proteoglycans, and other extracellular matrix components. This forms a provisional matrix that provides structural support and guides tissue repair.

   c. **Epithelialization**: Epithelial cells at the wound edges proliferate and migrate across the wound bed to form a new epithelial layer, sealing the wound.

Tissue Remodeling Phase:

1. The tissue remodeling phase involves the maturation and remodeling of the newly formed tissue. Key events during this phase include:

   a. **Collagen Remodeling**: The provisional matrix laid down during the proliferation phase is gradually replaced by mature collagen fibers through the action of matrix metalloproteinases (MMPs) and tissue inhibitors of metalloproteinases (TIMPs). This process strengthens and remodels the tissue, improving its tensile strength and flexibility.

   b. **Scar Formation**: While scar tissue lacks the specialized structure and function of the original tissue, it provides structural support and helps restore tissue integrity. Scar formation involves the deposition and organization of collagen fibers, which may lead to scar contracture and remodeling over time.

c. **Wound Contraction**: Myofibroblasts, specialized contractile cells derived from fibroblasts, exert mechanical forces that cause the wound edges to contract, reducing the wound size.

These basic principles of wound healing in the skin highlight the coordinated sequence of events involved in restoring tissue integrity following injury. Dysregulation of any phase of the wound healing process can lead to delayed healing, chronic wounds, or excessive scarring. Therefore, understanding the mechanisms underlying wound healing is essential for the development of effective therapeutic strategies to promote tissue repair and regeneration.

PATHOPHYSIOLOGY OF ATHEROSCLEROSIS

Atherosclerosis is a chronic inflammatory disease characterized by the buildup of plaques within the walls of arteries, leading to narrowing and obstruction of blood flow. The pathophysiology of atherosclerosis involves a complex interplay of various cellular and molecular mechanisms, including inflammation, lipid metabolism, endothelial dysfunction, and smooth muscle cell proliferation. Here's a detailed overview of the basic mechanisms involved:

Endothelial Dysfunction:

a. Atherosclerosis typically begins with damage or dysfunction of the endothelial cells lining the arterial walls. Various risk factors such as hypertension, hyperlipidemia, smoking, and diabetes can impair endothelial function. Endothelial dysfunction leads to increased expression of adhesion molecules (e.g., VCAM-1, ICAM-1), decreased production of vasodilators (e.g., nitric oxide), and enhanced permeability, promoting the recruitment of circulating immune cells and the retention of lipoproteins within the arterial wall.

Formation of Fatty Streaks:

Endothelial dysfunction allows low-density lipoprotein (LDL) particles to penetrate the arterial intima and become oxidized. Oxidized LDL (oxLDL) is recognized by scavenger receptors on macrophages, leading to their activation and the formation of foam cells. Foam cells, along with infiltrating T lymphocytes, contribute to the development of early lesions called fatty streaks, which are the hallmark of early atherosclerosis.

Inflammatory Response:

The accumulation of foam cells, T lymphocytes, and other immune cells within the arterial wall triggers an inflammatory response. Various pro-inflammatory cytokines, such as TNF-α, IL-1β, and IL-6, are released, perpetuating inflammation and promoting further recruitment of immune cells. Inflammatory mediators also stimulate the proliferation and migration of vascular smooth muscle cells from the media to the intima.

Formation of Atherosclerotic Plaques:

Over time, the inflammatory process leads to the formation of atherosclerotic plaques, consisting of a lipid-rich necrotic core surrounded by a fibrous cap composed of smooth muscle cells, collagen, and extracellular matrix. The plaques may undergo calcification, contributing to their stability or increasing their vulnerability to rupture.

Plaque Rupture and Thrombosis:

Atherosclerotic plaques can undergo structural changes, leading to plaque rupture or erosion. Plaque rupture exposes the highly thrombogenic lipid core to the bloodstream, triggering platelet activation and thrombus formation. Thrombus formation may partially or completely occlude the arterial lumen, leading to acute ischemic events such as myocardial infarction or stroke.

Fibrous Cap Degradation and Vulnerability:

Advanced plaques may exhibit features of vulnerability, including thinning or rupture of the fibrous cap, increased inflammation, and intraplaque hemorrhage. Matrix metalloproteinases (MMPs) secreted by activated macrophages and smooth muscle cells degrade the fibrous cap, increasing the risk of plaque rupture and thrombosis.

The pathophysiology of atherosclerosis involves a complex interplay of inflammatory, lipid metabolism, and vascular remodeling processes. Targeting key mechanisms involved in atherosclerosis, such as inflammation and lipid accumulation, is the basis for therapeutic strategies aimed at preventing or treating this disease.

Multiple-Choice Questions

1. What initiates the inflammatory response according to the text?
   A) Neurological signals
   B) Immune cell recognition of pathogens
   C) Recognition of tissue damage or pathogens by the immune system
   D) Blood vessel contraction

2. Which cells are the first to migrate to the site of inflammation?
   A) Lymphocytes
   B) Macrophages
   C) Neutrophils
   D) Eosinophils

3. What is the role of fibroblasts during the tissue repair process?
   A) Release histamine
   B) Phagocytose pathogens
   C) Synthesize extracellular matrix components
   D) Trigger inflammation

4. Which mediator is responsible for pain sensation during inflammation?
   A) Prostaglandins
   B) Bradykinin
   C) Leukotrienes
   D) Lipoxins

5. What leads to the redness (rubor) during inflammation?

A) Decreased blood flow

B) Neutrophil activity

C) Vasodilation

D) Lymphocyte activation

6. Which phase involves angiogenesis during wound healing?

A) Inflammatory phase

B) Proliferation phase

C) Remodeling phase

D) Maturation phase

7. What triggers acute inflammation?

A) Chronic irritation

B) Persistent infections

C) Tissue necrosis or pathogens

D) Autoimmune reactions

8. What characterizes chronic inflammation histologically?

A) Presence of neutrophils

B) Presence of lymphocytes and macrophages

C) Quick resolution

D) Short duration

9. Which type of inflammation involves the formation of granulomas?

A) Acute

B) Chronic

C) Granulomatous

D) Allergic

10. What is the main trigger for allergic inflammation?

A) Bacterial infections

B) Allergens

C) Autoantibodies

D) Viruses

11. What defines vasodilation during inflammation?

A) Narrowing of blood vessels

B) Widening of blood vessels

C) Leakage of blood cells

D) Decrease in blood flow

12. What is a consequence of increased vascular permeability during inflammation?

A) Blood vessel constriction

B) Reduced blood flow

C) Fluid accumulation in tissue

D) Decreased leukocyte activity

13. What does chemotaxis involve during the inflammation process?

A) Movement of immune cells towards a chemical gradient

B) Adhesion of immune cells to vessel walls

C) Blood cells becoming less permeable

D) Decrease in immune cell function

14. What are lipoxins involved in?

A) Promoting inflammation

B) Resolving inflammation

C) Initiating immune response

D) Destroying pathogens

15. What type of inflammation is characterized by autoimmunity?

A) Acute

B) Chronic

C) Autoimmune

D) Sterile

16. Which cells play a central role in the resolution phase of inflammation?

A) Neutrophils

B) Eosinophils

C) Macrophages

D) Platelets

17. What role does bradykinin play in inflammation?

A) Promotes blood clotting

B) Decreases vascular permeability

C) Induces pain and increases vascular permeability

D) Reduces immune cell migration

18. What is a characteristic feature of granulomatous inflammation?

A) Rapid resolution

B) Formation of granulomas

C) Absence of immune cells

D) Limited to dermal layers

19. What is the primary function of cytokines in inflammation?

A) Inhibit all immune responses

B) Transport oxygen to tissues

C) Regulate immune responses and mediate intercellular communication

D) Directly destroy pathogens

20. What triggers the formation of atherosclerotic plaques?

A) High levels of high-density lipoprotein

B) Endothelial dysfunction and lipid accumulation

C) Excessive calcium intake

D) High antioxidant levels

Short Answer Type Questions

1. What triggers the initial recognition of tissue damage or infection in inflammation?

2. Name two primary immune cells involved in the migration to the site of inflammation.

3. What role do prostaglandins play in the inflammatory process?

4. Describe the function of neutrophils during the inflammation process.

5. How do cytokines influence the inflammation process?

6. What are lipoxins and what role do they play in inflammation?

7. What are the classic signs of inflammation observed in clinical settings?

8. Explain how vasodilation contributes to the signs of inflammation.

9. What histological features characterize acute inflammation?

10. Differentiate between acute and chronic inflammation.

11. What is the main cause of granulomatous inflammation?

12. Describe how allergic inflammation is triggered.

13. What mechanisms lead to the formation of atherosclerotic plaques?

14. How do endothelial cells contribute to atherosclerosis?

15. What is the role of matrix metalloproteinases in atherosclerosis?

16. Describe the role of fibroblasts in the proliferation phase of wound healing.

17. What is the significance of chemotaxis in the inflammatory response?

18. How do leukocytes adhere to endothelial cells during inflammation?

19. Explain the process and significance of diapedesis in inflammation.

20. What are the consequences of dysregulated complement activation?

Long Answer Type Questions

1. Discuss the role of cytokines and chemokines in the regulation and progression of the inflammatory response, highlighting their functions and types.

2. Explain the vascular changes that occur during inflammation, focusing on the roles of histamine, prostaglandins, and nitric oxide in vasodilation and increased vascular permeability.

3. Describe the sequence of cellular events from the recognition of pathogens to the resolution of inflammation, emphasizing the roles of specific immune cells and mediators.

4. Discuss the pathophysiological mechanisms underlying chronic inflammation and how it differs from acute inflammation in terms of cellular involvement and clinical manifestations.

5. Explain the formation and consequences of granulomatous inflammation, including the types of diseases associated with this form of inflammation.

6. Detail the allergic response from the initial exposure to allergens to the development of symptoms, emphasizing the role of mast cells and IgE.

7. Outline the steps involved in wound healing in the skin, from the inflammatory phase to the remodeling phase, and discuss the roles of various cells and mediators in these processes.

8. Describe the pathophysiology of atherosclerosis from endothelial dysfunction to plaque rupture, focusing on the role of immune cells and inflammatory mediators.

9. Discuss the role of leukocyte extravasation in the inflammatory response, including the mechanisms of rolling adhesion, tight adhesion, and transmigration.

10. Analyze the role of lipid mediators in inflammation, detailing the functions of prostaglandins, leukotrienes, and specialized pro-resolving mediators in the regulation and resolution of inflammation.

Answer Key

1. C) Recognition of tissue damage or pathogens by the immune system
2. C) Neutrophils
3. C) Synthesize extracellular matrix components
4. B) Bradykinin
5. C) Vasodilation
6. B) Proliferation phase
7. C) Tissue necrosis or pathogens
8. B) Presence of lymphocytes and macrophages

9. C) Granulomatous

10.B) Allergens

11.B) Widening of blood vessels

12.C) Fluid accumulation in tissue

13.A) Movement of immune cells towards a chemical gradient

14.B) Resolving inflammation

15.C) Autoimmune

16.C) Macrophages

17.C) Induces pain and increases vascular permeability

18.B) Formation of granulomas

19.C) Regulate immune responses and mediate intercellular communication

20.B) Endothelial dysfunction and lipid accumulation

CHAPTER - 3

CARDIOVASCULAR AND RESPIRATORY SYSTEM

CARDIOVASCULAR SYSTEM

The cardiovascular system, also known as the circulatory system, is a complex network of organs and vessels responsible for transporting blood, oxygen, nutrients, hormones, and waste products throughout the body. It plays a vital role in maintaining homeostasis, which is the body's equilibrium or stable internal environment. Here's a detailed introduction to the cardiovascular system:

1. **Heart**: The heart is the central organ of the cardiovascular system. It's a muscular pump that contracts and relaxes rhythmically to propel blood throughout the body. The human heart consists of four chambers: two atria (upper chambers) and two ventricles (lower chambers). The right side of the heart receives deoxygenated blood from the body and pumps it to the lungs for oxygenation, while the left side receives oxygenated blood from the lungs and pumps it to the rest of the body.

2. **Blood Vessels**: Blood vessels are the conduits through which blood travels. There are three main types of blood vessels:

   a. **Arteries**: Arteries carry oxygen-rich blood away from the heart to the body's tissues and organs. The largest artery in the body is the aorta, which originates from the left ventricle of the heart.

   b. **Veins**: Veins carry oxygen-depleted blood back to the heart from the body's tissues and organs. The largest vein in the body is the vena cava, which returns blood to the right atrium of the heart.

   c. **Capillaries**: Capillaries are tiny, thin-walled vessels that connect arteries and veins. They facilitate the exchange of oxygen, nutrients, and waste products between the blood and the body's cells.

3. **Blood**: Blood is a specialized connective tissue consisting of cells suspended in a liquid matrix called plasma. The main components of blood include red blood cells (erythrocytes), white blood cells (leukocytes), and platelets (thrombocytes). Red blood cells carry oxygen from the lungs to the body's tissues, while white blood cells are involved in immune responses, and platelets play a crucial role in blood clotting.

4. **Circulation:** There are two main circulation pathways in the cardiovascular system:

    a. **Pulmonary Circulation**: This pathway transports deoxygenated blood from the heart to the lungs for oxygenation and returns oxygenated blood to the heart. It involves the right side of the heart and the pulmonary arteries and veins.

    b. **Systemic Circulation**: This pathway delivers oxygenated blood from the heart to the body's tissues and organs and returns deoxygenated blood to the heart. It involves the left side of the heart, arteries that branch out to various body parts, and veins that return blood to the heart.

5. **Regulation:** The cardiovascular system is regulated by various mechanisms to maintain blood pressure, heart rate, and blood flow to meet the body's demands. Regulation occurs through the autonomic nervous system, hormonal control (e.g., adrenaline and noradrenaline), and local mechanisms such as the release of vasodilators and vasoconstrictors.

6. **Diseases and Disorders**: The cardiovascular system is susceptible to various diseases and disorders, including hypertension (high blood pressure), coronary artery disease, heart failure, stroke, and arrhythmias (irregular heart rhythms). Lifestyle factors such as diet, exercise, smoking, and stress can significantly impact cardiovascular health.

Cardiovascular diseases (CVDs) encompass a range of conditions that affect the heart and blood vessels. They are generally classified into several main categories:

1. Coronary Artery Disease (CAD): This occurs when the blood vessels that supply blood to the heart become narrowed or blocked due to a buildup of cholesterol and other substances (atherosclerosis). It can lead to angina (chest pain) or heart attacks.

2. Hypertensive Heart Disease: High blood pressure (hypertension) can cause the heart to work harder to pump blood, leading to conditions such as hypertrophy (thickening) of the heart muscle, heart failure, or coronary artery disease.

3. Cardiomyopathy: This refers to diseases of the heart muscle, where the heart becomes enlarged, thickened, or stiff, affecting its ability to pump blood effectively.

4. Arrhythmias: These are irregular heartbeats, which can range from harmless to life-threatening. They include conditions such as atrial fibrillation, ventricular tachycardia, and bradycardia.

5. Valvular Heart Disease: This involves problems with the heart valves, which control the flow of blood through the heart. Conditions include valve stenosis (narrowing) or regurgitation (leakage).

6. Peripheral Artery Disease (PAD): This occurs when the blood vessels outside of the heart (usually those supplying the limbs) become narrowed or blocked, leading to reduced blood flow and potentially causing pain, numbness, or tissue damage.

7. Congenital Heart Disease: These are heart defects present at birth, which can affect the heart's structure and function.

8. Rheumatic Heart Disease: This is a complication of rheumatic fever, a condition caused by untreated strep throat infections. It can lead to damage and scarring of the heart valves.

HYPERTENSION

Hypertension, commonly known as high blood pressure, is a chronic medical condition characterized by elevated blood pressure levels in the arteries. It is a significant risk factor for cardiovascular diseases such as heart disease, stroke, and peripheral artery disease. Here's a detailed overview of hypertension in the context of the cardiovascular system:

Hypertension, commonly known as high blood pressure, is a chronic medical condition where the blood pressure in the arteries is consistently elevated. Blood pressure is measured in millimeters of mercury (mmHg) and is expressed as two numbers:

1. **Systolic pressure**: The top number represents the pressure in the arteries when the heart beats and pumps blood out (systole).

2. **Diastolic pressure**: The bottom number represents the pressure in the arteries when the heart is at rest between beats (diastole).

Normal blood pressure is typically defined as a systolic pressure below 120 mmHg and a diastolic pressure below 80 mmHg, often expressed as "120 over 80" (120/80 mmHg). However, blood pressure ranges can vary slightly depending on factors like age, gender, and overall health.

Hypertension is classified into several categories based on blood pressure readings:

1. **Normal**: Systolic pressure below 120 mmHg and diastolic pressure below 80 mmHg.

2. **Elevated**: Systolic pressure between 120-129 mmHg and diastolic pressure below 80 mmHg.

3. **Hypertension Stage 1**: Systolic pressure between 130-139 mmHg or diastolic pressure between 80-89 mmHg.

4. **Hypertension Stage 2**: Systolic pressure 140 mmHg or higher or diastolic pressure 90 mmHg or higher.

5. **Hypertensive Crisis**: A severe condition where blood pressure readings are higher than 180/120 mmHg. Emergency medical attention is typically required.

These categories help healthcare professionals determine the severity of hypertension and guide treatment decisions. Individuals with elevated or high blood pressure are at increased risk of various health complications, including heart disease, stroke, kidney disease, and other vascular problems.

Management of hypertension often involves lifestyle changes such as adopting a healthy diet, regular exercise, weight management, reducing salt intake, limiting alcohol consumption, and quitting smoking. In addition to lifestyle modifications, medications may also be prescribed to lower blood pressure and reduce the risk of complications. Medications can include diuretics, beta-blockers, ACE inhibitors, calcium channel blockers, and others, depending on individual health needs and factors. Regular monitoring of blood pressure and follow-up with healthcare providers are crucial for effectively managing hypertension.

Causes of Hypertension:

1. **Primary (essential) hypertension**: The exact cause is often multifactorial, involving a combination of genetic, environmental, and lifestyle factors. These may include family history, obesity, sedentary lifestyle, high salt intake, excessive alcohol consumption, stress, and aging.

2. **Secondary hypertension**: This type of hypertension arises as a result of an underlying medical condition or certain medications. Contributing factors may include kidney disease, adrenal gland disorders (such as

primary aldosteronism or pheochromocytoma), thyroid disorders, obstructive sleep apnea, certain medications (such as nonsteroidal anti-inflammatory drugs or birth control pills), and illegal drugs (like cocaine).

Effects on the Cardiovascular System:

1. **Increased workload on the heart**: Hypertension forces the heart to pump blood against higher resistance in the arteries, leading to increased strain on the heart muscle. Over time, this can result in left ventricular hypertrophy (LVH), a condition where the walls of the heart's main pumping chamber thicken. LVH can impair heart function and increase the risk of heart failure, arrhythmias, and sudden cardiac death.

2. **Atherosclerosis**: Chronic hypertension damages the inner lining of arteries, promoting the accumulation of fatty deposits (plaques) along arterial walls. Atherosclerosis narrows the arteries and restricts blood flow, predisposing individuals to coronary artery disease (CAD), stroke, peripheral artery disease (PAD), and renal artery disease.

3. **Coronary artery disease (CAD)**: Hypertension is a major risk factor for CAD, a condition characterized by the narrowing or blockage of the coronary arteries supplying oxygen-rich blood to the heart muscle. Reduced blood flow to the heart can cause angina (chest pain) or result in a heart attack (myocardial infarction).

4. **Stroke:** Hypertension increases the risk of stroke by damaging blood vessels in the brain and promoting the formation of blood clots or weakened vessel walls. Ischemic stroke, caused by a blockage in a cerebral artery, and hemorrhagic stroke, caused by bleeding into the brain, are both associated with hypertension.

5. **Peripheral artery disease (PAD):** Hypertension contributes to the development of PAD, a condition where narrowed arteries reduce blood flow to the extremities, particularly the legs. PAD can cause leg pain,

cramping, and impaired wound healing, and it increases the risk of limb amputation.

DIAGNOSIS OF HYPERTENSION:

Diagnosis of hypertension typically involves measuring blood pressure using a sphygmomanometer or automatic blood pressure monitor. The American Heart Association (AHA) and other guidelines define hypertension as a systolic blood pressure (SBP) ≥130 mmHg or a diastolic blood pressure (DBP) ≥80 mmHg. Diagnosis may also involve assessing for signs of end-organ damage and evaluating for secondary causes of hypertension through laboratory tests, imaging studies, and specialized assessments.

Treatment of Hypertension:

1. **Lifestyle modifications**: These include adopting a heart-healthy diet (such as the DASH diet), engaging in regular physical activity, maintaining a healthy weight, limiting alcohol consumption, reducing sodium intake, and managing stress.

2. **Medications**: Antihypertensive medications may be prescribed to lower blood pressure and reduce cardiovascular risk. These include diuretics, ACE inhibitors, angiotensin II receptor blockers (ARBs), beta-blockers, calcium channel blockers, and others. The choice of medication depends on factors such as the patient's age, comorbidities, and medication tolerability.

3. **Regular monitoring and follow-up**: Patients with hypertension should undergo regular blood pressure monitoring and follow-up with healthcare providers to assess treatment efficacy, adjust medications if needed, and address any complications or concerns.

CONGESTIVE HEART FAILURE

Congestive heart failure (CHF), also known simply as heart failure, is a chronic condition in which the heart is unable to pump blood effectively to meet the body's needs. This leads to fluid buildup (congestion) in various parts of the body, particularly the lungs and lower extremities. Here's a detailed overview of congestive heart failure within the context of the cardiovascular system: Understanding heart function and the types of heart failure is crucial in grasping the complexities of congestive heart failure (CHF).

Heart Function:

The heart is a muscular organ responsible for pumping blood throughout the body. It consists of four chambers: the left and right atria (upper chambers) and the left and right ventricles (lower chambers). Blood low in oxygen returns to the right atrium from the body and is then pumped into the right ventricle, which sends it to the lungs for oxygenation. Oxygen-rich blood returns to the left atrium from the lungs and is pumped into the left ventricle, which delivers it to the rest of the body.

Types of Heart Failure:

1. **Systolic Heart Failure**: Also known as heart failure with reduced ejection fraction (HFrEF), systolic heart failure occurs when the heart's ability to contract and pump blood out to the body is impaired. This can result from conditions such as myocardial infarction (heart attack), dilated cardiomyopathy, or long-standing hypertension. As a result, the heart's ejection fraction (EF), which measures the percentage of blood pumped out of the left ventricle with each heartbeat, is reduced.

2. **Diastolic Heart Failure**: Also called heart failure with preserved ejection fraction (HFpEF), diastolic heart failure occurs when the heart's ability to relax and fill with blood during the diastolic phase of the cardiac cycle is impaired. This leads to increased stiffness of the ventricles, hindering their ability to fill properly. Diastolic heart failure is commonly associated with conditions such as hypertensive heart disease, restrictive cardiomyopathy, or aging.

CONGESTIVE HEART FAILURE (CHF):

Congestive heart failure occurs when the heart is unable to pump blood effectively, leading to a buildup of fluid (congestion) in various parts of the body. This can result from either systolic or diastolic dysfunction, and it often manifests with symptoms such as:

a. Shortness of breath (dyspnea), especially during exertion or when lying flat.

b. Fatigue and weakness.

c. Swelling (edema) in the legs, ankles, feet, or abdomen.

d. Rapid or irregular heartbeat (palpitations).

e. Persistent cough or wheezing, especially when lying down.

f. Sudden weight gain due to fluid retention.

Mechanisms of Congestion:

1. **Fluid Retention**: As the heart's pumping ability weakens, blood flow to the kidneys may decrease. This prompts the kidneys to retain sodium and water, leading to fluid buildup in the body's tissues.

2. **Elevated Pressures**: Increased pressure within the heart's chambers and blood vessels can cause fluid to leak into surrounding tissues, leading to congestion in the lungs (pulmonary congestion) or peripheral edema.

Management of CHF:

Management of congestive heart failure aims to alleviate symptoms, improve quality of life, and reduce the risk of complications. This typically involves:

1. **Medications**: Diuretics to reduce fluid retention, ACE inhibitors or ARBs to dilate blood vessels and reduce blood pressure, beta-blockers to slow heart rate and improve heart function, and other medications depending on the underlying cause and symptoms.

2. **Lifestyle Modifications**: Including dietary changes (low-sodium diet), regular physical activity, weight management, smoking cessation, and limiting alcohol consumption.

3. **Monitoring and Follow-up**: Regular check-ups with healthcare providers to assess symptoms, adjust medications, monitor fluid status, and address any concerns or complications.

4. **Devices and Procedures**: In some cases, devices such as implantable cardioverter-defibrillators (ICDs) or cardiac resynchronization therapy (CRT) devices may be recommended to improve heart function and reduce the risk of arrhythmias.

5. **Surgical Interventions**: In severe cases, heart transplantation or left ventricular assist device (LVAD) implantation may be considered for eligible patients.

Congestive heart failure

Congestive heart failure (CHF) is a chronic condition in which the heart is unable to pump blood efficiently, leading to a buildup of fluid in the body's tissues. Understanding its causes and symptoms is crucial for early detection and management.

Causes of Congestive Heart Failure:

1. **Coronary Artery Disease (CAD):** Atherosclerosis, the buildup of plaque in the coronary arteries, can lead to heart attacks (myocardial infarctions) and subsequent damage to the heart muscle, impairing its ability to pump effectively.

2. **Hypertension (High Blood Pressure)**: Chronic high blood pressure can cause the heart to work harder to pump blood, leading to left ventricular hypertrophy (LVH) and eventually heart failure.

3. **Cardiomyopathy**: Conditions that directly affect the heart muscle, such as dilated cardiomyopathy, hypertrophic cardiomyopathy, or restrictive cardiomyopathy, can weaken the heart's pumping ability and lead to heart failure.

4. **Valvular Heart Disease**: Conditions such as mitral valve regurgitation or aortic stenosis can disrupt the normal flow of blood through the heart,

leading to increased pressure and volume overload, which can eventually cause heart failure.

5. **Myocarditi**s: Inflammation of the heart muscle, often due to viral infections or autoimmune disorders, can weaken the heart and impair its function, leading to heart failure.

6. **Congenital Heart Defects**: Structural abnormalities present at birth can affect the heart's function and lead to heart failure, especially if left untreated or poorly managed.

7. Ar**rhythmia**s: Abnormal heart rhythms, such as atrial fibrillation or ventricular tachycardia, can disrupt the heart's pumping action and contribute to heart failure.

8. **Other Factors**: Other factors such as diabetes, obesity, thyroid disorders, chronic lung diseases, and certain medications (such as nonsteroidal anti-inflammatory drugs or chemotherapeutic agents) can also contribute to the development or exacerbation of heart failure.

Symptoms of Congestive Heart Failure:

a. **Shortness of Breath (Dyspnea)**: Difficulty breathing, especially during exertion or when lying flat (orthopnea), is a hallmark symptom of heart failure. Patients may also experience paroxysmal nocturnal dyspnea (PND), sudden episodes of severe shortness of breath during sleep.

b. **Fatigue and Weakness**: Reduced blood flow and oxygen delivery to the body's tissues can lead to generalized fatigue, weakness, and reduced exercise tolerance.

c. **Swelling (Edema):** Fluid retention in the body's tissues can lead to swelling, particularly in the legs, ankles, feet, or abdomen. This can be caused by increased pressure in the veins and capillaries due to impaired heart function.

d. **Rapid Weight Gain**: Sudden weight gain due to fluid retention is common in patients with heart failure.

e. **Persistent Cough or Wheezing**: Fluid accumulation in the lungs can cause coughing, wheezing, or a frothy sputum, especially when lying down or during physical activity.

f. **Reduced Appetite and Digestive Symptoms**: Patients may experience nausea, abdominal pain, or a feeling of fullness due to fluid accumulation in the abdomen (ascites) or liver congestion.

g. **Increased Heart Rate (Tachycardia)**: The heart may beat faster to compensate for reduced cardiac output, leading to palpitations or a sensation of rapid or irregular heartbeat.

h. **Cyanosis:** In severe cases, inadequate oxygenation of the blood can lead to bluish discoloration of the lips, fingers, or toes (cyanosis).

Complications of congestive heart failure:

a. Fluid Overload: Progressive fluid retention can lead to pulmonary edema (fluid accumulation in the lungs), peripheral edema (swelling in the legs, ankles, and feet), and ascites (fluid accumulation in the abdomen), causing discomfort and increasing the risk of respiratory distress and organ dysfunction.

b. Arrhythmias: Heart failure can disrupt the heart's electrical system, leading to abnormal heart rhythms (arrhythmias) such as atrial fibrillation, ventricular tachycardia, or ventricular fibrillation. Arrhythmias can impair cardiac function, increase the risk of blood clots and stroke, and potentially lead to sudden cardiac death.

c. Renal Dysfunction: Reduced cardiac output and poor perfusion can impair kidney function, leading to acute kidney injury or chronic kidney disease. Fluid retention and electrolyte imbalances further exacerbate renal dysfunction, creating a vicious cycle.

d. Hepatic Congestion: Congestion of the liver due to impaired blood flow can lead to hepatic dysfunction, manifested by elevated liver enzymes, jaundice, and hepatomegaly (enlarged liver). Severe hepatic congestion may result in liver failure.

e. Pulmonary Embolism: Chronic heart failure increases the risk of blood clots forming in the veins of the legs (deep vein thrombosis), which can travel to the lungs and cause a pulmonary embolism, a life-threatening condition.

f. Cardiogenic Shock: In severe cases of heart failure, the heart may become so weak that it fails to pump enough blood to meet the body's demands, leading to cardiogenic shock. This is a medical emergency requiring immediate intervention to restore circulation and stabilize the patient.

Diagnosis of Congestive Heart Failure:

1) Medical History and Physical Examination: Healthcare providers will assess symptoms, medical history, risk factors, and perform a thorough physical examination, including listening to the heart and lungs, checking for signs of fluid retention, and evaluating overall health status.

2) Blood Tests: Blood tests may be ordered to assess kidney function, liver function, electrolyte levels, and biomarkers such as brain natriuretic peptide (BNP) or N-terminal pro-B-type natriuretic peptide (NT-proBNP), which are elevated in heart failure.

3) Imaging Studies:

   a) Echocardiogram: This ultrasound test provides detailed images of the heart's structure and function, including its size, shape, and pumping ability (ejection fraction).

   b) Chest X-ray: X-rays can reveal signs of fluid buildup in the lungs (pulmonary congestion) or enlargement of the heart.

   c) Electrocardiogram (ECG): This test measures the heart's electrical activity and can detect abnormal rhythms, signs of prior heart attacks, or other cardiac abnormalities.

4) Other Tests: Additional tests such as stress tests, cardiac catheterization, or cardiac MRI may be performed to further evaluate heart function, assess coronary artery disease, or identify other contributing factors.

Treatment of Congestive Heart Failure:

1) Medications:

   a) Diuretics: These medications help reduce fluid buildup and relieve symptoms of congestion.

   b) Angiotensin-Converting Enzyme (ACE) Inhibitors or Angiotensin II Receptor Blockers (ARBs): These drugs help dilate blood vessels, reduce blood pressure, and improve heart function.

   c) Beta-Blockers: These medications slow the heart rate, reduce blood pressure, and improve cardiac function.

   d) Aldosterone Antagonists: Drugs like spironolactone or eplerenone can help reduce fluid retention and improve heart function.

   e) Sacubitril/Valsartan (Entresto): This combination medication has been shown to reduce mortality and hospitalizations in patients with heart failure with reduced ejection fraction.

   f) Digoxin: In some cases, digoxin may be used to improve heart function and reduce symptoms.

2) Lifestyle Modifications:

   a) Low-Sodium Diet: Restricting sodium intake helps reduce fluid retention and manage symptoms.

   b) Fluid Restriction: Limiting fluid intake may be necessary for patients with severe fluid overload.

   c) Regular Exercise: Supervised exercise programs can improve cardiovascular fitness and overall health.

   d) Smoking Cessation: Quitting smoking is essential to reduce the risk of further heart damage.

3) Devices and Procedures:

a) Implantable Cardioverter-Defibrillator (ICD): For patients at high risk of sudden cardiac death due to arrhythmias.

b) Cardiac Resynchronization Therapy (CRT): This involves the placement of a specialized pacemaker to improve coordination of heart contractions in patients with certain types of heart failure.

c) Left Ventricular Assist Devices (LVAD): These mechanical pumps can help support heart function in advanced heart failure or as a bridge to heart transplantation.

4) Surgical Interventions:

a) Coronary Artery Bypass Grafting (CABG): For patients with significant coronary artery disease.

b) Heart Valve Repair or Replacement: To address valvular heart disease contributing to heart failure.

c) Heart Transplantation: For select patients with end-stage heart failure who have failed medical therapy and are suitable candidates for transplantation.

ISCHEMIC HEART DISEASE (ANGINA, MYOCARDIAL INFARCTION, ATHEROSCLEROSIS AND ARTERIOSCLEROSIS)

Ischemic heart disease (IHD) encompasses a range of conditions characterized by inadequate blood supply to the heart muscle due to the narrowing or blockage of coronary arteries. This lack of blood flow deprives the heart muscle of oxygen and nutrients, leading to various complications such as angina (chest pain), myocardial infarction (heart attack), atherosclerosis, and arteriosclerosis. Let's explore each of these components in detail:

Atherosclerosis and arteriosclerosis are both forms of cardiovascular disease that contribute to ischemic heart disease, including conditions like angina (chest pain) and myocardial infarction (heart attack). Let's delve into each of these terms and their implications in detail:

Atherosclerosis:

Atherosclerosis is a specific type of arteriosclerosis characterized by the buildup of plaque within the walls of arteries. This plaque consists of fatty deposits, cholesterol, calcium, and other substances. Over time, plaque can narrow and harden the arteries, restricting blood flow to vital organs, including the heart.

Causes and Progression:

a. **Endothelial Dysfunction**: Atherosclerosis often begins with damage to the endothelial cells lining the arteries, typically caused by factors like high blood pressure, smoking, diabetes, or high levels of LDL cholesterol.

b. **Plaque Formation**: In response to endothelial injury, LDL cholesterol and other substances can accumulate in the arterial wall, triggering an inflammatory response. Immune cells, such as macrophages, engulf the LDL cholesterol, leading to the formation of fatty streaks and eventually plaques.

c. **Plaque Rupture and Thrombosis**: Advanced plaques can become unstable and prone to rupture. When a plaque ruptures, it exposes the underlying tissue to blood, leading to platelet activation and blood clot formation (thrombosis). A blood clot can partially or completely block blood flow, causing ischemia or infarction.

Implications in Ischemic Heart Disease:

a. **Angina**: In stable angina, atherosclerosis narrows the coronary arteries, reducing blood flow to the heart muscle during periods of increased demand (e.g., exercise or stress). This mismatch between oxygen supply and demand causes chest pain or discomfort.

b. **Myocardial Infarction (Heart Attack)**: If an atherosclerotic plaque ruptures and causes a complete blockage of a coronary artery, it can lead to a myocardial infarction. Without adequate blood supply, a portion of the heart muscle becomes damaged or dies, resulting in chest pain, shortness of breath, and other symptoms.

Arteriosclerosis:

Arteriosclerosis is a broader term referring to the thickening and hardening of arterial walls, which occurs as a natural part of aging. It encompasses various types of arterial stiffening, including atherosclerosis, but also involves other processes such as calcification and fibrosis.

Types of Arteriosclerosis:

a. **Atherosclerosis**: As described earlier, atherosclerosis specifically involves the buildup of plaque within arterial walls.

b. **Monckeberg's Medial Calcific Sclerosis**: This type of arteriosclerosis involves the calcification of the middle layer (media) of arteries, particularly in the arteries of the extremities. It typically does not cause significant narrowing of the arteries or symptoms but may be detected incidentally on imaging studies.

Implications in Ischemic Heart Disease:

While arteriosclerosis itself may not directly cause ischemic heart disease, it contributes to reduced arterial elasticity and compliance, which can exacerbate the effects of atherosclerosis. Arteriosclerosis may also affect blood pressure regulation and increase the workload on the heart, potentially leading to hypertension and left ventricular hypertrophy, both of which are risk factors for ischemic heart disease.

Angina:

Angina is a common symptom of ischemic heart disease characterized by chest pain or discomfort due to reduced blood flow to the heart muscle (myocardium). It occurs when the demand for oxygen-rich blood exceeds the supply available through the coronary arteries. Angina is often described as a pressure, squeezing, tightness, or burning sensation in the chest, but it can also manifest as discomfort in the arms, shoulders, neck, jaw, or back.

Types of Angina:

a. **Stable Angina**: Typically triggered by physical exertion, stress, or other factors that increase the heart's workload. The chest pain or discomfort is predictable and usually subsides with rest or medication.

b. **Unstable Angina**: Characterized by chest pain or discomfort that occurs at rest or with minimal exertion and may be more severe or prolonged than stable angina. Unstable angina is considered a medical emergency as it may precede a heart attack.

c. **Variant (Prinzmetal's) Angina**: Caused by coronary artery spasms rather than by physical exertion or emotional stress. It often occurs at rest and may be associated with certain triggers or circadian rhythms.

Mechanism of Angina:

Angina typically occurs due to atherosclerosis, where fatty deposits (plaque) build up within the coronary arteries, narrowing their diameter and reducing blood flow to the heart muscle. During periods of increased demand (such as exercise), the narrowed arteries cannot supply enough oxygen-rich blood to meet the heart's needs, resulting in ischemia and the characteristic symptoms of angina.

Myocardial Infarction (Heart Attack):

A myocardial infarction (MI), commonly known as a heart attack, occurs when blood flow to a part of the heart muscle is severely reduced or completely blocked, leading to tissue damage or death (infarction) of the affected area. It is a medical emergency that requires prompt treatment to minimize damage and prevent complications.

Types of Myocardial Infarction:

a. **ST-Segment Elevation Myocardial Infarction (STEMI)**: This type of heart attack is characterized by an elevation of the ST segment on an electrocardiogram (ECG). It indicates complete blockage of a coronary artery and requires immediate reperfusion therapy, such as angioplasty with stent placement or thrombolytic therapy, to restore blood flow to the affected area.

b. **Non-ST-Segment Elevation Myocardial Infarction (NSTEMI)**: In NSTEMI, there may be partial blockage or temporary cessation of blood flow in a coronary artery. It is diagnosed based on elevated cardiac biomarkers (such as troponin) in the blood and may not always show significant changes on the ECG. Treatment involves medications to stabilize the patient and restore blood flow as appropriate.

Mechanism of Myocardial Infarction:

Myocardial infarction typically occurs due to the rupture of an atherosclerotic plaque within a coronary artery, leading to the formation of a blood clot (thrombus) that obstructs blood flow. The lack of oxygen and nutrients causes irreversible damage to the heart muscle, leading to cell death and tissue necrosis. The extent and severity of the infarction depend on factors such as the size of the blocked artery, the duration of the blockage, and the presence of collateral blood flow.

RESPIRATORY SYSTEM

The respiratory system is a complex network of organs and tissues responsible for the exchange of gases between the body and the environment. It facilitates the intake of oxygen from the air and the removal of carbon dioxide, a waste product of cellular metabolism. Here's a detailed introduction to the respiratory system:

1) **Organs of the Respiratory System:**

   a) **Nose and Nasal Cavity**: The nose is the primary entry point for air into the respiratory system. It contains nasal passages lined with mucous membranes and tiny hair-like structures called cilia, which help filter, humidify, and warm the air.

b) **Pharynx**: The pharynx, or throat, is a muscular tube located behind the nasal cavity and mouth. It serves as a passageway for air and food.

c) **Larynx**: The larynx, or voice box, is located at the top of the trachea. It contains the vocal cords, which vibrate to produce sound during speech.

d) **Trachea:** The trachea, or windpipe, is a rigid tube composed of cartilage rings. It conducts air from the larynx to the bronchi.

e) **Bronchi and Bronchioles**: The trachea branches into two bronchi, each leading to a lung. Inside the lungs, the bronchi further divide into smaller bronchioles, which eventually terminate in tiny air sacs called alveoli.

f) **Lungs:** The lungs are the main organs of respiration. They are soft, spongy organs enclosed within the thoracic cavity. The right lung has three lobes, while the left lung has two lobes to accommodate the heart.

g) **Alveoli:** Alveoli are microscopic air sacs located at the end of the bronchioles. They are the site of gas exchange, where oxygen from inhaled air diffuses into the bloodstream, and carbon dioxide from the bloodstream diffuses into the alveoli to be exhaled.

2) Mechanics of Breathing:

a) Breathing, or ventilation, is the process of inhaling and exhaling air. It involves the coordination of respiratory muscles, primarily the diaphragm and intercostal muscles.

b) During inhalation (inspiration), the diaphragm contracts and moves downward, while the intercostal muscles contract, causing the ribcage to expand. This increases the volume of the thoracic cavity, leading to a decrease in air pressure within the lungs. Air rushes in from the higher-pressure environment outside the body.

c) During exhalation (expiration), the diaphragm relaxes and moves upward, and the intercostal muscles relax, causing the ribcage to recoil. This decreases the volume of the thoracic cavity, leading to an increase in air pressure within the lungs. Air is forced out of the lungs to equalize the pressure with the external environment.

3) **Gas Exchange:**
   a) Gas exchange occurs in the alveoli, where oxygen from inhaled air diffuses across the alveolar membrane into the bloodstream, while carbon dioxide diffuses from the bloodstream into the alveoli to be exhaled.
   b) Oxygen is transported in the bloodstream bound to hemoglobin molecules in red blood cells, while carbon dioxide is transported primarily as bicarbonate ions and dissolved in plasma.

4) **Regulation of Breathing:**
   a) Breathing is regulated by the respiratory control centers in the brainstem, primarily the medulla oblongata and the pons.
   b) The respiratory centers monitor levels of oxygen, carbon dioxide, and pH (acidity) in the blood and adjust breathing rate and depth accordingly to maintain homeostasis.
   c) Peripheral chemoreceptors, located in the carotid bodies and aortic bodies, also play a role in detecting changes in blood oxygen and carbon dioxide levels and signaling the respiratory centers to adjust breathing.

5) **Respiratory Disorders:**
   a) Respiratory disorders can affect any part of the respiratory system and may include conditions such as asthma, chronic obstructive pulmonary disease (COPD), pneumonia, bronchitis, emphysema, lung cancer, and respiratory infections.
   b) Risk factors for respiratory disorders include smoking, air pollution, occupational exposures, genetics, and lifestyle factors.

Types of Respiratory disease:

Respiratory diseases affect the organs and tissues involved in breathing, including the lungs, airways, and respiratory muscles. They can vary widely in severity and include acute conditions as well as chronic diseases. Here are some common types:

1. Infectious Respiratory Diseases:
    a. Pneumonia: An infection of the lungs, often caused by bacteria, viruses, or fungi.
    b. Influenza (Flu): A viral infection that affects the respiratory system and can range from mild to severe.
    c. Tuberculosis (TB): A bacterial infection caused by Mycobacterium tuberculosis, usually affecting the lungs but can also involve other organs.
    d. Bronchitis: Inflammation of the bronchial tubes, often due to viral infections.
2. Chronic Obstructive Pulmonary Disease (COPD): A group of progressive lung diseases that obstruct airflow, including chronic bronchitis and emphysema.
3. Asthma: A chronic inflammatory condition of the airways that can cause episodes of wheezing, breathlessness, chest tightness, and coughing.
4. Interstitial Lung Diseases (ILDs): A group of diseases that cause inflammation and scarring of the lung tissue, leading to stiffness of the lungs and difficulty breathing. Examples include idiopathic pulmonary fibrosis (IPF) and sarcoidosis.
5. Lung Cancer: Abnormal cell growth in the lungs, often linked to smoking but can also occur in non-smokers.
6. Obstructive Sleep Apnea (OSA): A condition characterized by repetitive episodes of complete or partial upper airway obstruction during sleep, leading to disrupted breathing patterns and reduced oxygen levels.

7. Pulmonary Embolism (PE): A blockage in one of the pulmonary arteries in the lungs, usually caused by blood clots that travel from elsewhere in the body.

8. Cystic Fibrosis (CF): A genetic disorder that affects the lungs and digestive system, causing thick and sticky mucus to build up in the airways.

9. Chronic Respiratory Failure: A condition in which the respiratory system fails to adequately oxygenate the blood or remove carbon dioxide from the body, often seen in advanced stages of various respiratory diseases.

ASTHMA

Asthma is a chronic respiratory condition characterized by inflammation and narrowing of the airways, leading to recurrent episodes of wheezing, breathlessness, chest tightness, and coughing. It is a common condition that affects people of all ages, but it often begins in childhood and can persist into adulthood. Here's a detailed overview of asthma within the context of the respiratory system:

Asthma is a chronic respiratory condition characterized by inflammation and narrowing of the airways, resulting in symptoms such as wheezing, shortness of breath, chest tightness, and coughing. Understanding the pathophysiology and different types of asthma is crucial for effective management and treatment.

Pathophysiology of Asthma:

1) **Airway Inflammation**: Asthma is primarily driven by inflammation in the airways, which leads to swelling and narrowing of the bronchial tubes. This inflammation is characterized by the infiltration of immune cells, including eosinophils, mast cells, and T lymphocytes, into the airway walls.

2) **Bronchial Hyper-responsiveness**: Inflammation in the airways makes them more sensitive to various triggers, such as allergens, pollutants, exercise, cold air, or respiratory infections. When exposed to these triggers, the

airways become hyper responsive and constrict more readily, leading to asthma symptoms.

3) **Airway Remodeling**: Chronic inflammation and repeated episodes of bronchoconstriction can lead to structural changes in the airway walls, known as airway remodeling. This includes thickening of the smooth muscle layer, increased mucus production, and deposition of collagen and fibrous tissue. Airway remodeling contributes to the persistence and severity of asthma symptoms over time.

Types of Asthma:

1) **Allergic (Extrinsic) Asthma**: This type of asthma is triggered by exposure to allergens such as pollen, pet dander, mold, or dust mites. Allergic asthma often develops in childhood and may be associated with other allergic conditions such as hay fever or eczema. It is characterized by the production of IgE antibodies and an eosinophilic inflammatory response in the airways.

2) **Non-Allergic (Intrinsic) Asthma**: Non-allergic asthma is not triggered by allergens but may be provoked by other factors such as respiratory infections, exercise, cold air, stress, or irritants like smoke or strong odors. Non-allergic asthma can develop at any age and may be associated with eosinophilic or neutrophilic inflammation in the airways.

3) **Occupational Asthma**: This type of asthma is caused by exposure to allergens or irritants in the workplace, such as chemicals, dust, fumes, or animal dander. Occupational asthma can develop in individuals with or without a prior history of asthma and may improve with avoidance of the triggering substances.

4) **Exercise-Induced Bronchoconstriction (EIB)**: Some individuals experience asthma symptoms, such as coughing, wheezing, or shortness of breath, during or after exercise. Exercise-induced bronchoconstriction is more common in people with asthma but can also occur in individuals without a history of asthma.

5) **Steroid-Resistant Asthma**: In some cases, asthma symptoms may not respond well to corticosteroid medications, which are commonly used to control inflammation in the airways. Steroid-resistant asthma may require alternative treatments, such as biologic therapies targeting specific inflammatory pathways.

6) **Severe or Difficult-to-Treat Asthma**: Severe asthma is characterized by frequent symptoms, exacerbations, or persistent airflow limitation despite optimal treatment with high-dose medications. It may be associated with significant airway inflammation, airway hyperresponsiveness, and airway remodeling.

Symptoms of Asthma:

1) **Shortness of Breath (Dyspnea)**: Difficulty breathing is a hallmark symptom of asthma. It may range from mild to severe and can be triggered by various factors, including physical activity, exposure to allergens, or changes in weather.

2) **Wheezing**: Wheezing is a high-pitched whistling sound produced during breathing and is caused by airflow obstruction in the smaller airways of the lungs. It is a common symptom of asthma, especially during exhalation.

3) **Chest Tightness**: People with asthma often describe a sensation of tightness or pressure in the chest, which may feel like someone is squeezing or sitting on their chest.

4) **Coughing**: Persistent coughing, particularly at night or in the early morning, is common in asthma. The cough may be dry or productive and may worsen in response to triggers such as cold air, exercise, or exposure to allergens.

5) **Increased Respiratory Rate**: During asthma exacerbations or episodes of bronchoconstriction, individuals may experience rapid or shallow breathing as they struggle to get enough air into their lungs.

6) **Difficulty Sleeping**: Asthma symptoms can disrupt sleep, leading to frequent awakenings, restlessness, or difficulty falling asleep due to coughing, wheezing, or shortness of breath.

7) **Fatigue**: Persistent asthma symptoms, particularly if inadequately controlled, can lead to fatigue and decreased energy levels due to the extra effort required to breathe.

Diagnosis of Asthma:

1) **Medical History**: Healthcare providers will review the patient's medical history, including past respiratory symptoms, family history of asthma or allergies, exposure to potential triggers, and response to previous treatments.

2) **Physical Examination**: A thorough physical examination may be performed to assess respiratory function, listen for wheezing or other abnormal lung sounds, and evaluate for signs of nasal congestion, allergic rhinitis, or eczema.

3) **Lung Function Tests:**

   a) **Spirometry**: This test measures how much air a person can exhale and how quickly they can do so. It helps assess airflow obstruction and bronchial hyperresponsiveness, both characteristic features of asthma.

   b) **Peak Expiratory Flow (PEF) Measurement**: PEF monitoring involves using a handheld device called a peak flow meter to measure the maximum speed at which a person can exhale air. It is often used to monitor asthma control and assess response to treatment.

4) **Bronchial Provocation Tests**: In cases where spirometry results are inconclusive, bronchial provocation tests may be performed to assess airway hyperresponsiveness. These tests involve inhaling a substance (such as methacholine or histamine) that triggers bronchoconstriction in people with asthma.

5) **Allergy Testing:** Allergy testing may be recommended to identify specific allergens that trigger asthma symptoms, such as pollen, dust mites, pet dander, or mold.

6) **Exhaled Nitric Oxide (FeNO) Measurement:** FeNO testing measures the levels of nitric oxide in exhaled breath, which can be elevated in people with allergic or eosinophilic asthma. It helps assess airway inflammation and guide treatment decisions.

7) **Imaging Studies**: Chest X-rays or CT scans may be ordered to rule out other respiratory conditions or assess for complications of asthma, such as pneumothorax or pneumonia.

Treatment and Management of Asthma:

1) **Medications:**

   a) **Inhaled Corticosteroids (ICS)**: These anti-inflammatory medications are the cornerstone of asthma treatment and help reduce airway inflammation, prevent symptoms, and improve lung function.

   b) **Short-Acting Beta-Agonists (SABAs)**: These bronchodilator medications provide rapid relief of asthma symptoms by relaxing the muscles around the airways and improving airflow. They are used as rescue medications during acute asthma attacks.

   c) **Long-Acting Beta-Agonists (LABAs)**: LABAs are bronchodilators that provide sustained relief of asthma symptoms when used in combination with ICS. They are typically prescribed for patients with moderate to severe asthma.

   d) **Combination Inhalers**: Combination inhalers containing both an ICS and a LABA are available for the maintenance treatment of asthma and provide both anti-inflammatory and bronchodilator effects.

   e) **Leukotriene Receptor Antagonists**: These medications block the action of leukotrienes, inflammatory substances that contribute to asthma symptoms. They are used as alternative or adjunctive therapy in some patients.

f) **Biologic Therapies**: Biologic medications, such as monoclonal antibodies targeting specific inflammatory pathways (e.g., IgE, IL-5), are used in severe asthma to reduce exacerbations and improve symptoms.

g) **Oral Corticosteroids**: In severe asthma exacerbations or uncontrolled asthma, short courses of oral corticosteroids may be prescribed to reduce inflammation and improve lung function.

2) **Rescue Medications:**

a) **Short-Acting Beta-Agonists (SABAs)**: These medications, such as albuterol or levalbuterol, provide rapid relief of acute asthma symptoms and are used on an as-needed basis during asthma attacks or exacerbations.

b) **Oral Corticosteroids**: In severe exacerbations, oral corticosteroids may be prescribed to reduce airway inflammation and improve symptoms.

3) **Controller Medications:**

a) **Inhaled Corticosteroids (ICS)**: These medications are used on a daily basis to control airway inflammation and prevent asthma symptoms.

b) **Long-Acting Beta-Agonists (LABAs)**: LABAs are used in combination with ICS as maintenance therapy to provide long-term control of asthma symptoms and improve lung function.

c) **Leukotriene Receptor Antagonists**: These medications may be used as alternative or adjunctive therapy for patients who cannot tolerate or do not respond well to ICS.

4) **Allergy Management:**

a) **Allergen Avoidance**: Identifying and avoiding triggers such as pollen, dust mites, pet dander, mold, or certain foods can help reduce asthma symptoms.

b) **Allergen Immunotherapy (Allergy Shots)**: Allergy shots may be recommended for individuals with allergic asthma to desensitize the immune system to specific allergens and reduce asthma symptoms over time.

5) **Lifestyle Modifications:**

   a) **Smoking Cessation**: Smoking and exposure to secondhand smoke can worsen asthma symptoms and increase the risk of exacerbations. Quitting smoking is essential for improving asthma control.

   b) **Physical Activity**: Regular exercise is beneficial for overall health but may trigger asthma symptoms in some individuals. Proper warm-up, appropriate medication use, and avoiding exercise in cold or polluted environments can help minimize symptoms.

6) **Education and Self-Management:**

   a) **Asthma Action Plan**: A written asthma action plan provides guidance on how to manage asthma symptoms, adjust medications, and recognize when to seek medical help during exacerbations.

   b) **Peak Flow Monitoring**: Regular monitoring of peak expiratory flow (PEF) using a peak flow meter can help assess asthma control, identify worsening symptoms, and guide treatment adjustments.

Prevention of Asthma:

1) **Identifying and Avoiding Triggers**: Identifying and avoiding allergens, irritants, or other triggers that worsen asthma symptoms can help prevent exacerbations.

2) **Allergen Control Measures**: Implementing measures to reduce exposure to common allergens, such as using allergen-proof mattress and pillow covers, regularly cleaning carpets and upholstery, and maintaining low humidity levels indoors.

3) **Vaccinations**: Annual influenza vaccinations and pneumococcal vaccinations are recommended for individuals with asthma to reduce the risk of respiratory infections and exacerbations.

4) **Smoking Cessation**: Avoiding smoking and exposure to secondhand smoke is crucial for preventing asthma exacerbations and improving lung health.

5) **Regular Follow-Up and Monitoring**: Regular follow-up visits with healthcare providers, adherence to prescribed medications, and monitoring asthma symptoms and lung function are essential for maintaining asthma control and preventing exacerbations.

CHRONIC OBSTRUCTIVE AIRWAYS DISEASES

Chronic obstructive pulmonary disease (COPD) is a group of progressive respiratory conditions characterized by persistent airflow limitation and difficulty breathing. The two main types of COPD are chronic bronchitis and emphysema, often occurring together in individuals with the disease. Here's a detailed overview of COPD within the context of the respiratory system:

Chronic obstructive pulmonary disease (COPD) is a progressive lung disease characterized by airflow limitation that is not fully reversible. The two main subtypes of COPD are chronic bronchitis and emphysema, which often coexist and share overlapping features, though they have distinct pathophysiological mechanisms and clinical manifestations.

Chronic Bronchitis:

Chronic bronchitis is defined as the presence of chronic cough and sputum production for at least three months in two consecutive years in the absence of any other identifiable cause. It is characterized by inflammation and narrowing of the airways, excessive mucus production, and recurrent respiratory infections.

Pathophysiology:

1) **Airway Inflammation and Mucus Hypersecretion**: Chronic exposure to irritants such as cigarette smoke, air pollution, or occupational dust leads to

inflammation and damage to the airway epithelium. This stimulates the secretion of mucus-producing cells (goblet cells) and increases mucus production, leading to airway obstruction.

2) **Airway Remodeling**: Chronic inflammation in the airways triggers structural changes, including thickening of the bronchial walls, hypertrophy of mucous glands, and narrowing of the airway lumen. These changes further contribute to airflow limitation and airflow obstruction.

3) **Impaired Mucociliary Clearance**: In chronic bronchitis, impairment of the mucociliary clearance mechanism reduces the ability of the respiratory tract to clear mucus and debris, leading to mucus plugging, airway obstruction, and recurrent respiratory infections.

Clinical Manifestations:

1) **Chronic Cough**: Persistent cough lasting for at least three months is the hallmark symptom of chronic bronchitis. The cough is often productive, with the production of thick, tenacious sputum.

2) **Sputum Production**: Chronic bronchitis is characterized by excessive sputum production, particularly in the morning upon waking or during exacerbations of symptoms.

3) **Dyspnea**: Shortness of breath, initially on exertion but progressively worsening over time, is common in chronic bronchitis due to airflow limitation and decreased lung function.

4) **Frequent Respiratory Infections**: Individuals with chronic bronchitis are more susceptible to respiratory infections, including viral and bacterial infections, due to impaired mucociliary clearance and airway inflammation.

Emphysema:

Emphysema is characterized by the destruction of the lung parenchyma, particularly the alveolar walls, leading to enlargement of the airspaces and loss of elastic recoil. This results in airflow limitation and decreased gas exchange capacity.

Pathophysiology:

1) **Alveolar Damage**: Emphysema is primarily caused by exposure to cigarette smoke or other noxious inh**alants**, leading to inflammation and damage to the alveolar walls. This damage results in the destruction of alveolar septae and enlargement of airspaces (alveolar dilation), reducing the surface area available for gas exchange.

2) **Loss of Elastic Recoil**: Destruction of the alveolar walls and loss of elastic fibers in the lung parenchyma lead to decreased lung recoil and compliance. This impairs the ability of the lungs to recoil during expiration, resulting in air trapping and hyperinflation.

3) **Ventilation-Perfusion Mismatch**: Emphysema causes regional variations in ventilation and perfusion within the lungs, leading to inefficient gas exchange and hypoxemia. Areas of emphysematous destruction may have reduced ventilation but maintain perfusion, resulting in a ventilation-perfusion mismatch.

Clinical Manifestations:

1) **Dyspnea**: Shortness of breath, particularly during exertion, is a common symptom of emphysema. Dyspnea is typically progressive and may become more severe as the disease advances.

2) **Chronic Cough**: Some individuals with emphysema may experience a chronic cough, although it is often less prominent compared to chronic bronchitis.

3) **Barrel Chest:** Severe emphysema may result in hyperinflation of the lungs and a characteristic barrel-shaped chest, with an increased anteroposterior diameter.

4) **Weight Loss**: Advanced emphysema can lead to weight loss and muscle wasting, partly due to increased energy expenditure associated with labored breathing and reduced physical activity.

5) **Hypoxemia and Hypercapnia**: As emphysema progresses, impaired gas exchange leads to hypoxemia (low blood oxygen levels) and, in later stages, hypercapnia (high blood carbon dioxide levels).

Pathophysiology of COPD:

Chronic Bronchitis:

1) **Airway Inflammation**: Chronic exposure to irritants such as cigarette smoke, air pollution, or occupational dust leads to inflammation and damage to the airway epithelium.

2) **Mucus Hypersecretion**: Inflammatory mediators stimulate the production of mucus-producing cells (goblet cells), leading to excessive mucus production and airway obstruction.

3) **Airway Remodeling**: Chronic inflammation triggers structural changes in the airways, including thickening of the bronchial walls, hypertrophy of mucous glands, and narrowing of the airway lumen.

4) **Impaired Mucociliary Clearance**: Inflammation and mucus hypersecretion impair the mucociliary clearance mechanism, reducing the ability of the respiratory tract to clear mucus and debris.

Emphysema:

1) **Alveolar Damage**: Exposure to cigarette smoke or other noxious inhalants leads to inflammation and damage to the alveolar walls.

2) **Loss of Elastic Recoil**: Destruction of the alveolar walls and loss of elastic fibers in the lung parenchyma result in decreased lung recoil and compliance.

3) **Airspace Enlargement**: Destruction of alveolar septae leads to enlargement of the airspaces (alveolar dilation) and reduction in the surface area available for gas exchange.

4) **Ventilation-Perfusion Mismatch**: Emphysema causes regional variations in ventilation and perfusion within the lungs, leading to inefficient gas exchange and hypoxemia.

Risk Factors for COPD:

1) **Cigarette Smoking**: Tobacco smoking is the most significant risk factor for COPD, accounting for the majority of cases. Both active smoking and exposure to secondhand smoke increase the risk of developing COPD.

2) **Occupational Exposure**: Exposure to occupational hazards such as dust, chemicals, fumes, and gases increases the risk of developing COPD. Industries such as mining, construction, agriculture, and manufacturing carry a higher risk of occupational exposure.

3) **Environmental Factors**: Long-term exposure to indoor and outdoor air pollution, including biomass fuel combustion, vehicle emissions, and industrial pollutants, contributes to the development and progression of COPD.

4) **Genetic Factors**: Genetic predisposition plays a role in COPD susceptibility, although it is not as well-defined as in other respiratory conditions such as alpha-1 antitrypsin deficiency (AATD). AATD is a rare genetic disorder that predisposes individuals to early-onset emphysema, particularly in nonsmokers.

5) **Age**: Advanced age is a risk factor for COPD, with the prevalence and severity of the disease increasing with age.

6) **Respiratory Infections**: Recurrent respiratory infections, particularly during childhood, can impair lung development and increase the risk of developing COPD later in life.

7) **Socioeconomic Factors**: Socioeconomic status, including factors such as lower education level, poverty, and limited access to healthcare, is associated with an increased risk of COPD and poorer outcomes.

Diagnosis of COPD:

1) **Medical History and Physical Examination**: Healthcare providers will assess symptoms such as chronic cough, sputum production, dyspnea, and exposure to risk factors such as smoking or occupational hazards.

2) **Pulmonary Function Tests (PFTs):**

   a) **Spirometry**: Spirometry is the primary diagnostic test for COPD and measures lung function parameters such as forced expiratory volume in one second ($FEV1$) and forced vital capacity (FVC). It helps assess airflow limitation and severity of obstruction.

   b) **Post-Bronchodilator Testing**: Performing spirometry before and after administration of a bronchodilator helps differentiate reversible from irreversible airflow limitation, a hallmark feature of COPD.

3) **Imaging Studies:**

   a) **Chest X-ray:** Chest X-ray may be performed to assess for signs of hyperinflation, lung hyperlucency, or other abnormalities suggestive of COPD or complications such as pneumonia or pneumothorax.

   b) **Computed Tomography (CT) Scan**: High-resolution CT scanning can provide detailed imaging of the lungs and may be used to evaluate for emphysema, bronchiectasis, or other structural abnormalities.

4) **Arterial Blood Gas (ABG) Analysis**: Arterial blood gas sampling may be performed to assess for hypoxemia (low blood oxygen levels) and hypercapnia (high blood carbon dioxide levels), particularly in individuals with advanced COPD or acute exacerbations.

5) **Laboratory Tests**: Blood tests may be conducted to assess for other conditions that may mimic or exacerbate COPD, such as alpha-1 antitrypsin deficiency (AATD) or respiratory infections.

Treatment of COPD:

1) **Smoking Cessation**: Smoking cessation is the single most effective intervention for slowing the progression of COPD and reducing symptoms. Healthcare providers should offer counseling, behavioral interventions, and pharmacotherapy (e.g., nicotine replacement therapy, varenicline, bupropion) to support smoking cessation efforts.

2) **Medications:**

a) **Bronchodilators**: Short-acting or long-acting bronchodilators, such as beta-agonists or anticholinergics, are used to relieve bronchospasm and improve airflow. They may be administered via inhalers (metered-dose inhalers or dry powder inhalers) or nebulizers.

b) **Inhaled Corticosteroids (ICS)**: Inhaled corticosteroids may be used in combination with long-acting bronchodilators for individuals with frequent exacerbations or persistent symptoms despite bronchodilator therapy.

c) **Phosphodiesterase-4 (PDE4) Inhibitors**: PDE4 inhibitors such as roflumilast may be prescribed for individuals with severe COPD and chronic bronchitis to reduce exacerbations and improve lung function.

3) **Pulmonary Rehabilitation**: Pulmonary rehabilitation programs incorporate exercise training, education, and psychosocial support to improve symptoms, exercise tolerance, and quality of life in individuals with COPD.

4) **Oxygen Therapy**: Long-term oxygen therapy (LTOT) is indicated for individuals with severe COPD and persistent hypoxemia to improve survival, alleviate symptoms, and enhance exercise capacity.

5) **Surgery**: In select cases of severe emphysema, surgical interventions such as lung volume reduction surgery (LVRS) or lung transplantation may be considered to improve lung function and quality of life.

Prevention of COPD:

1) **Smoking Prevention and Cessation**: Public health initiatives aimed at reducing tobacco use, implementing smoke-free policies, and providing smoking cessation support can help prevent COPD and reduce the burden of the disease.

2) **Occupational Safety Measures**: Implementing workplace safety measures, such as proper ventilation, personal protective equipment (e.g., respirators), and exposure monitoring, can reduce the risk of occupational lung diseases, including COPD.

3) **Environmental Interventions**: Addressing environmental factors such as indoor and outdoor air pollution, biomass fuel combustion, and other environmental pollutants can help prevent COPD and mitigate its impact on public health.

4) **Vaccinations**: Annual influenza vaccinations and pneumococcal vaccinations are recommended for individuals with COPD to reduce the risk of respiratory infections and exacerbations.

5) **Early Detection and Treatment**: Early detection of COPD through screening programs, spirometry testing, and targeted interventions can help identify at-risk individuals and initiate appropriate treatment to prevent disease progression and complications.

RENAL SYSTEM: ACUTE AND CHRONIC RENAL FAILURE

It seems like there might be a slight mix-up with the systems here. Acute and chronic renal failure are conditions that affect the kidneys, not the respiratory system. However, I can provide detailed explanations of acute and chronic renal failure within the context of the renal system:

Certainly, let's delve into acute renal failure (ARF) and chronic renal failure (CRF) in detail, focusing on the renal system and the distinctions between these conditions.

Acute Renal Failure (ARF):

Definition:

Acute renal failure, also known as acute kidney injury (AKI), refers to a sudden and rapid decline in kidney function over a short period. ARF is characterized by a rapid rise in serum creatinine levels, a decrease in urine output, and disturbances in fluid and electrolyte balance.

Causes:

1) **Prerenal Causes**: Reduced blood flow to the kidneys due to hypovolemia (e.g., dehydration, hemorrhage), decreased cardiac output (e.g., heart failure, shock), or renal artery obstruction (e.g., renal artery stenosis).

2) **Intrinsic Causes**: Direct damage to the kidney tissue, such as acute tubular necrosis (ATN) due to ischemia, nephrotoxic drugs (e.g., aminoglycosides, contrast agents), or acute glomerulonephritis.

3) **Postrenal Causes**: Obstruction of the urinary tract, such as by kidney stones, tumors, or enlarged prostate, leading to urinary stasis and subsequent kidney injury.

Clinical Features:

1) **Decreased Urine Output (Oliguria)**: Reduced urine output is a common feature of ARF, although some individuals may experience polyuria or normal urine output in certain cases.

2) **Fluid and Electrolyte Imbalance**: ARF can lead to disturbances in fluid and electrolyte balance, such as hyperkalemia, metabolic acidosis, hyperphosphatemia, and fluid overload.

3) **Azotemia**: Elevated blood urea nitrogen (BUN) and serum creatinine levels are characteristic of ARF due to decreased glomerular filtration rate (GFR).

4) **Symptoms of Uremia**: Uremic symptoms may develop as waste products accumulate in the blood, including nausea, vomiting, fatigue, confusion, and pruritus.

Management:

Treatment of ARF involves addressing the underlying cause, optimizing fluid and electrolyte balance, and preventing complications such as metabolic acidosis and uremia. Management strategies may include fluid resuscitation, diuretics, vasopressors (in cases of hypotension or shock), discontinuation of nephrotoxic medications, and renal replacement therapy (e.g., dialysis) in severe cases.

Chronic Renal Failure (CRF):

Definition:

Chronic renal failure, also known as chronic kidney disease (CKD), refers to progressive and irreversible loss of kidney function over a period of months to years. CRF is characterized by persistent elevation of serum creatinine levels, decreased GFR, and structural changes in the kidneys.

Causes:

1) **Diabetes Mellitus:** Diabetes is the leading cause of CKD worldwide, leading to diabetic nephropathy characterized by glomerulosclerosis and progressive loss of kidney function.

2) **Hypertension**: Chronic uncontrolled hypertension can damage the small blood vessels in the kidneys, leading to renal arteriosclerosis and CKD.

3) **Glomerulonephrit**is: Inflammatory conditions affecting the glomeruli can lead to glomerular damage and CKD.

4) **Polycystic Kidney Disease (PKD**): Inherited disorders such as PKD can lead to the formation of cysts in the kidneys, causing progressive kidney damage.

5) **Autoimmune Diseases**: Conditions such as systemic lupus erythematosus (SLE) and vasculitis can cause inflammation and damage to the kidneys over time.

Clinical Features:

1) **Asymptomatic Early Stages**: CKD may be asymptomatic in the early stages, with symptoms becoming more apparent as kidney function declines.

2) **Fluid and Electrolyte Imbalance**: Similar to ARF, CKD can lead to fluid and electrolyte disturbances, including hyperkalemia, metabolic acidosis, and fluid overload.

3) **Anemia:** Decreased production of erythropoietin by the kidneys can lead to anemia, resulting in fatigue, weakness, and dyspnea.

4) **Bone and Mineral Disorders**: CKD can lead to abnormalities in calcium, phosphate, and vitamin D metabolism, resulting in renal osteodystrophy and increased risk of fractures.

Management:

The management of CKD aims to slow the progression of kidney damage, manage complications, and preserve kidney function for as long as possible. Treatment strategies may include blood pressure control (e.g., renin-angiotensin-aldosterone system inhibitors), glycemic control (in diabetic patients), dietary modifications (e.g., restriction of protein, sodium, and phosphate intake), management of anemia (e.g., erythropoiesis-stimulating agents), and avoidance of nephrotoxic medications. In advanced stages of CKD, renal replacement therapy (e.g., dialysis or kidney transplantation) may be necessary to sustain life.

Prevention:

Preventive measures for both ARF and CRF include:

1) Management of underlying conditions such as diabetes and hypertension.

2) Avoidance of nephrotoxic drugs and substances.

3) Maintenance of a healthy lifestyle, including regular exercise and a balanced diet.

4) Early detection and treatment of kidney disease through regular monitoring of kidney function and screening tests in high-risk individuals.

Acute renal failure (ARF) and chronic renal failure (CRF) represent distinct entities within the spectrum of kidney diseases, characterized by different etiologies, clinical features, and management strategies. While ARF is characterized by a sudden decline in kidney function, often reversible with prompt intervention, CRF involves

CHAPTER - 4

HAEMATOLOGICAL DISEASE AND ENDOCRINE SYSTEM

HEMATOLOGICAL DISEASES

Hematological diseases are disorders that affect the blood and blood-forming tissues, including the bone marrow, lymph nodes, spleen, and blood vessels. These diseases can involve abnormalities in the production, function, or lifespan of blood cells, leading to various symptoms and complications. Here's a detailed introduction to some common hematological diseases:

1. **Anemia:** Anemia is a condition characterized by a deficiency of red blood cells (RBCs) or hemoglobin in the blood. This results in reduced oxygen-carrying capacity, leading to symptoms such as fatigue, weakness, pale skin, shortness of breath, and dizziness. Causes of anemia include nutritional deficiencies (such as iron, vitamin B12, or folate deficiency), chronic diseases, bone marrow disorders, and genetic conditions like sickle cell anemia and thalassemia.

2. **Leukemia**: Leukemia is a type of cancer that affects the bone marrow and results in the abnormal proliferation of immature white blood cells (leukocytes). These abnormal cells crowd out normal blood cells, leading to symptoms such as fatigue, weakness, frequent infections, easy bruising or bleeding, swollen lymph nodes, and bone pain. Leukemia can be acute or chronic and is classified based on the type of white blood cell affected (lymphoid or myeloid) and the rate of disease progression.

3. **Lymphoma**: Lymphoma is a cancer that originates in the lymphatic system, which includes the lymph nodes, spleen, thymus, and bone marrow. It arises from abnormal lymphocytes, a type of white blood cell, and can be categorized as Hodgkin lymphoma or non-Hodgkin

lymphoma based on the presence or absence of Reed-Sternberg cells. Symptoms of lymphoma may include swollen lymph nodes, fever, weight loss, night sweats, fatigue, and itching.

4. **Multiple Myeloma**: Multiple myeloma is a cancer of plasma cells, a type of white blood cell responsible for producing antibodies. In multiple myeloma, abnormal plasma cells accumulate in the bone marrow and form tumors, which can lead to bone pain, weakness, anemia, kidney problems, frequent infections, and elevated blood calcium levels.

5. **Hemophilia**: Hemophilia is a genetic disorder characterized by deficient or defective blood clotting proteins, which results in prolonged bleeding and difficulty forming blood clots. It is usually inherited in an X-linked recessive manner and primarily affects males. Symptoms include easy bruising, prolonged bleeding from minor cuts or injuries, joint pain and swelling (in severe cases), and spontaneous bleeding into joints or muscles.

6. **Thrombocytopenia:** Thrombocytopenia is a condition characterized by a low platelet count in the blood, which impairs the blood's ability to clot properly. It can be caused by factors such as autoimmune disorders, certain medications, infections, bone marrow disorders, or inherited conditions. Symptoms of thrombocytopenia may include easy bruising, prolonged bleeding from minor cuts or injuries, nosebleeds, and petechiae (small red or purple spots on the skin).

7. **Sickle Cell Disease**: Sickle cell disease is a genetic disorder that affects hemoglobin, the molecule in red blood cells responsible for carrying oxygen. In individuals with sickle cell disease, abnormal hemoglobin causes red blood cells to become rigid and take on a crescent or sickle shape, leading to various complications such as pain crises, anemia, infections, stroke, organ damage, and impaired blood flow.

These are just a few examples of hematological diseases, and there are many other conditions that can affect the blood and its components. Treatment for hematological diseases varies depending on the specific condition and may include medications, blood transfusions, bone marrow or stem cell transplantation, chemotherapy, radiation therapy, and supportive care measures. Early diagnosis and appropriate management are crucial for improving outcomes and quality of life for individuals with hematological diseases.

Iron deficiency

Iron deficiency is a common hematological disorder characterized by low levels of iron in the body, leading to a decrease in the production of red blood cells and hemoglobin. It can occur as a primary condition or as a secondary complication of other underlying diseases. Here's a detailed overview of iron deficiency in hematological diseases:

1. **Causes**: Iron deficiency can occur due to various reasons, including:
    a) Inadequate dietary intake of iron: Not consuming enough iron-rich foods, such as meat, poultry, fish, beans, lentils, and iron-fortified foods.
    b) **Blood loss**: Chronic blood loss from conditions such as gastrointestinal bleeding (e.g., ulcers, gastritis, colorectal cancer), menstrual bleeding (in women with heavy periods), urinary tract bleeding, or frequent blood donation.
    c) **Poor absorption of iron:** Conditions that affect the absorption of iron in the gastrointestinal tract, such as celiac disease, inflammatory bowel disease (Crohn's disease, ulcerative colitis), or gastric bypass surgery.
    d) **Increased iron requirements**: During periods of rapid growth (infancy, adolescence, pregnancy), or in conditions associated with increased red blood cell turnover (hemolysis) or iron utilization (e.g., chronic infections, certain cancers).

2. **Symptoms**: Iron deficiency can manifest with a variety of symptoms, which may vary in severity depending on the extent of iron depletion and the underlying cause. Common symptoms include:

   a) Fatigue and weakness

   b) Pale skin and mucous membranes (pallor)

   c) Shortness of breath

   d) Dizziness or lightheadedness

   e) Headaches

   f) Cold hands and feet

   g) Brittle nails

   h) Restless leg syndrome (uncomfortable sensations in the legs, especially at night)

   i) Pica (craving for non-food items like ice, dirt, or starch)

3. **Diagnosis**: Iron deficiency is typically diagnosed through a combination of medical history, physical examination, and laboratory tests, including:

   a) **Complete blood count (CBC):** Blood tests to evaluate the levels of hemoglobin, hematocrit, mean corpuscular volume (MCV), and red blood cell indices. In iron deficiency, these values are typically low.

   b) **Serum iron and ferritin levels**: Serum iron measures the amount of iron in the blood, while ferritin is a protein that stores iron. Low levels of serum iron and ferritin are indicative of iron deficiency.

   c) **Total iron-binding capacity (TIBC):** A measure of the body's capacity to bind and transport iron in the blood. Elevated TIBC levels are seen in iron deficiency.

   d) **Peripheral blood smear**: Examination of blood under a microscope to assess the morphology of red blood cells. In iron deficiency, red blood cells may appear hypochromic (pale) and microcytic (small).

4. **Treatment**: The treatment of iron deficiency aims to replenish iron stores and correct the underlying cause. Treatment modalities may include:

   a) **Iron supplementation**: Oral iron supplements, such as ferrous sulfate, ferrous gluconate, or ferrous fumarate, are commonly prescribed to increase iron levels in the body. These supplements are usually taken with vitamin C to enhance iron absorption.

   b) **Dietary changes**: Increasing the intake of iron-rich foods in the diet, such as red meat, poultry, fish, leafy green vegetables, fortified cereals, beans, and lentils.

   c) **Treating underlying conditions**: Addressing the underlying cause of iron deficiency, such as treating gastrointestinal bleeding, managing inflammatory bowel disease, or correcting malabsorption disorders.

   d) **Blood transfusions**: In severe cases of iron deficiency anemia or when rapid correction is needed, blood transfusions may be necessary to replenish iron and red blood cell levels.

5. **Prevention**: Preventive measures for iron deficiency include consuming a balanced diet rich in iron, ensuring adequate intake of vitamins and minerals that enhance iron absorption (such as vitamin C), and addressing risk factors for chronic blood loss or malabsorption.

Megaloblastic anemia (Vit B$_{12}$ and folic acid)

Megaloblastic anemia is a type of anemia characterized by the presence of unusually large and immature red blood cells (megaloblasts) in the bone marrow. This condition is typically caused by deficiencies in vitamin B12 (cobalamin) or folate (folic acid), both of which are essential for the production of normal red blood cells. Here's a detailed overview of megaloblastic anemia, focusing on its association with vitamin B12 and folate deficiencies:

1. **Causes:**

a. **Vitamin B12 deficiency**: Vitamin B12 is essential for the synthesis of DNA and the formation of red blood cells in the bone marrow. Deficiency of vitamin B12 can occur due to:

   i. Inadequate dietary intake, especially in individuals following a vegan or vegetarian diet without adequate supplementation.

   ii. Malabsorption disorders affecting the gastrointestinal tract, such as pernicious anemia (autoimmune destruction of intrinsic factor-producing cells in the stomach), gastric bypass surgery, inflammatory bowel disease, or celiac disease.

   iii. Certain medications that interfere with vitamin B12 absorption, such as proton pump inhibitors (PPIs) or metformin.

   iv. Genetic conditions affecting vitamin B12 metabolism, such as congenital pernicious anemia or transcobalamin deficiency.

b. **Folate deficiency**: Folate is a B-vitamin that plays a crucial role in DNA synthesis and cell division. Folate deficiency can occur due to:

   i. Inadequate dietary intake of folate-rich foods, such as leafy green vegetables, fruits, beans, and fortified cereals.

   ii. Malabsorption disorders affecting the small intestine, such as celiac disease or inflammatory bowel disease.

   iii. Increased requirements during periods of rapid growth (pregnancy, infancy, adolescence) or in conditions associated with increased red blood cell turnover (hemolysis).

2. **Symptoms:**

a) Fatigue and weakness

b) Shortness of breath

c) Pale skin (pallor)

d) Dizziness or lightheadedness

e) Rapid heartbeat (tachycardia)

f) Headaches

g) Glossitis (inflammation of the tongue)

h) Numbness or tingling in the hands and feet (paresthesia)

i) Difficulty concentrating or memory problems

j) Jaundice (yellowing of the skin and eyes) in severe cases

3. **Diagnosis:**

a) **Blood tests**: A complete blood count (CBC) may reveal characteristic findings, including macrocytic (large) red blood cells, an elevated mean corpuscular volume (MCV), and a low hemoglobin level. Peripheral blood smear examination may show hypersegmented neutrophils.

b) **Serum levels of vitamin B12 and folate:** Low levels of vitamin B12 and/or folate confirm the respective deficiencies.

c) **Other tests**: Additional tests may be performed to evaluate the underlying cause of deficiency, such as testing for antibodies against intrinsic factor or parietal cells in pernicious anemia, or assessing markers of malabsorption.

4. **Treatment:**

a) **Vitamin B12 supplementation**: For vitamin B12 deficiency, treatment typically involves intramuscular injections of vitamin B12 or high-dose oral supplements. In cases of pernicious anemia or malabsorption disorders, lifelong supplementation may be necessary.

b) **Folate supplementation**: Folate deficiency is treated with oral folic acid supplements. It's important to identify and address the underlying cause of deficiency to prevent recurrence.

c) **Dietary changes**: Increasing intake of foods rich in vitamin B12 and folate, such as meat, fish, poultry, dairy products, fortified cereals, leafy green vegetables, and legumes.

5. **Prevention:**

a) Consuming a balanced diet rich in vitamin B12 and folate.

b) Consideration of vitamin B12 supplementation in individuals at risk of deficiency, such as older adults, vegetarians/vegans, and individuals with malabsorption disorders.

c) Folic acid supplementation for women of childbearing age to prevent neural tube defects during pregnancy.

Megaloblastic anemia due to vitamin B12 or folate deficiency is a treatable condition, and prompt diagnosis and appropriate management are essential to alleviate symptoms and prevent complications such as neurological damage or irreversible hematological changes. Regular monitoring and addressing underlying causes are crucial for long-term management and prevention of recurrence.

Sickle cell anemia

Sickle cell anemia is a hereditary blood disorder characterized by the presence of abnormal hemoglobin, known as hemoglobin S (HbS), in red blood cells. This genetic mutation causes the red blood cells to take on a rigid, sickle-like shape under certain conditions, leading to various complications. Here's a detailed overview of sickle cell anemia:

1. **Genetics:**

a) Sickle cell anemia is an autosomal recessive genetic disorder, meaning that individuals must inherit two copies of the abnormal hemoglobin gene (one from each parent) to develop the disease.

b) The abnormal gene responsible for sickle cell anemia is called the HBB gene, which encodes the beta-globin subunit of hemoglobin. A single nucleotide substitution results in the production of hemoglobin S instead of normal hemoglobin A.

2. **Pathophysiology:**

a) Hemoglobin S tends to polymerize and form long, rigid structures inside red blood cells when exposed to low oxygen levels or other stressors.

b) The polymerization of hemoglobin S distorts the shape of red blood cells, causing them to become stiff and assume a characteristic sickle shape.

c) Sickle cells are less flexible and have a shorter lifespan than normal red blood cells, leading to chronic hemolysis (destruction of red blood cells) and anemia.

3. **Clinical Manifestations:**

a) **Anemia**: Chronic hemolysis and decreased red blood cell lifespan lead to anemia, characterized by fatigue, weakness, pallor, and shortness of breath.

b) **Vaso-occlusive crises:** Sickle cells can block small blood vessels, leading to episodes of severe pain, known as vaso-occlusive crises. These crises can occur anywhere in the body and may require hospitalization for pain management.

c) **Acute chest syndrome**: Blockage of blood vessels in the lungs can cause acute chest syndrome, characterized by chest pain, cough, fever, and difficulty breathing. It is a life-threatening complication of sickle cell disease.

d) **Stroke**: Sickle cell anemia increases the risk of stroke, particularly in children, due to blockage of blood vessels in the brain.

e) **Organ damage**: Chronic vaso-occlusion and impaired blood flow can lead to damage to various organs, including the spleen, liver, kidneys, bones, and eyes.

f) **Infections**: Individuals with sickle cell anemia are at increased risk of infections, particularly those caused by encapsulated bacteria such as Streptococcus pneumoniae, due to functional asplenia (loss of spleen function).

4. **Diagnosis:**

a) Sickle cell anemia is typically diagnosed through blood tests, including hemoglobin electrophoresis or high-performance liquid chromatography (HPLC), which can identify the presence of hemoglobin S.

b) Additional tests may be performed to assess complications and monitor disease progression, such as complete blood count (CBC), reticulocyte count, bilirubin levels, and imaging studies.

5. **Treatment:**

a) **Symptomatic management**: Treatment aims to relieve symptoms and prevent complications. This may include pain management during vaso-occlusive crises, hydration, and supplemental oxygen during acute chest syndrome episodes.

b) **Hydroxyurea**: This medication can help reduce the frequency and severity of vaso-occlusive crises and acute chest syndrome by increasing the production of fetal hemoglobin (HbF), which interferes with the polymerization of hemoglobin S.

c) **Blood transfusions**: Regular transfusions may be necessary to treat severe anemia or prevent complications such as stroke.

d) **Bone marrow or stem cell transplantation**: Curative treatment options may be considered for eligible individuals, particularly children with severe disease.

6. **Prevention:**

   a) **Genetic counseling**: Individuals with sickle cell trait or a family history of sickle cell disease should consider genetic counseling to understand the risk of passing the disease to their children.

   b) **Newborn screening**: Many countries have implemented newborn screening programs to identify infants with sickle cell disease early, allowing for early intervention and treatment.

Sickle cell anemia is a chronic condition that requires comprehensive medical management and supportive care to improve quality of life and reduce complications. Ongoing research efforts aim to develop new treatments and therapies to further improve outcomes for individuals with this condition.

Thalassemia

Thalassemia is a group of inherited blood disorders characterized by abnormal hemoglobin production, leading to reduced synthesis of normal hemoglobin chains. This results in anemia and various complications due to inadequate oxygen transport by red blood cells. Thalassemia is classified into two main types: alpha thalassemia and beta thalassemia. Here's a detailed overview:

1. **Genetics:**

   a) Thalassemia is inherited in an autosomal recessive pattern, meaning that individuals must inherit two abnormal copies of the hemoglobin gene (one from each parent) to develop the disorder.

   b) The genes responsible for thalassemia are the HBA1, HBA2 (alpha globin genes), and HBB (beta globin gene).

c) Mutations in these genes result in reduced or absent production of alpha or beta globin chains, leading to imbalanced hemoglobin synthesis and thalassemia.

2. **Types:**

   a) **Alpha thalassemia**: Alpha thalassemia results from mutations in the alpha globin genes (HBA1 and HBA2). It can be classified into four subtypes based on the number of affected alpha globin genes: silent carrier, alpha thalassemia trait, hemoglobin H disease, and Bart's hydrops fetalis.

   b) **Beta thalassemia**: Beta thalassemia occurs due to mutations in the beta globin gene (HBB). It can be classified into thalassemia minor (beta thalassemia trait), thalassemia intermedia, and thalassemia major (also known as Cooley's anemia).

3. **Pathophysiology:**

   a) Reduced or absent synthesis of alpha or beta globin chains leads to an imbalance in the production of hemoglobin subunits.

   b) In alpha thalassemia, excess beta globin chains form unstable tetramers, leading to hemolysis (destruction of red blood cells) and ineffective erythropoiesis (inefficient production of red blood cells).

   c) In beta thalassemia, excess alpha globin chains precipitate within red blood cells, causing damage to the cell membrane and leading to hemolysis and anemia.

4. **Clinical Manifestations:**

   a) **Anemia**: Thalassemia causes varying degrees of anemia, depending on the severity of the disease.

   b) Fatigue, weakness, and pallor due to decreased oxygen-carrying capacity of the blood.

c) Growth retardation and delayed puberty, especially in individuals with severe forms of thalassemia.

d) Skeletal abnormalities, such as bone deformities and osteoporosis, due to increased bone marrow activity.

e) Splenomegaly (enlarged spleen) and hepatomegaly (enlarged liver) due to extramedullary hematopoiesis and hemolysis.

f) Jaundice and gallstones due to increased bilirubin production from hemolysis.

g) Thalassemia major may present with severe anemia in infancy, requiring regular blood transfusions for survival.

5. **Diagnosis:**

a) Thalassemia is diagnosed through a combination of clinical evaluation, blood tests, and genetic testing.

b) Complete blood count (CBC) may show microcytic (small cell size) hypochromic (pale) red blood cells, low hemoglobin, and elevated levels of red blood cell indices such as mean corpuscular volume (MCV).

c) Hemoglobin electrophoresis or high-performance liquid chromatography (HPLC) can identify abnormal hemoglobin variants and quantify their levels.

d) Genetic testing can confirm the presence of specific mutations in the alpha or beta globin genes.

6. **Treatment:**

a. Management of thalassemia aims to alleviate symptoms, prevent complications, and improve quality of life.

b. Treatment modalities include:

   i. **Blood transfusions**: Regular transfusions to maintain hemoglobin levels within a target range and prevent anemia-related complications.

ii. **Iron chelation therapy**: To remove excess iron from the body, which accumulates due to frequent blood transfusions.

iii. **Folic acid supplementation**: To support red blood cell production.

iv. Splenectomy: In some cases of severe splenomegaly or hypersplenism.

v. **Bone marrow or stem cell transplantation**: Curative treatment for select individuals, particularly those with severe thalassemia major.

7. **Prevention:**

a) Genetic counseling and prenatal testing for carriers of thalassemia to assess the risk of having affected offspring.

b) Preimplantation genetic diagnosis (PGD) for couples undergoing in vitro fertilization (IVF) to select embryos without thalassemia mutations.

c) Public health programs for carrier screening and education in populations with a high prevalence of thalassemia.

Thalassemia is a chronic condition that requires lifelong management and support from a multidisciplinary healthcare team, including hematologists, genetic counselors, and specialized nurses. Early diagnosis, appropriate treatment, and genetic counseling are essential for improving outcomes and quality of life for individuals affected by thalassemia.

Hereditary acquired anemia

"Hereditary acquired anemia" seems like a contradictory term. Anemia can either be hereditary or acquired. Hereditary anemias are those that are inherited due to genetic mutations affecting red blood cell production, structure, or function. Acquired anemias, on the other hand, develop later in life due to various factors such as nutritional deficiencies, chronic diseases, medications, or environmental exposures. However, I can provide an overview of both hereditary anemias and acquired anemias separately:

Hereditary Anemias:

1. **Sickle Cell Anemia**: As discussed earlier, sickle cell anemia is a hereditary blood disorder caused by a mutation in the beta-globin gene, leading to the production of abnormal hemoglobin known as hemoglobin S. This results in the characteristic sickle-shaped red blood cells, chronic hemolysis, anemia, and various complications.

2. **Thalassemia**: Thalassemia encompasses a group of inherited blood disorders characterized by reduced or absent synthesis of normal hemoglobin chains, leading to anemia and other complications. Alpha thalassemia and beta thalassemia are the two main types, each with different subtypes and clinical manifestations.

3. **Hereditary Spherocytosis**: This is a genetic disorder characterized by defects in proteins involved in the structure and stability of red blood cell membranes, leading to spherical-shaped red blood cells (spherocytes), chronic hemolysis, and anemia.

4. **Hereditary Elliptocytosis**: Another inherited disorder affecting red blood cell shape, characterized by elliptical-shaped red blood cells (elliptocytes), which are prone to hemolysis and can lead to anemia.

Acquired Anemias:

1. **Iron Deficiency Anemia**: The most common type of anemia worldwide, caused by inadequate dietary intake of iron, chronic blood loss (such as gastrointestinal bleeding or menstruation), malabsorption disorders, or increased iron requirements (e.g., during pregnancy or rapid growth periods).

2. **Vitamin Deficiency Anemias**: Anemias resulting from deficiencies in specific vitamins essential for red blood cell production, such as vitamin B12 deficiency (pernicious anemia) and folate deficiency. These

deficiencies can occur due to inadequate dietary intake, malabsorption disorders, or other factors.

3. **Anemia of Chronic Disease**: Anemia that develops in the context of chronic inflammatory conditions such as chronic infections, autoimmune diseases, cancer, or chronic kidney disease. It is characterized by impaired iron utilization, decreased red blood cell lifespan, and altered production of erythropoietin.

4. **Hemolytic Anemias**: Anemias caused by increased destruction (hemolysis) of red blood cells, either due to intrinsic defects in the red blood cells (e.g., hereditary spherocytosis, glucose-6-phosphate dehydrogenase deficiency) or extrinsic factors (e.g., autoimmune hemolytic anemia, certain infections or medications).

5. **Aplastic Anemia**: A rare but severe form of anemia characterized by bone marrow failure, resulting in decreased production of red blood cells, white blood cells, and platelets. It can be acquired due to exposure to toxins, certain medications, infections, or autoimmune conditions.

Each type of hereditary or acquired anemia requires specific diagnostic tests, management strategies, and targeted treatments. Treatment may include dietary modifications, supplementation, medications, blood transfusions, or other interventions aimed at addressing the underlying cause and alleviating symptoms. Early diagnosis and appropriate management are essential for improving outcomes and quality of life for individuals with anemia.

Hemophilia

Hemophilia is a rare genetic disorder characterized by a deficiency or dysfunction of clotting factors in the blood, leading to prolonged bleeding and impaired blood clotting. It primarily affects males, as it is inherited in an X-linked recessive pattern. Here's a detailed overview of hemophilia:

1. **Genetics:**

a) Hemophilia is caused by mutations in the genes responsible for producing clotting factors, particularly factor VIII (hemophilia A) or factor IX (hemophilia B).

b) Because the genes for these clotting factors are located on the X chromosome, hemophilia primarily affects males. Females can be carriers of the hemophilia gene and may exhibit mild symptoms or be asymptomatic carriers.

2. **Clotting Factor Deficiency:**

a) **Hemophilia A:** This type of hemophilia is caused by a deficiency or dysfunction of factor VIII, a protein essential for blood clot formation. It is the most common type, accounting for about 80-85% of cases.

b) **Hemophilia B (Christmas disease):** Hemophilia B is caused by a deficiency or dysfunction of factor IX, another clotting protein involved in the coagulation cascade. It accounts for the remaining 15-20% of cases.

3. **Pathophysiology:**

a) In individuals with hemophilia, the deficiency or dysfunction of clotting factors impairs the formation of stable blood clots.

b) As a result, even minor injuries or trauma can lead to prolonged bleeding episodes, which may be spontaneous or occur after surgery, dental procedures, or trauma.

c) Bleeding can occur internally (into joints, muscles, or organs) or externally (from cuts, wounds, or mucous membranes).

4. **Clinical Manifestations:**

a) **Prolonged bleeding**: The hallmark symptom of hemophilia is prolonged bleeding, which may present as excessive bleeding from minor cuts or injuries, nosebleeds, or bleeding gums.

b) **Easy bruising:** Individuals with hemophilia may bruise easily due to the tendency to bleed beneath the skin (hematoma formation).

c) **Joint bleeding**: Recurrent bleeding into joints, particularly weight-bearing joints such as the knees, ankles, and elbows, can lead to chronic joint pain, swelling, and eventually, joint damage (hemophilic arthropathy).

d) **Muscle bleeding**: Bleeding into muscles can cause swelling, pain, and reduced range of motion in affected muscles.

5. Diagnosis:

a) Diagnosis of hemophilia involves a combination of medical history, physical examination, and laboratory tests.

b) Clotting factor assays: Blood tests to measure the levels of factor VIII or factor IX activity. Reduced activity levels indicate hemophilia.

c) Genetic testing: To identify specific mutations in the factor VIII or factor IX genes, particularly in cases where the diagnosis is uncertain or for carrier detection in female relatives.

6. Treatment:

a) **Replacement therapy**: The mainstay of treatment for hemophilia involves replacing the deficient clotting factor through intravenous infusion of clotting factor concentrates. Recombinant clotting factor concentrates are now widely used to reduce the risk of transmitting blood-borne infections.

b) **Prophylactic therapy**: Regular prophylactic infusions of clotting factor concentrates to prevent bleeding episodes, particularly in individuals with severe hemophilia or a history of frequent bleeds.

c) **On-demand therapy**: Treatment of acute bleeding episodes with clotting factor concentrates as needed.

d) **Desmopressin (DDAVP)**: In some cases of mild hemophilia A, desmopressin may be used to stimulate the release of stored factor VIII from endothelial cells.

e) **Hemostatic agents**: In addition to clotting factor replacement, other hemostatic agents such as fibrin sealants or tranexamic acid may be used to control bleeding.

7. **Complications and Management:**

a) **Joint damage**: Chronic joint bleeding can lead to hemophilic arthropathy, characterized by pain, stiffness, and reduced range of motion in affected joints. Physical therapy and joint protection techniques are essential to manage joint complications.

b) **Inhibitor development**: Some individuals with hemophilia may develop inhibitors (antibodies) against clotting factor concentrates, which can complicate treatment and increase the risk of bleeding.

c) **Comprehensive care**: Management of hemophilia requires a multidisciplinary approach involving hematologists, orthopedic specialists, physical therapists, social workers, and genetic counselors to address the complex medical, psychological, and social aspects of the condition.

8. **Prevention:**

a) **Genetic counseling**: Providing information and support to individuals and families affected by hemophilia, including carrier testing and family planning options.

b) **Avoidance of high-risk activities**: Encouraging individuals with hemophilia to avoid activities with a high risk of injury or trauma to prevent bleeding episodes.

c) **Prophylactic treatment**: Early initiation of prophylactic clotting factor replacement therapy to prevent joint damage and improve quality of life for individuals with severe hemophilia.

Hemophilia is a chronic condition that requires lifelong management, but with appropriate treatment and comprehensive care, individuals with hemophilia can lead fulfilling lives with reduced risk of bleeding complications. Ongoing research into gene therapy and other innovative treatments holds promise for further improving outcomes and quality of life for individuals with hemophilia.

ENDOCRINE SYSTEM:

The endocrine system is a complex network of glands and organs that produce and secrete hormones to regulate various physiological processes in the body, including metabolism, growth and development, reproduction, mood regulation, and response to stress. Here's a detailed introduction to the endocrine system:

1. **Components of the Endocrine System:**
   a) **Glands:** The primary components of the endocrine system are glands, which are specialized organs that produce and secrete hormones directly into the bloodstream. Major endocrine glands include the pituitary gland, thyroid gland, adrenal glands, pancreas, ovaries (in females), and testes (in males).
   b) **Hormones**: Hormones are chemical messengers produced by endocrine glands that travel through the bloodstream to target cells or organs, where they exert their effects. Hormones regulate various physiological processes, including metabolism, growth and development, stress response, reproduction, and mood regulation.

2. **Key Endocrine Glands and Hormones:**
   a) **Pituitary Gland**: Often referred to as the "master gland," the pituitary gland is located at the base of the brain and produces several important hormones that regulate other endocrine glands, including growth hormone, thyroid-stimulating hormone,

adrenocorticotropic hormone, and gonadotropins (follicle-stimulating hormone and luteinizing hormone).

b) **Thyroid Gland**: The thyroid gland, located in the neck, produces thyroid hormones (thyroxine and triiodothyronine) that regulate metabolism, growth, and energy expenditure.

c) **Adrenal Glands**: The adrenal glands, situated on top of the kidneys, produce hormones such as cortisol (stress hormone), aldosterone (regulates salt and water balance), and adrenaline (epinephrine, involved in the fight-or-flight response).

d) **Pancreas**: The pancreas secretes insulin and glucagon, which regulate blood sugar levels by controlling glucose metabolism and storage.

e) **Gonads**: The ovaries (in females) produce estrogen and progesterone, which regulate menstrual cycles, pregnancy, and secondary sexual characteristics. The testes (in males) produce testosterone, which is responsible for male reproductive functions and secondary sexual characteristics.

3. **Hormone Action:**

a) Hormones act by binding to specific receptors on target cells or organs, triggering a series of biochemical and physiological responses.

b) Hormones can exert their effects through various mechanisms, including altering gene expression, activating enzyme cascades, modifying cell membrane permeability, and regulating protein synthesis.

4. **Regulation of Hormone Secretion:**

a) Hormone secretion is tightly regulated by feedback mechanisms involving the endocrine glands, target organs, and the central nervous system.

b) Negative feedback loops help maintain hormone levels within a narrow physiological range by inhibiting further hormone secretion when levels are elevated and stimulating secretion when levels are low.

5. **Endocrine Disorders:**

   a) Dysfunction of the endocrine system can lead to various disorders, including hormone deficiencies, excess hormone production, and impaired hormone action.

   b) Common endocrine disorders include diabetes mellitus (caused by insulin deficiency or resistance), thyroid disorders (such as hypothyroidism and hyperthyroidism), adrenal disorders (such as Addison's disease and Cushing's syndrome), and reproductive hormone imbalances (such as polycystic ovary syndrome and hypogonadism).

6. **Diagnostic Tests:**

   a) Diagnosis of endocrine disorders often involves a combination of medical history, physical examination, and laboratory tests to measure hormone levels, assess organ function, and identify underlying causes.

   b) Imaging studies such as ultrasound, CT scans, and MRI may be used to visualize endocrine glands and detect structural abnormalities.

7. **Treatment:**

   a) Treatment of endocrine disorders depends on the specific condition and may include hormone replacement therapy, medications to regulate hormone levels, lifestyle modifications, and surgical interventions (such as gland removal or tumor resection).

   b) Management of chronic endocrine disorders often requires long-term monitoring and multidisciplinary care involving endocrinologists, primary care physicians, nurses, dietitians, and other healthcare professionals.

Overall, the endocrine system plays a vital role in maintaining homeostasis and coordinating physiological functions throughout the body. Dysfunction of the endocrine system can have profound effects on health and wellbeing, highlighting the importance of early detection, diagnosis, and management of endocrine disorders.

Types of Endocrine diseases:

Endocrine diseases are disorders that affect the endocrine system, which consists of glands that produce hormones to regulate various bodily functions. Here are some common types of endocrine diseases:

1. Diabetes Mellitus:
    a. Type 1 Diabetes: An autoimmune condition where the immune system attacks and destroys insulin-producing beta cells in the pancreas, leading to insulin deficiency.
    b. Type 2 Diabetes: Characterized by insulin resistance, where cells fail to respond properly to insulin, and eventually, insulin production may decrease.
    c. Gestational Diabetes: Occurs during pregnancy and is characterized by high blood sugar levels that may affect both the mother and the baby.
2. Thyroid Disorders:
    a. Hypothyroidism: A condition where the thyroid gland does not produce enough thyroid hormone, leading to symptoms such as fatigue, weight gain, and cold intolerance.
    b. Hyperthyroidism: Characterized by an overactive thyroid gland that produces excessive amounts of thyroid hormone, leading to

symptoms such as weight loss, rapid heartbeat, and heat intolerance.

    c. Thyroid Nodules and Thyroid Cancer: Abnormal growths in the thyroid gland that can be benign or malignant.

3. Adrenal Disorders:

    a. Cushing's Syndrome: Resulting from prolonged exposure to high levels of cortisol, either due to excessive production by the adrenal glands or prolonged use of corticosteroid medications.

    b. Addison's Disease: Occurs when the adrenal glands do not produce enough cortisol and aldosterone, leading to symptoms such as fatigue, weight loss, and low blood pressure.

4. Polycystic Ovary Syndrome (PCOS): A hormonal disorder common among women of reproductive age, characterized by irregular menstrual periods, excess androgen levels, and polycystic ovaries.

5. Hypopituitarism: A condition where the pituitary gland fails to produce one or more of its hormones, leading to various symptoms depending on which hormones are deficient.

6. Hyperparathyroidism and Hypoparathyroidism: Disorders of the parathyroid glands, which regulate calcium and phosphate levels in the body. Hyperparathyroidism involves excessive production of parathyroid hormone, while hypoparathyroidism involves insufficient production.

7. Growth Hormone Disorders:

    a. Growth Hormone Deficiency: Characterized by inadequate production of growth hormone, leading to short stature in children and potential metabolic abnormalities in adults.

    b. Acromegaly: Resulting from excessive production of growth hormone in adults, leading to enlargement of bones and tissues.

8. Multiple Endocrine Neoplasia (MEN) Syndromes: Rare genetic disorders characterized by the development of tumors in multiple endocrine glands, leading to hormonal imbalances.

Diabetes

Diabetes mellitus is a chronic metabolic disorder characterized by high blood sugar levels (hyperglycemia) resulting from defects in insulin secretion, insulin action, or both. It is one of the most prevalent endocrine disorders globally and has significant implications for health and wellbeing. Here's a detailed overview of diabetes:

1. **Types of Diabetes:**

   a) **Type 1 Diabetes**: Type 1 diabetes, previously known as insulin-dependent diabetes or juvenile-onset diabetes, is characterized by autoimmune destruction of pancreatic beta cells, leading to absolute insulin deficiency. Individuals with type 1 diabetes require lifelong insulin therapy for survival.

   b) **Type 2 Diabetes**: Type 2 diabetes, formerly known as non-insulin-dependent diabetes or adult-onset diabetes, is the most common form of diabetes. It is characterized by insulin resistance, where the body's cells become resistant to the effects of insulin, and impaired insulin secretion by pancreatic beta cells. Type 2 diabetes can often be managed with lifestyle modifications, oral medications, and/or insulin therapy.

   c) **Gestational Diabetes**: Gestational diabetes occurs during pregnancy and is characterized by elevated blood sugar levels that develop or are first recognized during pregnancy. It increases the risk of complications for both the mother and the baby and may resolve after childbirth, but it also predisposes women to develop type 2 diabetes later in life.

d) **Other Forms of Diabetes**: Other forms of diabetes include monogenic diabetes (caused by mutations in a single gene), secondary diabetes (resulting from other medical conditions or medications), and diabetes of pancreatic origin (due to pancreatic diseases or surgery).

2. Pathophysiology:

a) **Type 1 Diabetes**: In type 1 diabetes, autoimmune destruction of pancreatic beta cells results in an absolute deficiency of insulin production. Without sufficient insulin, glucose cannot enter cells to be used for energy, leading to hyperglycemia. Individuals with type 1 diabetes require exogenous insulin replacement to regulate blood sugar levels.

b) **Type 2 Diabetes**: Type 2 diabetes develops due to a combination of insulin resistance and impaired insulin secretion. Insulin resistance occurs when cells fail to respond adequately to insulin, leading to elevated blood sugar levels. Over time, pancreatic beta cells may become exhausted and fail to produce enough insulin to overcome insulin resistance, further contributing to hyperglycemia.

c) **Gestational Diabetes**: Gestational diabetes results from hormonal changes during pregnancy that increase insulin resistance, coupled with inadequate compensatory insulin secretion. This leads to elevated blood sugar levels during pregnancy, which can increase the risk of complications for both the mother and the baby.

3. Clinical Manifestations:

a) Common symptoms of diabetes include increased thirst, frequent urination (polyuria), excessive hunger (polyphagia), unexplained weight loss, fatigue, blurred vision, slow wound healing, and recurrent infections.

b) In some cases, especially in type 2 diabetes, individuals may be asymptomatic or have mild symptoms that go unnoticed for years, leading to delayed diagnosis and increased risk of complications.

4. Diagnosis:

a) Diagnosis of diabetes is typically based on blood tests that measure fasting blood glucose levels, oral glucose tolerance test (OGTT), or HbA1c levels (glycated hemoglobin), which provide an average of blood sugar levels over the past 2-3 months.

b) Diagnosis of gestational diabetes is based on glucose tolerance testing performed during pregnancy.

5. Complications:

a) Chronic hyperglycemia in diabetes can lead to various long-term complications affecting multiple organ systems, including the eyes (diabetic retinopathy), kidneys (diabetic nephropathy), nerves (diabetic neuropathy), and cardiovascular system (heart disease, stroke, peripheral vascular disease).

b) Other complications may include diabetic foot ulcers, skin conditions, dental problems, and sexual dysfunction.

6. Treatment:

a) Treatment of diabetes aims to achieve and maintain blood sugar levels within a target range to prevent complications and improve quality of life.

b) Treatment modalities may include lifestyle modifications (such as healthy diet, regular exercise, weight management), oral medications (e.g., metformin, sulfonylureas, DPP-4 inhibitors), injectable medications (e.g., insulin, GLP-1 receptor agonists), and, in some cases, bariatric surgery.

c) Management of gestational diabetes involves dietary changes, monitoring blood sugar levels, and sometimes insulin therapy to maintain blood sugar levels within target ranges during pregnancy.

7. Prevention:

a) Prevention of type 1 diabetes is not currently possible, as it is primarily an autoimmune condition with genetic and environmental factors.

b) Prevention of type 2 diabetes and gestational diabetes involves lifestyle interventions aimed at promoting healthy eating habits, regular physical activity, weight management, and avoidance of tobacco use.

c) Early detection and management of prediabetes can help prevent or delay the onset of type 2 diabetes through lifestyle modifications and, in some cases, medications such as metformin.

8. Monitoring and Management:

a) Individuals with diabetes require regular monitoring of blood sugar levels, periodic assessment of HbA1c levels, and screening for diabetes-related complications.

b) Diabetes management should be individualized and may require adjustments over time based on changes in health status, medication efficacy, and lifestyle factors.

c) Patient education and self-management are integral components of diabetes care, empowering individuals to actively participate in their treatment and make informed decisions about their health.

Overall, diabetes is a complex and chronic condition that requires comprehensive management to prevent complications and optimize health outcomes. A multidisciplinary approach involving healthcare professionals, including endocrinologists, primary care physicians, nurses, dietitians, and diabetes educators, is essential for providing personalized care and support to individuals with diabetes.

Thyroid diseases

Thyroid diseases encompass a range of disorders that affect the structure or function of the thyroid gland, a butterfly-shaped gland located in the front of the neck. The thyroid gland plays a crucial role in regulating metabolism, growth, and energy expenditure by producing and secreting thyroid hormones. Here's a detailed overview of thyroid diseases:

1. **Anatomy and Function of the Thyroid Gland:**
   a) The thyroid gland produces two main hormones: thyroxine (T4) and triiodothyronine (T3), which regulate metabolism, heart rate, body temperature, and other physiological processes.
   b) Thyroid hormone synthesis is regulated by thyroid-stimulating hormone (TSH), which is produced by the pituitary gland. TSH stimulates the thyroid gland to produce and release thyroid hormones in response to the body's metabolic needs.

2. **Thyroid Disorders:**
   a) **Hypothyroidism:** Hypothyroidism occurs when the thyroid gland fails to produce sufficient thyroid hormones, leading to a slowdown in metabolic processes. Causes of hypothyroidism include autoimmune thyroiditis (Hashimoto's thyroiditis), thyroid surgery or radiation therapy, iodine deficiency, medications, and congenital defects.
   b) **Hyperthyroidism:** Hyperthyroidism is characterized by excessive production of thyroid hormones, resulting in an overactive metabolism. Common causes include autoimmune hyperthyroidism (Graves' disease), toxic multinodular goiter, thyroid nodules or adenomas, thyroiditis, and excessive iodine intake.

c) **Thyroid Nodules**: Thyroid nodules are lumps or growths that develop within the thyroid gland. While most thyroid nodules are benign (non-cancerous), some may be malignant (cancerous). Risk factors for thyroid nodules include age, gender (more common in women), family history, radiation exposure, and iodine deficiency.

d) **Thyroid Cancer**: Thyroid cancer is relatively uncommon but can occur in individuals with thyroid nodules. Types of thyroid cancer include papillary carcinoma, follicular carcinoma, medullary carcinoma, and anaplastic carcinoma. Treatment typically involves surgery, radioactive iodine therapy, and sometimes, external beam radiation therapy or chemotherapy.

e) **Thyroiditis:** Thyroiditis refers to inflammation of the thyroid gland, which can result in temporary hyperthyroidism (due to leakage of thyroid hormones) followed by hypothyroidism as the thyroid gland becomes depleted of hormones. Types of thyroiditis include Hashimoto's thyroiditis (an autoimmune condition), subacute thyroiditis, postpartum thyroiditis, and drug-induced thyroiditis.

3. Clinical Manifestations:

a) **Hypothyroidism**: Symptoms of hypothyroidism may include fatigue, weight gain, cold intolerance, constipation, dry skin, brittle nails, hair loss, depression, memory impairment, and menstrual irregularities.

b) **Hyperthyroidism**: Hyperthyroidism is characterized by symptoms such as weight loss, increased appetite, heat intolerance, sweating, palpitations, tremors, anxiety, irritability, insomnia, frequent bowel movements, and menstrual irregularities.

c) **Thyroid Nodules:** Thyroid nodules are often asymptomatic and discovered incidentally during physical examination or imaging studies. However, larger nodules may cause symptoms such as neck swelling, difficulty swallowing, hoarseness, or voice changes.

d) **Thyroid Cancer:** Symptoms of thyroid cancer may include a painless lump or swelling in the neck, hoarseness, difficulty swallowing, enlarged lymph nodes in the neck, and sometimes, symptoms of hyperthyroidism or hypothyroidism.

e) **Thyroiditis**: Symptoms of thyroiditis vary depending on the underlying cause but may include neck pain, tenderness, fever, fatigue, and symptoms of hyperthyroidism or hypothyroidism during the acute phase.

4. **Diagnosis:**

a) Diagnosis of thyroid disorders involves a combination of medical history, physical examination, laboratory tests, and imaging studies.

b) Blood tests such as thyroid-stimulating hormone (TSH), free thyroxine (T4), free triiodothyronine (T3), and thyroid antibodies (anti-TPO, anti-thyroglobulin) are commonly used to assess thyroid function and detect autoimmune thyroid disorders.

c) Imaging studies such as ultrasound, thyroid scan (radioiodine uptake), or fine-needle aspiration biopsy may be performed to evaluate thyroid nodules and detect thyroid cancer.

5. **Treatment:**

a) Treatment of thyroid disorders depends on the specific condition and may include medication, radioactive iodine therapy, surgery, or a combination of these approaches.

b) Hypothyroidism is typically treated with synthetic thyroid hormone replacement therapy (levothyroxine) to restore normal thyroid hormone levels.

c) Hyperthyroidism may be managed with antithyroid medications (such as methimazole or propylthiouracil), radioactive iodine therapy, or thyroidectomy (surgical removal of the thyroid gland).

d) Thyroid nodules and thyroid cancer may require surgical removal of the affected thyroid tissue (thyroidectomy), radioactive iodine therapy, external beam radiation therapy, or targeted therapy with medications such as tyrosine

Disorders of sex hormones

Disorders of sex hormones encompass a broad spectrum of conditions that affect the production, regulation, or action of hormones involved in sexual development and function. These disorders can arise from genetic abnormalities, hormonal imbalances, tumors, medications, or environmental factors. Here's a detailed overview:

1. **Sex Hormones:**

   a) **Androgens**: Androgens are male sex hormones primarily produced by the testes in males and, to a lesser extent, by the adrenal glands in both sexes. The most well-known androgen is testosterone, which plays a key role in male sexual development, reproductive function, muscle mass, bone density, and mood regulation.

   b) **Estrogens:** Estrogens are female sex hormones primarily produced by the ovaries in females and, to a lesser extent, by the adrenal glands in both sexes. The main types of estrogen include estradiol, estrone, and estriol. Estrogens are involved in female sexual development, reproductive function, menstrual cycle regulation, bone health, and cardiovascular health.

2. **Disorders of Androgens:**

   a) **Hypogonadism**: Hypogonadism refers to reduced or absent function of the testes or ovaries, leading to insufficient production of sex hormones. It can be classified as primary (due to testicular or ovarian dysfunction) or secondary (due to hypothalamic-pituitary dysfunction). Symptoms of hypogonadism may include decreased libido, erectile dysfunction (in males), menstrual irregularities (in females), infertility, fatigue, and reduced bone density.

b) **Hyperandrogenis**m: Hyperandrogenism refers to excessive production of androgens, leading to symptoms such as hirsutism (excessive hair growth), acne, male-pattern baldness, menstrual irregularities, and infertility. Common causes include polycystic ovary syndrome (PCOS), congenital adrenal hyperplasia (CAH), and androgen-secreting tumors.

3. **Disorders of Estrogens:**

a) **Hypoestrogenism**: Hypoestrogenism refers to low levels of estrogen, which can occur in conditions such as menopause, premature ovarian failure, hypothalamic-pituitary dysfunction, or surgical removal of the ovaries. Symptoms may include hot flashes, vaginal dryness, mood changes, insomnia, and bone loss (osteoporosis).

b) **Hyperestrogenism**: Hyperestrogenism refers to elevated levels of estrogen, which can result from conditions such as estrogen-producing tumors (e.g., ovarian tumors), hormone replacement therapy, obesity (due to increased conversion of androgens to estrogens in adipose tissue), or certain medications. Symptoms may include abnormal uterine bleeding, breast tenderness, bloating, mood changes, and increased risk of blood clots.

4. **Intersex Disorders:**

a) Intersex disorders, also known as disorders of sexual development (DSD), encompass a range of conditions where individuals are born with variations in sex characteristics that do not fit typical definitions of male or female. These variations can involve chromosomal, gonadal, or anatomical differences, leading to ambiguous genitalia, atypical hormone levels, or differences in internal reproductive organs.

b) Examples of intersex disorders include androgen insensitivity syndrome (AIS), congenital adrenal hyperplasia (CAH), 5-alpha-reductase deficiency, and mixed gonadal dysgenesis. Management of intersex disorders may involve medical, surgical, and psychosocial interventions aimed at optimizing physical and psychological health outcomes.

5. **Diagnosis and Treatment:**

a) Diagnosis of sex hormone disorders typically involves a combination of medical history, physical examination, laboratory tests (including hormone levels and imaging studies), and genetic testing.

b) Treatment of sex hormone disorders depends on the underlying cause and may include hormone replacement therapy (e.g., testosterone or estrogen replacement), medications to suppress or block hormone production (e.g., antiandrogens), surgery (e.g., gonadectomy or gonadal reconstruction), and supportive therapies (e.g., fertility treatment or psychotherapy).

c) Management of sex hormone disorders often requires a multidisciplinary approach involving endocrinologists, gynecologists, urologists, geneticists, psychologists, and other healthcare professionals to address the complex medical, psychological, and social aspects of these conditions.

6. **Prevention and Support:**

a) Prevention of sex hormone disorders may involve genetic counseling, prenatal screening, and early detection and treatment of hormonal imbalances or congenital conditions.

b) Individuals with sex hormone disorders may benefit from support groups, educational resources, and counseling services to help cope with the physical, emotional, and social challenges associated with these conditions.

Overall, disorders of sex hormones can have profound effects on sexual development, reproductive function, and overall health. Early diagnosis, appropriate treatment, and comprehensive care are essential for optimizing outcomes and quality of life for individuals affected by these conditions.

Multiple Choice Questions (Objective)

1. What is the primary symptom of anemia?

    A) Fever

    B) Fatigue

    C) Nausea

    D) Headache

2. Which type of cancer originates in the lymphatic system?

    A) Leukemia

    B) Lymphoma

    C) Multiple Myeloma

    D) Hemophilia

3. What is the characteristic shape of red blood cells in sickle cell anemia?

    A) Oval

    B) Crescent

    C) Round

    D) Irregular

4. Which gland is referred to as the "master gland" in the endocrine system?

A) Adrenal gland

B) Thyroid gland

C) Pituitary gland

D) Pancreas

5. What is a common treatment for hypothyroidism?

A) Insulin injections

B) Thyroid hormone replacement

C) Antithyroid medications

D) Blood transfusions

6. Which hormone is primarily involved in type 1 diabetes?

A) Cortisol

B) Insulin

C) Adrenaline

D) Thyroxine

7. What does hemophilia primarily affect?

A) Blood clotting

B) Oxygen transport

C) Immune response

D) Hormone production

8. Which type of thyroiditis is an autoimmune condition?

A) Subacute thyroiditis

B) Postpartum thyroiditis

C) Drug-induced thyroiditis

9. D) Hashimoto's thyroiditis

10. What is a key feature of Type 2 Diabetes?

A) Absolute insulin deficiency

B) Autoimmune destruction of beta cells

C) Insulin resistance

D) Temporary hyperglycemia

11. Which is not a typical treatment for iron deficiency anemia?

A) Iron supplementation

B) Blood transfusions

C) High protein diet

D) Dietary changes

12. What distinguishes Hodgkin lymphoma from non-Hodgkin lymphoma?

A) Presence of Reed-Sternberg cells

B) Involvement of white blood cells

C) Formation of tumors in lymph nodes

D) Development in children

13. What is a common cause of acquired anemia?

A) Genetic mutation

B) Nutritional deficiencies

C) Bone marrow hyperplasia

D) Overproduction of red blood cells

14. Which vitamin deficiency can cause megaloblastic anemia?

A) Vitamin A

B) Vitamin C

C) Vitamin B12

D) Vitamin D

15. What is the primary role of the thyroid gland?

A) Regulate growth and metabolism

B) Produce blood cells

C) Regulate body temperature

D) Control blood sugar levels

16. What causes the blood cells in sickle cell anemia to have a sickle shape?

A) Lack of oxygen

B) High glucose levels

C) Abnormal haemoglobin

D) Infection

17. Which hormone does the pancreas produce to regulate blood sugar levels?

A) Cortisol

B) Insulin

C) Adrenaline

D) Thyroxine

18. What is the genetic inheritance pattern of thalassemia?

A) Autosomal dominant

B) X-linked recessive

C) Autosomal recessive

D) Mitochondrial

19. What type of hypersensitivity is involved in Type 1 Diabetes?

A) Type I

B) Type II

C) Type III

D) Type IV

20. What is the first choice of treatment for moderate to severe hypothyroidism?

A) Radioactive iodine

B) Surgical removal of the thyroid

C) Levothyroxine

D) Dietary iodine supplementation

21. What does effective management of diabetes primarily aim to achieve?

A) Cure the diabetes

B) Enhance insulin resistance

C) Maintain blood sugar levels within a target range

D) Increase blood sugar variability

Answer Key for MCQs:

1. B) Fatigue

2. B) Lymphoma

3. B) Crescent

4. C) Pituitary gland

5. B) Thyroid hormone replacement

6. B) Insulin

7. A) Blood clotting

8. D) Hashimoto's thyroiditis

9. C) Insulin resistance

10. C) High protein diet

11. A) Presence of Reed-Sternberg cells

12. B) Nutritional deficiencies

13. C) Vitamin B12

14. A) Regulate growth and metabolism

15. C) Abnormal hemoglobin

16. B) Insulin

17. C) Autosomal recessive

18. A) Type I

19. C) Levothyroxine

20. C) Maintain blood sugar levels within a target range

Short Answer Type Questions (Subjective)

1. What is the main function of red blood cells?

2. Describe the role of insulin in the human body.

3. What are the typical symptoms of hyperthyroidism?

4. How is gestational diabetes diagnosed?

5. What genetic mutation is associated with sickle cell anemia?

6. Which dietary changes are recommended for managing hypothyroidism?

7. What are the primary symptoms of iron deficiency anemia?

8. Explain the significance of TSH in thyroid health.

9. What are the common complications associated with diabetes?

10. How does hemophilia affect blood clotting?

11. What is the primary treatment for thalassemia major?

12. Describe the genetic basis of hereditary spherocytosis.

13. What is the impact of untreated hypothyroidism on the body?

14. How is hypogonadism diagnosed?

15. What is the role of hemoglobin in the body?

16. Describe the typical progression of symptoms in Type 1 Diabetes.

17. What causes the thyroid gland to produce too much hormone?

18. How are thyroid nodules typically discovered?

19. What is the importance of folate in red blood cell production?

20. Explain how hyperestrogenism might present in females.

Long Answer Type Questions (Subjective)

1. Discuss the pathophysiology of Type 1 Diabetes and its implications for management.

2. Explain the diagnostic criteria for hypothyroidism and the rationale behind the use of levothyroxine as a treatment.

3. Describe the impact of sickle cell anemia on the body and outline the treatment options available.

4. Analyze the causes of Type 2 Diabetes and discuss the lifestyle interventions recommended for its management.

5. Explain how genetic factors contribute to the development of thalassemia and the potential complications of this condition.

6. Describe the role of the endocrine system in regulating metabolism and how disorders such as hyperthyroidism can disrupt this process.

7. Discuss the clinical manifestations, diagnosis, and treatment options for hemophilia.

8. Explore the causes and consequences of iron deficiency anemia and outline the steps for diagnosis and treatment.

9. Describe the different types of thyroid cancer, their diagnostic process, and treatment approaches.

10. Analyze the role of hormonal imbalances in reproductive health disorders and their management strategies.

CHAPTER - 5

NERVOUS SYSTEM AND GASTRO INTESTINE SYSTEM

NERVOUS SYSTEM

The nervous system is one of the most intricate and essential systems in the human body, responsible for coordinating all bodily functions and enabling interactions with the external environment. Comprised of the brain, spinal cord, and peripheral nerves, it serves as the body's communication network, allowing for the transmission of signals between various parts of the body and the brain. The components and functions of the nervous system in more detail:

1. **Central Nervous System (CNS):**
   a) The CNS consists of the brain and spinal cord, which are encased in protective structures such as the skull and vertebral column.
   b) **Brain**: The brain is the command center of the nervous system, responsible for processing sensory information, initiating motor responses, and coordinating higher cognitive functions such as thinking, learning, and memory.
   c) **Spinal Cord**: The spinal cord serves as a conduit for transmitting signals between the brain and the rest of the body. It also plays a crucial role in reflex actions, which are rapid, involuntary responses to stimuli.

2. **Peripheral Nervous System (PNS):**
   a) The PNS includes all nerves outside the CNS and is further divided into the somatic nervous system and the autonomic nervous system.
   b) **Somatic Nervous System (SNS):** The SNS controls voluntary movements and transmits sensory information from the body to the CNS. It consists of sensory neurons that convey information to the

CNS and motor neurons that carry commands from the CNS to muscles and glands.

c) **Autonomic Nervous System (ANS):** The ANS regulates involuntary bodily functions such as heart rate, digestion, and breathing. It comprises sympathetic and parasympathetic divisions, which often have opposing effects on physiological processes, maintaining a balance known as homeostasis.

3. **Neurons:**

   a) Neurons are the basic structural and functional units of the nervous system, specialized for transmitting electrical and chemical signals.

   b) They consist of three main parts: the cell body (soma), dendrites, and axon. Dendrites receive signals from other neurons, while the axon transmits signals to other neurons or effector cells.

   c) Neurons communicate with each other via synapses, specialized junctions where neurotransmitters are released from one neuron and received by another.

4. **Supporting Cells:**

   a) Supporting cells, or neuroglia, provide structural support, insulation, and nourishment to neurons.

   b) The main types of neuroglia include astrocytes, oligodendrocytes (in the CNS), Schwann cells (in the PNS), and microglia.

5. **Functions:**

   a) **Sensory Function**: The nervous system receives information from sensory receptors and transmits it to the CNS for processing.

   b) **Integrative Function**: The CNS processes sensory information, initiates appropriate responses, and integrates higher cognitive functions.

c) **Motor Function**: The nervous system sends motor commands from the CNS to muscles and glands, resulting in voluntary and involuntary movements and physiological responses.

Types of nervous diseases:

Nervous system diseases, also known as neurological disorders, affect the brain, spinal cord, and nerves throughout the body. They can vary widely in severity and symptoms. Here are some common types:

1) Neurodegenerative Diseases:
   a) Alzheimer's Disease: A progressive brain disorder that affects memory, thinking skills, and eventually, the ability to carry out simple tasks.
   b) Parkinson's Disease: A progressive disorder of the nervous system that affects movement, causing tremors, stiffness, and difficulty with balance and coordination.
   c) Amyotrophic Lateral Sclerosis (ALS): A progressive neurodegenerative disease that affects nerve cells in the brain and spinal cord, leading to muscle weakness, paralysis, and eventually respiratory failure.
   d) Huntington's Disease: A hereditary disorder that causes progressive degeneration of nerve cells in the brain, leading to movement, cognitive, and psychiatric symptoms.
2) Stroke: A sudden interruption of blood flow to the brain, leading to brain damage and symptoms such as paralysis, speech difficulties, and cognitive impairment.
3) Epilepsy: A neurological disorder characterized by recurrent seizures, which are caused by abnormal electrical activity in the brain.
4) Multiple Sclerosis (MS): An autoimmune disease that affects the central nervous system, causing damage to the myelin sheath that covers nerve

fibers, leading to symptoms such as fatigue, weakness, and difficulty with coordination and balance.

5) Migraine: A type of headache disorder characterized by recurrent moderate to severe headaches, often accompanied by other symptoms such as nausea, vomiting, and sensitivity to light and sound.

6) Neuropathy: Damage or dysfunction of one or more nerves, leading to symptoms such as pain, numbness, tingling, and weakness, often in the hands and feet.

7) Cerebral Palsy: A group of permanent movement disorders that appear in early childhood, affecting muscle coordination and posture, often caused by damage to the developing brain.

8) Traumatic Brain Injury (TBI): Damage to the brain caused by an external force, leading to a wide range of symptoms depending on the severity and location of the injury.

9) Peripheral Nerve Disorders: Conditions that affect the peripheral nerves, such as Guillain-Barré syndrome, Charcot-Marie-Tooth disease, and diabetic neuropathy.

10) Neurodevelopmental Disorders: Conditions that affect the development of the nervous system, such as autism spectrum disorder, attention-deficit/hyperactivity disorder (ADHD), and intellectual disability.

Epilepsy

Epilepsy is a neurological disorder characterized by recurrent seizures, which are caused by abnormal electrical activity in the brain. It is one of the most common neurological disorders, affecting people of all ages, though it often manifests in childhood or adolescence. Let's explore epilepsy in more detail:

1. Causes and Risk Factors:

a) Epilepsy can have various causes, including genetic factors, brain injury, infections (such as meningitis or encephalitis), developmental disorders, brain tumors, stroke, or prenatal injury.

b) In many cases, the cause of epilepsy remains unknown (idiopathic epilepsy).

c) Certain risk factors may increase the likelihood of developing epilepsy, including a family history of the disorder, head injuries, prenatal injury or exposure to toxins, and certain developmental or genetic disorders.

2. **Types of Seizures:**

   a. Seizures in epilepsy can vary widely in their presentation, severity, and duration. They are broadly categorized into two main types:

      i. **Generalized Seizures**: These seizures affect both hemispheres of the brain and typically involve loss of consciousness. Subtypes include tonic-clonic (formerly known as grand mal), absence (formerly known as petit mal), myoclonic, and atonic seizures.

      ii. **Focal (Partial) Seizures**: These seizures originate in one specific area of the brain and may or may not involve loss of consciousness. Subtypes include simple focal seizures (with preserved awareness) and complex focal seizures (with altered consciousness).

3. **Symptoms:**

   a) The symptoms of epilepsy depend on the type of seizure and the area of the brain affected.

   b) Generalized seizures may involve loss of consciousness, convulsions, muscle rigidity, sudden jerking movements, staring spells, or temporary confusion.

c) Focal seizures may present with unusual sensations or feelings (aura), involuntary movements, altered consciousness, repetitive movements, or automatic behaviors.

4. **Diagnosis:**

   a) Diagnosing epilepsy involves a thorough medical history, physical examination, and neurological evaluation.

   b) Diagnostic tests such as electroencephalogram (EEG), magnetic resonance imaging (MRI), and blood tests may be conducted to assess brain activity and identify potential underlying causes.

5. **Treatment:**

   a) The primary goal of epilepsy treatment is to control seizures while minimizing side effects and improving quality of life.

   b) Antiepileptic drugs (AEDs) are the most common treatment option and are prescribed based on the type and frequency of seizures.

   c) In cases where medication fails to adequately control seizures, other treatment options may include ketogenic diet, vagus nerve stimulation (VNS), responsive neurostimulation (RNS), or epilepsy surgery to remove or disconnect the seizure focus.

6. **Management and Support:**

   a) Managing epilepsy often requires ongoing medical care, lifestyle modifications (such as avoiding triggers like sleep deprivation or excessive stress), and adherence to treatment regimens.

   b) Education and support are crucial for individuals with epilepsy and their families to understand the condition, recognize seizure triggers, and know how to respond in case of a seizure emergency.

Overall, while epilepsy can be a challenging condition to manage, with proper diagnosis, treatment, and support, many individuals with epilepsy can lead fulfilling lives and effectively control their seizures. Ongoing research into the underlying mechanisms and treatments for epilepsy continues to improve outcomes and quality of life for those affected by the disorder.

Parkinson's disease

Parkinson's disease is a progressive neurological disorder that primarily affects movement. It is characterized by a loss of dopamine-producing neurons in the brain, particularly in a region called the substantia nigra. Dopamine is a neurotransmitter that plays a crucial role in regulating movement and coordination. As dopamine levels decrease, individuals with Parkinson's disease experience a range of motor and non-motor symptoms. Let's delve into Parkinson's disease in more detail:

1. **Causes and Risk Factors:**
   a) The exact cause of Parkinson's disease is not fully understood, but it is believed to involve a combination of genetic, environmental, and lifestyle factors.
   b) Genetic mutations, exposure to certain toxins or environmental factors, and aging are thought to contribute to the development of Parkinson's disease.
   c) Age is the most significant risk factor, with the majority of cases occurring in individuals over the age of 60.

2. **Pathophysiology:**
   a) Parkinson's disease is characterized by the accumulation of abnormal protein aggregates called Lewy bodies within neurons, particularly in the substantia nigra.
   b) The loss of dopamine-producing neurons leads to impaired communication between brain regions involved in movement control, resulting in motor symptoms characteristic of Parkinson's disease.

3. **Symptoms:**

a) Motor Symptoms:
   i. Bradykinesia (slowness of movement)
   ii. Tremors, especially at rest
   iii. Muscle rigidity
   iv. Postural instability (difficulty maintaining balance)

b) Non-Motor Symptoms:
   i. Depression and anxiety
   ii. Cognitive impairment (e.g., memory loss, executive dysfunction)
   iii. Sleep disturbances
   iv. Autonomic dysfunction (e.g., constipation, urinary problems)
   v. Loss of sense of smell (anosmia)
   vi. Psychiatric symptoms (e.g., hallucinations, delusions)

4. Diagnosis:

a) Diagnosis of Parkinson's disease is primarily based on clinical symptoms and medical history.

b) There is no specific test for Parkinson's disease, so diagnosis relies on the presence of characteristic motor symptoms and the exclusion of other conditions that may mimic Parkinsonism.

c) Neurological examinations, imaging studies (such as MRI or CT scans), and sometimes dopamine transporter imaging (DAT scan) may be used to support diagnosis and rule out other conditions.

5. Treatment:

a) The management of Parkinson's disease aims to alleviate symptoms, improve quality of life, and slow disease progression.

b) Medications that increase dopamine levels in the brain, such as levodopa/carbidopa, dopamine agonists, MAO-B inhibitors, and COMT inhibitors, are the mainstay of treatment.

c) Deep brain stimulation (DBS), a surgical procedure that involves implanting electrodes in specific brain regions to modulate abnormal neural activity, may be recommended for individuals with advanced Parkinson's disease who do not respond well to medication.

6. **Lifestyle and Supportive Care:**

   a) Regular exercise, physical therapy, and occupational therapy can help improve mobility, balance, and overall function in individuals with Parkinson's disease.

   b) Speech therapy and swallowing therapy may be beneficial for addressing speech and swallowing difficulties.

   c) Support groups and counseling can provide emotional support and practical advice for individuals with Parkinson's disease and their caregivers.

While Parkinson's disease is currently incurable, ongoing research continues to advance our understanding of the disease mechanisms and develop new treatment strategies aimed at slowing or halting disease progression and improving symptom management. Early diagnosis and comprehensive multidisciplinary care are key to optimizing outcomes for individuals living with Parkinson's disease.

Stroke

A stroke, also known as a cerebrovascular accident (CVA), is a medical emergency that occurs when blood flow to a part of the brain is interrupted or reduced, depriving brain cells of oxygen and nutrients. This can lead to rapid brain damage and neurological deficits. Strokes are a leading cause of disability and death worldwide. Let's explore strokes in more detail:

1. **Types of Stroke:**

a) **Ischemic Stroke**: This is the most common type of stroke, accounting for approximately 87% of all cases. It occurs when a blood clot blocks or narrows an artery supplying blood to the brain. The clot may form within the blood vessel (thrombotic stroke) or travel from elsewhere in the body and become lodged in a brain artery (embolic stroke).

b) **Hemorrhagic Stroke**: This type of stroke occurs when a blood vessel in the brain ruptures and causes bleeding into the surrounding brain tissue (intracerebral hemorrhage) or into the space surrounding the brain (subarachnoid hemorrhage).

2. **Risk Factors:**

a) Several risk factors increase the likelihood of experiencing a stroke, including:

   i. High blood pressure (hypertension)

   ii. Diabetes

   iii. High cholesterol

   iv. Smoking

   v. Obesity

   vi. Physical inactivity

   vii. Excessive alcohol consumption

   viii. Family history of stroke or transient ischemic attack (TIA)

3. **Symptoms:**

a) The symptoms of a stroke depend on the area of the brain affected and may include:

   i. Sudden numbness or weakness in the face, arm, or leg, typically on one side of the body

   ii. Confusion, trouble speaking, or difficulty understanding speech

   iii. Sudden trouble seeing in one or both eyes

iv. Severe headache with no known cause

v. Trouble walking, dizziness, loss of balance, or coordination

4. **Diagnosis:**

   a) Prompt diagnosis of a stroke is crucial for initiating appropriate treatment and minimizing brain damage.

   b) Diagnostic tests may include a neurological examination, brain imaging studies such as CT scan or MRI, and blood tests to assess clotting function and other risk factors.

5. **Treatment:**

   a) **Ischemic Stroke Treatment**: The goal of treatment for ischemic stroke is to restore blood flow to the affected area of the brain. This may involve administering clot-busting medications such as tissue plasminogen activator (tPA) or performing mechanical thrombectomy to remove the clot using a catheter-based procedure.

   b) **Hemorrhagic Stroke Treatment**: Treatment for hemorrhagic stroke focuses on controlling bleeding and reducing pressure on the brain. This may involve medications to lower blood pressure, surgery to repair ruptured blood vessels or remove blood clots, or endovascular procedures to seal off abnormal blood vessels.

6. **Rehabilitation and Recovery:**

   a) After the acute phase of stroke treatment, rehabilitation plays a crucial role in maximizing recovery and regaining lost function.

   b) Rehabilitation programs may include physical therapy, occupational therapy, speech therapy, and cognitive rehabilitation to address motor deficits, improve mobility and independence, and manage speech and language difficulties.

7. **Prevention:**

   a) Lifestyle modifications, including maintaining a healthy diet, exercising regularly, quitting smoking, limiting alcohol consumption, and managing chronic conditions such as hypertension and diabetes, can help reduce the risk of stroke.

b) Medications such as anticoagulants or antiplatelet drugs may be prescribed to prevent blood clots in individuals at high risk of stroke.

Psychiatric disorders

Psychiatric disorders, also known as mental disorders or mental illnesses, are conditions that affect a person's thoughts, emotions, behaviors, and overall mental well-being. While psychiatric disorders primarily involve disturbances in brain function and neurotransmitter systems, they can have complex interactions with various biological, psychological, and environmental factors. Let's explore psychiatric disorders in more detail:

1. **Classification:**

   a) Psychiatric disorders are classified in various ways, including the Diagnostic and Statistical Manual of Mental Disorders (DSM) published by the American Psychiatric Association and the International Classification of Diseases (ICD) published by the World Health Organization.

   b) Common categories of psychiatric disorders include mood disorders (e.g., depression, bipolar disorder), anxiety disorders (e.g., generalized anxiety disorder, panic disorder), psychotic disorders (e.g., schizophrenia, schizoaffective disorder), personality disorders (e.g., borderline personality disorder, narcissistic personality disorder), and neurodevelopmental disorders (e.g., attention-deficit/hyperactivity disorder, autism spectrum disorder).

2. **Causes:**

a) The exact causes of psychiatric disorders are often complex and multifactorial, involving interactions between genetic, biological, environmental, and psychosocial factors.

b) Genetic predisposition and family history play significant roles in many psychiatric disorders, but environmental stressors, trauma, substance abuse, and adverse childhood experiences can also contribute to their development.

c) Neurobiological factors, including imbalances in neurotransmitters (e.g., serotonin, dopamine), abnormalities in brain structure and function, and dysregulation of neural circuits, are implicated in the pathophysiology of many psychiatric disorders.

3. **Symptoms:**

a) Symptoms of psychiatric disorders vary widely depending on the specific condition but may include:

    i. Mood disturbances (e.g., sadness, irritability, euphoria)

    ii. Anxiety, fear, or excessive worry

    iii. Psychotic symptoms (e.g., hallucinations, delusions, disorganized thinking)

    iv. Changes in sleep patterns, appetite, or energy levels

    v. Impaired cognition, concentration, or memory

    vi. Impulsive or self-destructive behaviors

    vii. Social withdrawal or isolation

    viii. Changes in perception or reality testing

4. **Diagnosis and Treatment:**

a) Diagnosis of psychiatric disorders involves a comprehensive assessment by a mental health professional, including a clinical interview, observation of symptoms, and sometimes psychological testing or imaging studies.

b) Treatment approaches for psychiatric disorders may include:

i. Psychotherapy (e.g., cognitive-behavioral therapy, psychoanalysis, interpersonal therapy)

ii. Psychopharmacology (e.g., antidepressants, antipsychotics, mood stabilizers, anxiolytics)

iii. Hospitalization or intensive outpatient programs for severe or acute symptoms

iv. Electroconvulsive therapy (ECT) or transcranial magnetic stimulation (TMS) for treatment-resistant cases

v. Lifestyle modifications, social support, and complementary therapies (e.g., exercise, mindfulness, support groups)

5. **Impact and Stigma:**

   a) Psychiatric disorders can significantly impact individuals' functioning, relationships, and quality of life, leading to disability, unemployment, substance abuse, and increased risk of suicide.

   b) Stigma and discrimination surrounding mental illness can further exacerbate the challenges faced by individuals with psychiatric disorders, contributing to social isolation, low self-esteem, and barriers to seeking help.

6. **Prevention and Management:**

   a) Early intervention, education, and destigmatization efforts are essential for promoting mental health awareness, preventing psychiatric disorders, and improving access to timely and appropriate treatment.

   b) Comprehensive, holistic approaches that address biological, psychological, social, and environmental factors are often most effective in managing psychiatric disorders and promoting recovery.

Overall, psychiatric disorders are complex and heterogeneous conditions that require personalized, multidisciplinary interventions tailored to the individual's needs and circumstances. With proper diagnosis, treatment, and support, many individuals with psychiatric disorders can achieve symptom relief, functional improvement, and a better quality of life.

Depression

Depression is a common and debilitating mood disorder characterized by persistent feelings of sadness, hopelessness, and loss of interest or pleasure in activities. It affects how a person thinks, feels, and behaves, and can interfere with daily functioning and quality of life. Depression involves complex interactions between genetic, biological, psychological, and environmental factors, which affect brain function and neurotransmitter systems. Let's explore depression in more detail:

1. **Neurobiology of Depression:**
    a) **Neurotransmitter Imbalance**: One of the key theories regarding the neurobiology of depression involves disturbances in neurotransmitter systems, particularly serotonin, norepinephrine, and dopamine. These neurotransmitters play crucial roles in regulating mood, emotions, and motivation.
    b) **Dysfunction in Brain Circuits**: Depression is associated with alterations in brain circuits involved in emotion regulation, including the prefrontal cortex, amygdala, hippocampus, and thalamus. Dysfunction in these circuits can lead to negative biases in perception, cognition, and emotional processing.
    c) **Neuroendocrine Dysregulation:** Dysregulation of the hypothalamic-pituitary-adrenal (HPA) axis, which governs the body's stress response, is commonly observed in depression. Chronic stress can lead to hyperactivity of the HPA axis, resulting in elevated levels of cortisol and increased susceptibility to depressive symptoms.

d) **Neuroinflammation**: There is growing evidence implicating neuroinflammation and immune dysregulation in the pathophysiology of depression. Inflammatory cytokines released in response to stress or infection can trigger neuroinflammatory processes that contribute to depressive symptoms.

2. Risk Factors:

a) **Genetic Factors**: Family and twin studies suggest a genetic predisposition to depression, with heritability estimates ranging from 30% to 40%. Certain genetic variations may increase susceptibility to depression by influencing neurotransmitter function, stress reactivity, or neural circuitry.

b) **Biological Factors**: Other biological factors associated with an increased risk of depression include hormonal imbalances (e.g., thyroid dysfunction), chronic illnesses (e.g., cardiovascular disease, diabetes), and neurological conditions (e.g., Parkinson's disease, multiple sclerosis).

c) **Psychosocial Factors**: Psychosocial stressors such as trauma, abuse, loss of a loved one, relationship problems, financial difficulties, or chronic stress can precipitate or exacerbate depressive episodes.

3. Symptoms:

a) Depressive symptoms can vary in severity and duration but typically include:

   i. Persistent feelings of sadness, emptiness, or despair

   ii. Loss of interest or pleasure in previously enjoyed activities (anhedonia)

   iii. Changes in appetite or weight

   iv. Sleep disturbances (insomnia or hypersomnia)

   v. Fatigue or loss of energy

vi. Feelings of worthlessness or excessive guilt

vii. Difficulty concentrating, making decisions, or remembering

viii. Thoughts of death or suicide, suicide attempts

b) Diagnosis and Treatment:

a) Diagnosis of depression is based on a comprehensive clinical assessment, including a thorough medical history, psychiatric evaluation, and screening for depressive symptoms using standardized assessment tools such as the Patient Health Questionnaire (PHQ-9).

b) Treatment for depression typically involves a combination of psychotherapy, pharmacotherapy, and lifestyle modifications.

i. **Psychotherapy**: Cognitive-behavioral therapy (CBT), interpersonal therapy (IPT), and other evidence-based psychotherapies can help individuals identify and challenge negative thought patterns, improve coping skills, and address underlying emotional issues.

ii. **Pharmacotherapy:** Antidepressant medications, including selective serotonin reuptake inhibitors (SSRIs), serotonin-norepinephrine reuptake inhibitors (SNRIs), tricyclic antidepressants (TCAs), and monoamine oxidase inhibitors (MAOIs), are commonly prescribed to alleviate depressive symptoms and restore neurotransmitter balance.

iii. **Lifestyle Modifications**: Regular exercise, healthy diet, adequate sleep, stress management techniques, social support, and avoiding alcohol and substance abuse can help support overall mental health and complement other treatment modalities.

4. Prognosis and Management:

a) With appropriate treatment, many individuals with depression can experience significant symptom relief, functional improvement, and enhanced quality of life.

b) However, depression is a recurrent and chronic condition for some individuals, requiring ongoing maintenance treatment and management strategies to prevent relapse and promote long-term recovery.

c) Supportive interventions such as self-help groups, peer support, and community resources can provide additional support and encouragement for individuals living with depression.

Overall, depression is a complex and multifaceted disorder with profound implications for individual well-being and public health. Understanding the neurobiological underpinnings of depression and its interaction with genetic, environmental, and psychosocial factors is crucial for developing effective prevention, early intervention, and treatment strategies to alleviate suffering and improve outcomes for individuals affected by this debilitating condition.

Schizophrenia

Schizophrenia is a chronic and severe mental disorder characterized by a range of symptoms, including hallucinations, delusions, disorganized thinking, impaired cognition, and social dysfunction. It affects approximately 20 million people worldwide and typically emerges in late adolescence or early adulthood. Schizophrenia is considered a neurodevelopmental disorder with complex interactions between genetic, biological, environmental, and psychosocial factors. Let's explore schizophrenia in more detail:

1. **Neurobiology of Schizophrenia:**

   a) **Dopamine Dysregulation**: The dopamine hypothesis of schizophrenia proposes that dysregulation of dopamine neurotransmission in the brain contributes to the development of psychotic symptoms. Excessive dopamine activity, particularly in the mesolimbic pathway, is thought to underlie positive symptoms such as hallucinations and delusions, while decreased dopamine activity in the prefrontal cortex may contribute to negative symptoms and cognitive deficits.

b) **Glutamate Hypothesis**: Dysfunction in the glutamatergic neurotransmitter system, particularly involving N-methyl-D-aspartate (NMDA) receptors, has also been implicated in the pathophysiology of schizophrenia. Abnormalities in glutamate signaling may contribute to impaired synaptic plasticity, disrupted neural connectivity, and cognitive dysfunction observed in schizophrenia.

c) **Structural and Functional Brain Abnormalities**: Neuroimaging studies have identified structural and functional abnormalities in the brains of individuals with schizophrenia, including reduced gray matter volume, enlarged ventricles, altered white matter integrity, and aberrant activation patterns in cortical and subcortical regions. These abnormalities may contribute to the cognitive deficits, sensory processing abnormalities, and altered perception experienced by individuals with schizophrenia.

d) **Neurodevelopmental Factors**: Schizophrenia is considered a neurodevelopmental disorder, with evidence suggesting that disruptions in brain development during prenatal or early postnatal periods may increase susceptibility to the disorder. Genetic and environmental factors, such as prenatal exposure to infections, maternal stress, and obstetric complications, can influence neurodevelopmental processes and contribute to the risk of developing schizophrenia later in life.

2. Symptoms:

a) Schizophrenia is characterized by a range of symptoms that can be broadly categorized into positive, negative, and cognitive symptoms:

   i. **Positive Symptoms**: These include hallucinations (perceptions of sensory experiences that are not real, such as hearing voices), delusions (false beliefs that are firmly held despite evidence to the contrary), disorganized thinking, and grossly disorganized or abnormal motor behavior.

   ii. **Negative Symptoms**: Negative symptoms refer to deficits in emotional expression, motivation, social engagement, and self-care. These may include blunted affect (reduced emotional expression), avolition (lack of motivation or initiative), social withdrawal, and anhedonia (inability to experience pleasure).

   iii. **Cognitive Symptoms**: Cognitive deficits in schizophrenia typically involve impairments in attention, memory, executive function, and processing speed. These cognitive impairments can significantly impact daily functioning, academic and occupational performance, and social interactions.

3. **Diagnosis and Treatment:**

   a) Diagnosis of schizophrenia is based on a comprehensive psychiatric evaluation, including a clinical interview, observation of symptoms, and assessment using standardized diagnostic criteria such as those outlined in the DSM-5.

   b) Treatment for schizophrenia typically involves a combination of pharmacotherapy, psychotherapy, psychosocial interventions, and supportive services:

i. **Antipsychotic Medications**: Antipsychotic medications, such as first-generation (typical) and second-generation (atypical) antipsychotics, are the cornerstone of pharmacological treatment for schizophrenia. These medications help alleviate positive symptoms and reduce the risk of relapse but may have side effects such as weight gain, metabolic abnormalities, and extrapyramidal symptoms.

ii. **Psychotherapy**: Cognitive-behavioral therapy (CBT), supportive therapy, and family therapy can help individuals with schizophrenia cope with symptoms, manage stress, improve social skills, and enhance medication adherence.

iii. **Psychosocial Interventions**: Psychosocial interventions such as supported employment, vocational rehabilitation, housing assistance, and assertive community treatment (ACT) can help individuals with schizophrenia integrate into the community, enhance social functioning, and improve quality of life.

4. **Prognosis and Management:**

a) Schizophrenia is a chronic condition that requires long-term management and support. While symptoms may fluctuate over time, many individuals with schizophrenia experience persistent functional impairments and may require ongoing treatment and supervision.

b) Early intervention, comprehensive treatment planning, and a multidisciplinary approach involving psychiatrists, psychologists, social workers, and other mental health professionals are essential for optimizing outcomes and promoting recovery.

c) Supportive services, including case management, peer support, psychoeducation, and rehabilitation programs, can help individuals with schizophrenia and their families cope with the challenges of the disorder and achieve greater independence and quality of life.

Overall, schizophrenia is a complex and heterogeneous disorder with profound implications for individuals, families, and society. Understanding the neurobiological underpinnings of schizophrenia and its interaction with genetic, environmental, and psychosocial factors is crucial for developing effective prevention, early intervention, and treatment strategies to alleviate suffering and improve outcomes for individuals affected by this debilitating condition.

Alzheimer's disease

Alzheimer's disease is a progressive neurodegenerative disorder that primarily affects memory, cognition, and behavior. It is the most common cause of dementia, accounting for approximately 60-70% of all dementia cases. Alzheimer's disease typically develops slowly and gradually worsens over time, ultimately leading to severe impairment in daily functioning and quality of life. Let's explore Alzheimer's disease in more detail:

1. **Pathophysiology:**
   a) **Amyloid Plaque Formation**: Alzheimer's disease is characterized by the accumulation of abnormal protein aggregates called beta-amyloid plaques outside neurons in the brain. These plaques are formed from the buildup of beta-amyloid peptides, which are derived from the amyloid precursor protein (APP).
   b) **Neurofibrillary Tangle Formation**: Inside neurons, another hallmark feature of Alzheimer's disease is the accumulation of abnormal protein filaments known as neurofibrillary tangles. These tangles primarily consist of hyperphosphorylated tau protein, which disrupts the structure and function of neurons and interferes with intracellular transport.
   c) **Neuronal Dysfunction and Loss**: The accumulation of beta-amyloid plaques and neurofibrillary tangles disrupts neuronal

function, impairs synaptic communication, and ultimately leads to neuronal injury and cell death, particularly in brain regions critical for memory and cognition, such as the hippocampus and cerebral cortex.

d) **Neuroinflammation**: Inflammatory processes in the brain, involving activation of microglia and release of pro-inflammatory cytokines, contribute to the progression of Alzheimer's disease and exacerbate neuronal damage and cognitive decline.

2. **Risk Factors:**

a) **Age:** Advanced age is the single greatest risk factor for Alzheimer's disease, with the prevalence and incidence of the disease increasing significantly with age.

b) **Genetics**: While most cases of Alzheimer's disease occur sporadically, genetic factors can play a role in increasing susceptibility to the disease. Mutations in genes such as APP, presenilin 1 (PSEN1), and presenilin 2 (PSEN2) are associated with familial forms of early-onset Alzheimer's disease, whereas the apolipoprotein E (APOE) ε4 allele is a major genetic risk factor for late-onset Alzheimer's disease.

c) **Family History**: Individuals with a family history of Alzheimer's disease have an increased risk of developing the disease themselves, suggesting a potential genetic component.

d) **Other Risk Factors**: Other factors associated with an increased risk of Alzheimer's disease include cardiovascular risk factors (e.g., hypertension, diabetes, obesity), head trauma, low educational attainment, and lifestyle factors such as physical inactivity, smoking, and poor diet.

3. **Symptoms:**

a) Early symptoms of Alzheimer's disease may include mild memory lapses, difficulty recalling recent events or conversations, and challenges with problem-solving or planning.

b) As the disease progresses, individuals may experience worsening memory impairment, confusion, disorientation, language difficulties (e.g., word-finding problems), changes in mood or behavior, and difficulty performing routine tasks such as dressing or bathing.

c) In later stages, individuals with Alzheimer's disease may require assistance with all activities of daily living and may experience severe cognitive and functional decline, leading to dependency and loss of autonomy.

4. Diagnosis:

a) Diagnosis of Alzheimer's disease is based on a comprehensive evaluation, including a detailed medical history, physical examination, cognitive assessment, laboratory tests, and neuroimaging studies (e.g., MRI, PET scans).

b) Diagnostic criteria, such as those outlined in the National Institute on Aging and Alzheimer's Association (NIA-AA) guidelines, emphasize the presence of characteristic cognitive and functional impairments consistent with Alzheimer's disease, along with evidence of biomarker abnormalities such as beta-amyloid deposition and tau pathology.

5. Treatment:

a) While there is currently no cure for Alzheimer's disease, available treatments aim to alleviate symptoms, slow disease progression, and improve quality of life.

b) Medications such as cholinesterase inhibitors (e.g., donepezil, rivastigmine, galantamine) and the N-methyl-D-aspartate (NMDA) receptor antagonist memantine can help improve cognitive function and manage behavioral symptoms in some individuals with Alzheimer's disease.

    c) Non-pharmacological interventions, including cognitive stimulation, physical exercise, social engagement, and caregiver support, are also important components of Alzheimer's disease management.

6. Prognosis and Management:

    a) Alzheimer's disease is a progressive and ultimately fatal condition, with a variable course and rate of decline among individuals.

    b) Management of Alzheimer's disease involves ongoing monitoring, symptom management, and support for individuals with the disease and their caregivers.

    c) Advance care planning, including discussions about end-of-life care preferences and decisions, is important for ensuring that individuals with Alzheimer's disease receive appropriate care and support as their condition progresses.

GASTROINTESTINAL SYSTEM

The gastrointestinal (GI) system, also known as the digestive system, is a complex and vital organ system responsible for the ingestion, digestion, absorption, and elimination of food and waste products. It comprises a series of interconnected organs and structures that work together to process food, extract nutrients, and eliminate waste. Let's explore the components and functions of the gastrointestinal system in more detail:

1. Mouth and Salivary Glands:

    a) Digestion begins in the mouth, where food is mechanically broken down by chewing (mastication) and mixed with saliva produced by the salivary glands.

b) Saliva contains enzymes (such as amylase) that initiate the digestion of carbohydrates, as well as lubricating substances that facilitate swallowing.

2. Esophagus:

a) The esophagus is a muscular tube that connects the mouth to the stomach.

b) Its primary function is to transport food bolus from the mouth to the stomach through a series of coordinated muscle contractions known as peristalsis.

3. Stomach:

a) The stomach is a hollow, muscular organ located in the upper abdomen, beneath the rib cage.

b) It serves several functions, including mixing and storing ingested food, breaking down food into smaller particles, and initiating the digestion of proteins through the action of gastric juices containing hydrochloric acid and pepsin.

4. Small Intestine:

a) The small intestine is the longest part of the digestive tract, comprising three segments: the duodenum, jejunum, and ileum.

b) It is the primary site of nutrient absorption, where digestive enzymes from the pancreas and bile from the liver (via the gallbladder) further break down food particles, and nutrients are absorbed into the bloodstream through specialized structures called villi and microvilli lining the intestinal walls.

5. Liver, Gallbladder, and Pancreas:

a) The liver is a large, multifunctional organ located in the upper right abdomen. It plays a central role in metabolism, detoxification, and the production of bile, which is stored and concentrated in the gallbladder before being released into the small intestine to aid in fat digestion.

   b) The pancreas is a gland located behind the stomach that secretes digestive enzymes (such as amylase, lipase, and proteases) into the small intestine to further break down carbohydrates, fats, and proteins, as well as insulin and glucagon into the bloodstream to regulate blood sugar levels.

6. Large Intestine (Colon):

   a) The large intestine is the final segment of the digestive tract, consisting of the cecum, colon, rectum, and anus.

   b) Its primary functions include absorbing water and electrolytes from undigested food residues, forming and storing feces, and facilitating the elimination of waste products through defecation.

7. Rectum and Anus:

The rectum is the terminal portion of the large intestine that stores feces until they are expelled from the body through the anus during defecation.

The gastrointestinal system functions through the coordination of mechanical and chemical processes that break down food into nutrients, which are then absorbed into the bloodstream and transported to cells throughout the body for energy, growth, and repair. Proper functioning of the gastrointestinal system is essential for maintaining overall health and well-being, and disruptions or disorders within this system can lead to a wide range of digestive problems and nutritional deficiencies.

Type of Gastrointestinal (GI) diseases

Gastrointestinal (GI) diseases refer to disorders affecting the digestive system, which includes the esophagus, stomach, small intestine, large intestine (colon), liver, gallbladder, and pancreas. Here are some common types:

1) Gastroesophageal Reflux Disease (GERD): A chronic condition where stomach acid flows back into the esophagus, leading to symptoms such as heartburn, regurgitation, and chest pain.

2) Peptic Ulcer Disease: Open sores that develop on the lining of the stomach, small intestine, or esophagus, often caused by infection with Helicobacter pylori bacteria or long-term use of nonsteroidal anti-inflammatory drugs (NSAIDs).

3) Gastritis: Inflammation of the stomach lining, which can be acute or chronic and may result from infection, autoimmune disease, or irritants such as alcohol and NSAIDs.

4) Gastroenteritis: Inflammation of the stomach and intestines, commonly referred to as stomach flu, often caused by viral or bacterial infections, leading to symptoms such as diarrhea, vomiting, abdominal pain, and fever.

5) Inflammatory Bowel Disease (IBD):

   a) Crohn's Disease: A chronic inflammatory condition that can affect any part of the digestive tract, often leading to symptoms such as abdominal pain, diarrhea, weight loss, and fatigue.

   b) Ulcerative Colitis: A chronic inflammatory condition that primarily affects the colon and rectum, leading to symptoms such as bloody diarrhea, abdominal pain, and urgency to have bowel movements.

6) Irritable Bowel Syndrome (IBS): A functional gastrointestinal disorder characterized by abdominal pain or discomfort, bloating, and changes in bowel habits, without evidence of structural or biochemical abnormalities.

7) Diverticular Disease: Formation of small pouches (diverticula) in the colon wall, which can become inflamed or infected, leading to conditions such as diverticulitis or diverticular bleeding.

8) Hemorrhoids: Swollen and inflamed veins in the rectum and anus, often causing discomfort, itching, bleeding, and pain during bowel movements.

9) Celiac Disease: An autoimmune disorder triggered by the ingestion of gluten, a protein found in wheat, barley, and rye, leading to damage to the small intestine and malabsorption of nutrients.

10) Liver Diseases:

a) Hepatitis: Inflammation of the liver, often caused by viral infections (hepatitis A, B, C, etc.), alcohol abuse, autoimmune diseases, or certain medications.

b) Cirrhosis: Scarring of the liver tissue, usually resulting from long-term liver damage, leading to impaired liver function and potentially liver failure.

11) Pancreatitis: Inflammation of the pancreas, often caused by gallstones, alcohol abuse, or certain medications, leading to symptoms such as abdominal pain, nausea, vomiting, and fever.

Peptic Ulcer

A peptic ulcer is a sore or lesion that develops on the lining of the stomach (gastric ulcer), the first part of the small intestine (duodenal ulcer), or occasionally, in the esophagus. Peptic ulcers are commonly caused by an imbalance between stomach acid, an enzyme called pepsin, and the protective mechanisms of the gastrointestinal tract. Let's explore peptic ulcers in more detail:

1. **Causes:**

a) **Helicobacter pylori (H. pylori) Infection**: This bacterium is a major cause of peptic ulcers. It weakens the protective mucous layer of the stomach and duodenum, making them more susceptible to damage from stomach acid and pepsin.

b) **Non-Steroidal Anti-Inflammatory Drugs (NSAIDs)**: Regular use of NSAIDs, such as aspirin, ibuprofen, and naproxen, can irritate the stomach lining and increase the risk of developing peptic ulcers by inhibiting the production of prostaglandins, which help protect the stomach lining.

c) **Excessive Stomach Acid**: Factors that increase stomach acid production or decrease the effectiveness of the mucous lining can also contribute to peptic ulcer formation. These include stress, smoking, alcohol consumption, and certain medical conditions such as Zollinger-Ellison syndrome.

d) **Other Factors**: Less common causes of peptic ulcers include excessive alcohol consumption, radiation therapy, and certain medications (e.g., corticosteroids).

2. Symptoms:

a) The most common symptom of peptic ulcers is a burning or gnawing pain in the abdomen, typically located in the upper abdomen between the breastbone and the navel.

b) Other symptoms may include:

   i. Nausea

   ii. Vomiting

   iii. Loss of appetite

   iv. Bloating

   v. Belching

   vi. Unintended weight loss

   vii. Blood in the stool (which may appear dark or tarry) or vomiting blood (which may appear red or resemble coffee grounds) in severe cases.

3. Diagnosis:

Diagnosis of peptic ulcers typically involves a combination of medical history, physical examination, and diagnostic tests, such as:

i. **Endoscopy:** A procedure in which a flexible tube with a camera is inserted through the mouth to visualize the lining of the esophagus, stomach, and duodenum.

ii. **Upper GI Series (Barium Swallow):** A series of X-rays taken after drinking chalky liquid containing barium to help visualize the esophagus, stomach, and duodenum.

iii. Blood, stool, or breath tests to detect H. pylori infection.

4. Treatment:

Treatment of peptic ulcers aims to relieve symptoms, promote healing of the ulcer, and prevent complications. Depending on the cause of the ulcer, treatment may include:

i. **Antibiotics**: To eradicate H. pylori infection, if present.

ii. **Proton Pump Inhibitors (PPIs) or Histamine-2 (H2) Blockers**: To reduce stomach acid production and allow the ulcer to heal.

iii. **Antacids**: To neutralize stomach acid and provide symptomatic relief.

iv. **Cytoprotective Agents**: Medications such as sucralfate or misoprostol may be used to enhance the protective mucous layer of the stomach and duodenum.

v. Avoidance of NSAIDs and other ulcer-causing medications.

vi. Lifestyle modifications, such as avoiding smoking, alcohol, and spicy foods, and managing stress.

5. Complications:

Left untreated, peptic ulcers can lead to serious complications, including:

i. **Bleeding**: Ulcers can erode blood vessels in the stomach or duodenum, leading to gastrointestinal bleeding.

ii. **Perforation:** Ulcers can penetrate through the wall of the stomach or duodenum, causing a perforation that allows digestive juices and food to leak into the abdominal cavity, leading to peritonitis (inflammation of the abdominal lining).

iii. **Gastric Outlet Obstruction**: Large ulcers located near the pylorus (the opening between the stomach and the small intestine) can obstruct the passage of food from the stomach into the small intestine, leading to nausea, vomiting, and abdominal pain.

6. Prevention:

To reduce the risk of developing peptic ulcers, it's important to:

i. Avoid smoking and limit alcohol consumption.

ii. Use NSAIDs sparingly and at the lowest effective dose.

iii. Practice good hygiene to reduce the risk of H. pylori infection.

iv. Manage stress through relaxation techniques, exercise, and counseling.

Inflammatory bowel diseases

Inflammatory bowel diseases (IBD) are chronic inflammatory disorders of the gastrointestinal tract characterized by inflammation of the digestive tract lining. The two main types of IBD are Crohn's disease and ulcerative colitis. While they share some similarities, they also have distinct features in terms of location and nature of inflammation. Let's delve into each aspect of inflammatory bowel diseases in detail:

1. Crohn's Disease:

a) Crohn's disease can affect any part of the gastrointestinal tract, from the mouth to the anus, but it most commonly involves the end of the small intestine (ileum) and the beginning of the colon.

b) The inflammation in Crohn's disease is transmural, meaning it affects all layers of the intestinal wall, leading to thickening and scarring of the affected areas.

c) Symptoms of Crohn's disease can vary widely and may include abdominal pain, diarrhea, rectal bleeding, weight loss, fatigue, fever, and malnutrition.

d) Complications of Crohn's disease may include strictures (narrowing of the intestines), fistulas (abnormal connections between organs), abscesses, bowel obstruction, and nutritional deficiencies.

2. Ulcerative Colitis:

a) Ulcerative colitis primarily affects the colon and rectum, causing inflammation and ulcers in the innermost lining of the large intestine.

b) In contrast to Crohn's disease, the inflammation in ulcerative colitis is continuous and superficial, typically starting in the rectum and extending proximally through the colon in a continuous pattern.

c) Symptoms of ulcerative colitis may include bloody diarrhea, abdominal pain and cramping, urgency to have a bowel movement, tenesmus (the feeling of needing to pass stools even when the bowel is empty), fatigue, and weight loss.

d) Complications of ulcerative colitis may include severe bleeding, perforation of the colon, toxic megacolon (a life-threatening condition characterized by severe dilation of the colon), and an increased risk of colorectal cancer.

3. Etiology and Pathogenesis:

a) The exact cause of inflammatory bowel diseases is not fully understood, but they are believed to result from a combination of genetic, environmental, and immune factors.

b) **Genetic factors**: Certain genetic variations have been implicated in the development of IBD, particularly in genes related to the immune system and gut barrier function.

c) **Environmental factors**: Factors such as diet, smoking, infections, and changes in the gut microbiome may contribute to the development and exacerbation of IBD.

d) **Immune dysregulation**: IBD is characterized by an abnormal immune response in which the immune system mistakenly attacks the lining of the gastrointestinal tract, leading to chronic inflammation.

4. Diagnosis:

a) Diagnosis of inflammatory bowel diseases involves a combination of medical history, physical examination, laboratory tests, imaging studies, and endoscopic evaluation.

b) Blood tests may reveal signs of inflammation, anemia, and nutritional deficiencies.

c) Stool tests may be performed to check for infections and evaluate fecal calprotectin levels, which can indicate inflammation in the intestines.

d) Imaging studies such as X-rays, CT scans, or MRIs may be used to visualize the gastrointestinal tract and assess for complications.

e) Endoscopic procedures such as colonoscopy or sigmoidoscopy allow direct visualization of the colon and rectum, and biopsy samples may be taken for microscopic examination.

5. Treatment:

a) The goals of treatment for inflammatory bowel diseases are to induce and maintain remission, alleviate symptoms, prevent complications, and improve quality of life.

b) Treatment approaches may include:

    i. **Medications**: Depending on the severity and location of inflammation, medications such as aminosalicylates, corticosteroids, immunomodulators, biologic therapies (e.g., anti-TNF agents), and antibiotics may be used to reduce inflammation and suppress the immune response.

    ii. **Nutritional therapy**: In some cases, dietary modifications, nutritional supplements, or enteral nutrition may be recommended to manage symptoms and support healing of the intestines.

    iii. **Lifestyle modifications**: Strategies such as stress management, regular exercise, smoking cessation, and maintaining a healthy diet may help reduce symptoms and improve overall well-being.

    iv. **Surgery**: In severe cases or when complications arise, surgical intervention such as bowel resection, strictureplasty, or ostomy formation may be necessary to remove diseased portions of the intestines and alleviate symptoms.

6. **Prognosis and Management:**

a) Inflammatory bowel diseases are chronic conditions with a variable course and can have a significant impact on quality of life.

b) With proper management and adherence to treatment, many individuals with IBD can achieve long-term remission and lead fulfilling lives.

c) Regular monitoring, follow-up care, and collaboration with a multidisciplinary healthcare team, including gastroenterologists, nutritionists, and mental health professionals, are essential for optimizing outcomes and managing the complex needs of individuals with IBD.

Jaundice, hepatitis (A, B, C, D, E, F)

Jaundice is a condition characterized by yellowing of the skin, mucous membranes, and whites of the eyes due to elevated levels of bilirubin in the blood. Bilirubin is a yellow pigment produced during the breakdown of red blood cells and is normally processed by the liver and excreted in bile. When there is a disruption in the normal metabolism or excretion of bilirubin, it can accumulate in the body, leading to jaundice. Hepatitis refers to inflammation of the liver, which can be caused by various factors, including viral infections, alcohol consumption, autoimmune diseases, medications, and toxins. There are several types of viral hepatitis, including hepatitis A, B, C, D, and E, each caused by different viruses. Let's explore each in more detail:

1. **Jaundice:**
    a) Jaundice occurs when there is an excess of bilirubin in the bloodstream, leading to yellow discoloration of the skin, sclerae (whites of the eyes), and mucous membranes.
    b) **Causes of jaundice include:**
        i. Excessive breakdown of red blood cells (hemolysis)
        ii. Impaired liver function or bile excretion
        iii. Obstruction of bile ducts (e.g., gallstones, tumors)
    c) Symptoms of jaundice may include yellowing of the skin and eyes, dark urine, pale stools, abdominal pain, fatigue, itching (pruritus), and nausea.

2. **Hepatitis A:**
    a) Hepatitis A is caused by the hepatitis A virus (HAV), which is typically transmitted through the fecal-oral route, often via

contaminated food or water, or through close personal contact with an infected individual.

b) Symptoms of hepatitis A may include fever, fatigue, loss of appetite, nausea, vomiting, abdominal pain, dark urine, clay-colored stools, and jaundice.

c) Hepatitis A is usually a self-limiting illness that does not lead to chronic liver disease, and most individuals recover completely with supportive care.

3. **Hepatitis B:**

a) Hepatitis B is caused by the hepatitis B virus (HBV), which is transmitted through contact with infected blood, semen, or other bodily fluids, as well as from mother to child during childbirth.

b) Symptoms of hepatitis B may include fatigue, nausea, vomiting, abdominal pain, jaundice, dark urine, clay-colored stools, and joint pain.

c) Hepatitis B can lead to acute or chronic infection, and chronic hepatitis B infection increases the risk of liver cirrhosis, liver failure, and hepatocellular carcinoma (liver cancer).

4. **Hepatitis C:**

a) Hepatitis C is caused by the hepatitis C virus (HCV), which is primarily transmitted through exposure to infected blood, such as through injection drug use, blood transfusions (prior to screening of blood donations), and unsafe medical procedures.

b) Many people with hepatitis C infection are asymptomatic or have mild symptoms, but chronic hepatitis C infection can lead to progressive liver damage, cirrhosis, liver failure, and hepatocellular carcinoma.

c) Hepatitis C is often referred to as a "silent epidemic" because it can remain asymptomatic for years or even decades before complications develop.

5. Hepatitis D:

a) Hepatitis D, also known as delta hepatitis, is caused by the hepatitis D virus (HDV), which can only infect individuals who are already infected with hepatitis B virus (HBV).

b) Hepatitis D is transmitted through contact with infected blood or bodily fluids, similar to hepatitis B.

c) Hepatitis D infection can exacerbate the severity of hepatitis B infection and increase the risk of liver damage and complications.

6. Hepatitis E:

a) Hepatitis E is caused by the hepatitis E virus (HEV), which is transmitted primarily through the fecal-oral route, often via contaminated water in areas with poor sanitation.

b) Hepatitis E infection is usually self-limiting and resolves on its own within a few weeks to months, although it can be more severe in pregnant women and individuals with pre-existing liver disease.

c) Hepatitis E is more common in developing countries and is generally not a significant public health concern in developed countries.

7. Hepatitis F:

a) Hepatitis F is a hypothetical and controversial virus that has not been definitively identified or characterized.

b) Some researchers have suggested the existence of a novel hepatitis virus based on cases of hepatitis with unknown etiology, but conclusive evidence for the existence of hepatitis F virus is lacking.

Alcoholic liver disease

Alcoholic liver disease (ALD) is a spectrum of liver disorders caused by excessive alcohol consumption over an extended period. It encompasses a range of conditions, from fatty liver (steatosis) to alcoholic hepatitis and ultimately to cirrhosis, which is the advanced stage of liver scarring. ALD is a significant cause of liver-related morbidity and mortality worldwide. Let's explore ALD in more detail:

1. **Pathophysiology:**
    a) The exact mechanism by which alcohol damages the liver is complex and not fully understood, but it involves several key processes:
        i. **Metabolism of Alcohol**: Alcohol is metabolized primarily in the liver by enzymes such as alcohol dehydrogenase and cytochrome P450 2E1 (CYP2E1). This process produces toxic byproducts such as acetaldehyde and reactive oxygen species (ROS), which can damage liver cells and trigger inflammation.
        ii. **Hepatic Steatosis**: Chronic alcohol consumption disrupts lipid metabolism in the liver, leading to the accumulation of fat within hepatocytes (fatty liver or steatosis). Hepatic steatosis is reversible with abstinence from alcohol.
        iii. **Oxidative Stress and Inflammation**: Alcohol metabolism generates ROS and activates inflammatory pathways, leading to oxidative stress, inflammation, and tissue injury.
        iv. **Fibrosis and Cirrhosis**: Prolonged inflammation and liver damage can trigger the deposition of scar tissue (fibrosis) in the liver, eventually progressing to cirrhosis, characterized by widespread fibrosis and loss of liver function.

2. **Clinical Manifestations:**

a) The clinical presentation of ALD can vary depending on the stage and severity of liver damage:

   i. **Fatty Liver**: In the early stages, ALD may be asymptomatic or present with nonspecific symptoms such as fatigue, abdominal discomfort, or mild elevation of liver enzymes on blood tests.

   ii. **Alcoholic Hepatitis:** Alcoholic hepatitis is characterized by inflammation and necrosis of liver cells, leading to symptoms such as jaundice, abdominal pain, fever, nausea, vomiting, loss of appetite, and tender hepatomegaly.

   iii. **Cirrhosis:** Advanced ALD with cirrhosis can manifest with complications such as portal hypertension, ascites (fluid accumulation in the abdomen), hepatic encephalopathy (impaired brain function due to liver failure), variceal bleeding, and hepatocellular carcinoma (liver cancer).

3. Diagnosis:

a) Diagnosis of ALD involves a combination of medical history, physical examination, laboratory tests, imaging studies, and liver biopsy if necessary:

   i. Blood tests may reveal elevated liver enzymes (AST and ALT), elevated bilirubin levels, prolonged prothrombin time (indicative of impaired liver function), and other markers of liver injury and inflammation.

   ii. Imaging studies such as ultrasound, CT scan, or MRI may show evidence of liver steatosis, fibrosis, or cirrhosis.

   iii. Liver biopsy may be performed to assess the extent of liver damage and inflammation, although it is not always necessary for diagnosis.

4. Treatment:

a) The mainstay of treatment for ALD is abstinence from alcohol, which is essential to prevent further liver damage and promote liver regeneration.

b) Other treatment approaches may include:

    i. **Nutritional support**: Adequate nutrition, including supplementation with vitamins and minerals, is important to support liver function and promote healing.

    ii. **Medications**: In severe cases of alcoholic hepatitis, corticosteroids or pentoxifylline may be used to reduce inflammation, although their efficacy remains controversial.

    iii. Management of complications: Complications of ALD such as ascites, hepatic encephalopathy, variceal bleeding, and hepatocellular carcinoma require specific interventions and supportive care.

5. Prognosis and Prevention:

a) The prognosis of ALD depends on various factors, including the severity of liver damage, the presence of complications, and the individual's response to treatment.

b) Early detection and intervention, along with cessation of alcohol consumption, can improve outcomes and prevent progression to advanced liver disease.

c) Prevention of ALD involves promoting awareness of the risks of excessive alcohol consumption, implementing public health measures to reduce alcohol-related harm, and providing support and resources for individuals struggling with alcohol use disorders.

Multiple-Choice Questions (MCQs)

1. What is the primary function of the Central Nervous System (CNS)?

    A) Transmitting signals throughout the body

B) Regulating involuntary bodily functions

C) Processing sensory information and coordinating motor responses

D) Controlling voluntary movements

2. Epilepsy is characterized by:

    A) High blood pressure

    B) Recurrent seizures

    C) Memory loss

    D) Motor neuron degeneration

3. Which system is the autonomic nervous system (ANS) a part of?

    A) Peripheral Nervous System

    B) Central Nervous System

    C) Somatic Nervous System

    D) Spinal Cord

4. Parkinson's disease primarily affects:

    A) Sensory neurons

    B) Dopamine-producing neurons

    C) Peripheral nerves

    D) Astrocytes

5. The accumulation of what leads to Alzheimer's disease?

    A) Myelin

    B) Dopamine

    C) Beta-amyloid plaques

    D) Acetylcholine

6. What is the most common type of stroke?

    A) Hemorrhagic

    B) Ischemic

    C) Transient Ischemic Attack (TIA)

    D) Cerebral Stroke

7. Schizophrenia is characterized by all the following symptoms EXCEPT:

A) Hallucinations

B) Delusions

C) High blood sugar levels

D) Disorganized thinking

8. Which is NOT a function of the gastrointestinal system?

A) Nutrient absorption

B) Hormone secretion

C) Waste elimination

D) Blood cell formation

9. What causes peptic ulcers primarily?

A) Helicobacter pylori infection

B) High fiber diet

C) Excessive exercise

D) Low stomach acid production

10. Crohn's disease is a type of:

A) Cardiovascular disorder

B) Inflammatory bowel disease

C) Neurodegenerative disorder

D) Psychiatric disorder

11. Major depressive disorder is characterized by:

A) Excessive happiness

B) Loss of interest or pleasure in activities

C) Increased energy levels

D) Enhanced memory function

12. Hepatitis C is primarily transmitted through:

A) Contaminated water

B) Airborne pathogens

C) Infected blood

D) Insect bites

13. The main risk factor for developing Parkinson's disease is:

A) Gender

B) Diet

C) Age

D) Exercise frequency

14. An essential feature of Alzheimer's disease visible on neuroimaging is:

A) Enlarged ventricles

B) Bone fractures

C) Beta-amyloid plaques

D) Reduced gray matter volume

15. What does the substantia nigra relate to in Parkinson's disease?

A) It is responsible for memory formation.

B) It is where dopamine-producing neurons are lost.

C) It controls the autonomic nervous system.

D) It manages sensory information processing.

16. Which condition is an autoimmune disorder affecting the liver?

A) Hepatitis A

B) Hepatitis B

C) Hepatitis C

D) None of the above

17. Alcoholic liver disease progresses in which order?

A) Cirrhosis, fatty liver, alcoholic hepatitis

B) Fatty liver, alcoholic hepatitis, cirrhosis

C) Alcoholic hepatitis, cirrhosis, fatty liver

D) Cirrhosis, alcoholic hepatitis, fatty liver

18. Which is a preventive measure for peptic ulcers?

A) Regular use of NSAIDs

B) Smoking cessation

C) High alcohol intake

D) Frequent use of corticosteroids

19. What is the primary symptom of a stroke?

A) Nausea

B) Sudden numbness or weakness

C) Increased appetite

D) Gradual loss of movement

20. What is the main type of medication used to treat schizophrenia?

A) Antipyretics

B) Antibiotics

C) Antipsychotics

D) Antidepressants

Short Answer Type Questions (Subjective)

1. What is the primary function of the central nervous system?

2. Define epilepsy and describe its primary manifestation.

3. What roles do the somatic and autonomic nervous systems play in the human body?

4. Explain the significance of dopamine in Parkinson's disease.

5. Describe the pathological changes that occur in the brain in Alzheimer's disease.

6. What are the main types of strokes and their causes?

7. What are the typical symptoms associated with a peptic ulcer?

8. Explain the difference between Crohn's disease and ulcerative colitis.

9. What is jaundice, and what are its primary symptoms?

10. Describe the transmission routes for hepatitis A and hepatitis B.

11. What role does the liver play in the metabolism of alcohol?

12. What are the common symptoms of depression and their impact on daily life?

13. How does schizophrenia affect cognitive function?

14. What are the main components of the gastrointestinal system and their functions?

15. What leads to the development of alcoholic liver disease?

16. Explain the role of neurotransmitters in psychiatric disorders.

17. What is the impact of genetic factors on Alzheimer's disease?

18. Describe the emergency treatment for ischemic stroke.

19. How can lifestyle changes influence the risk of developing peptic ulcers?

20. What are Lewy bodies, and what role do they play in Parkinson's disease?

Long Answer Type Questions (Subjective)

1. Discuss the neurobiological factors involved in depression and how they contribute to the symptoms of the disorder.

2. Describe the diagnosis and treatment options available for epilepsy, focusing on how treatment is tailored to different types of seizures.

3. Explain the progression of Alzheimer's disease from early symptoms to the more severe stages and the impact on patient care.

4. Analyze the role of the immune system in the pathogenesis of inflammatory bowel diseases and the implications for treatment.

5. Discuss the mechanisms by which chronic alcohol consumption leads to liver disease, including the stages from steatosis to cirrhosis.

6. Outline the diagnostic process for schizophrenia and discuss the challenges in managing this mental disorder effectively.

7. Describe the functions of the gastrointestinal system and explain how disorders in this system can affect overall health.

8. Provide a detailed explanation of the pathophysiological changes that occur in the brain during a stroke and the resulting symptoms.

9. Discuss the impact of environmental and lifestyle factors on the incidence of psychiatric disorders and their management.

10.Explain the role of oxidative stress and inflammation in the progression of alcoholic liver disease and the potential interventions to mitigate these effects.

Answer Key

1. C) Processing sensory information and coordinating motor responses
2. B) Recurrent seizures
3. A) Peripheral Nervous System
4. B) Dopamine-producing neurons
5. C) Beta-amyloid plaques
6. B) Ischemic
7. C) High blood sugar levels
8. D) Blood cell formation
9. A) Helicobacter pylori infection
10.B) Inflammatory bowel disease
11.B) Loss of interest or pleasure in activities
12.C) Infected blood
13.C) Age
14.D) Reduced gray matter volume
15.B) It is where dopamine-producing neurons are lost.
16.D) None of the above
17.B) Fatty liver, alcoholic hepatitis, cirrhosis
18.B) Smoking cessation
19.B) Sudden numbness or weakness
20.C) Antipsychotics

CHAPTER - 6

DISEASE OF BONES AND JOINT AND CANCER

DISEASE OF BONES AND JOINTS

Diseases affecting bones and joints encompass a broad spectrum of conditions, ranging from degenerative disorders to inflammatory diseases and traumatic injuries. Here's a detailed introduction covering some of the most common diseases in this category:

1. **Osteoarthritis (OA):**
   a. OA is the most prevalent form of arthritis, characterized by the breakdown of cartilage in the joints.
   b. Risk factors include age, obesity, joint injury, and genetics.
   c. Symptoms include joint pain, stiffness, and reduced range of motion.
   d. Treatment may involve pain management, lifestyle modifications, physical therapy, and in severe cases, joint replacement surgery.

2. **Rheumatoid Arthritis (RA):**
   a. RA is an autoimmune disorder where the immune system attacks the synovium, leading to inflammation of the joint lining.
   b. It primarily affects the small joints of the hands and feet but can involve other joints as well.
   c. Symptoms include joint pain, swelling, stiffness, and fatigue.
   d. Treatment involves medications to suppress the immune response, physical therapy, and sometimes surgery to repair or replace damaged joints.

3. **Osteoporosis:**
   a. Osteoporosis is a condition characterized by low bone density and increased risk of fractures.

b. It is more common in older adults, especially postmenopausal women, but can occur in men as well.

c. Risk factors include age, gender, genetics, hormonal changes, inadequate calcium and vitamin D intake, and certain medications.

d. Treatment focuses on medications to improve bone density, calcium and vitamin D supplementation, and lifestyle changes to prevent falls and fractures.

4. Fractures:

a. Fractures occur when there is a break or crack in a bone.

b. They can result from trauma, such as falls, sports injuries, or car accidents, or from underlying bone diseases like osteoporosis.

c. Treatment depends on the severity and location of the fracture but may involve immobilization with casts or splints, surgical repair, and rehabilitation.

5. Gout:

a. Gout is a type of inflammatory arthritis caused by the buildup of uric acid crystals in the joints.

b. It typically affects the big toe but can involve other joints as well.

c. Risk factors include genetics, diet high in purines (found in red meat, seafood, and alcohol), obesity, and certain medical conditions.

d. Treatment involves medications to reduce inflammation and lower uric acid levels, dietary changes, and lifestyle modifications.

6. Ankylosing Spondylitis (AS):

a. AS is a type of inflammatory arthritis that primarily affects the spine, causing stiffness and fusion of the vertebrae.

b. It can also involve other joints and organs, such as the eyes and heart.

c. Symptoms include back pain, stiffness, and reduced flexibility.

d. Treatment includes medications to reduce inflammation and pain, physical therapy, and exercise to maintain mobility.

7. **Paget's Disease:**
   a. Paget's disease is a chronic bone disorder characterized by abnormal bone remodeling, leading to weakened, misshapen bones.
   b. It can affect any bone but commonly involves the spine, pelvis, skull, and long bones of the legs.
   c. Symptoms include bone pain, deformities, and fractures.
   d. Treatment may involve medications to regulate bone turnover and relieve pain, as well as surgery in severe cases.

Rheumatoid arthritis

Rheumatoid arthritis (RA) is a chronic autoimmune disorder that primarily affects the joints, causing inflammation, pain, and progressive joint damage. Here's a detailed overview:

Rheumatoid arthritis (RA) is a chronic autoimmune disorder characterized by inflammation of the synovium, the lining of the membranes that surround the joints. Here's a detailed overview of its autoimmune nature and symptoms:

Autoimmune Nature:

1. **Immune System Dysfunction:**
   a. In RA, the immune system mistakenly attacks the synovium, which leads to inflammation and damage to the joint tissues.
   b. The exact cause of this autoimmune response is not fully understood, but it is believed to involve a combination of genetic, environmental, and hormonal factors.
   c. Certain genetic variations, such as specific human leukocyte antigen (HLA) genes, have been associated with an increased risk of developing RA.

d. Environmental triggers, such as smoking, infections, and hormonal changes, may also contribute to the dysregulation of the immune system in susceptible individuals.

2. **Inflammatory Response:**
   a. Inflammation in RA is characterized by the infiltration of immune cells, particularly T cells, B cells, and macrophages, into the synovium.
   b. These immune cells release pro-inflammatory cytokines, such as tumor necrosis factor-alpha (TNF-alpha), interleukin-1 (IL-1), and interleukin-6 (IL-6), which contribute to the inflammatory process and tissue damage.
   c. Chronic inflammation in the synovium leads to the proliferation of synovial cells, formation of pannus (abnormal tissue overgrowth), and erosion of cartilage and bone within the joint.

3. **Autoantibodies:**
   a. Autoantibodies are antibodies produced by the immune system that mistakenly target self-antigens, leading to tissue damage.
   b. Rheumatoid factor (RF) and anti-cyclic citrullinated peptide (anti-CCP) antibodies are autoantibodies commonly found in the blood of individuals with RA.
   c. These autoantibodies may contribute to the pathogenesis of RA by promoting inflammation, activating immune cells, and causing tissue damage in the joints.

Symptoms:

1. **Joint Symptoms:**
   a. **Joint pain**: Persistent pain, often described as aching or throbbing, is a hallmark symptom of RA. Pain may be worse in the morning or after periods of inactivity.

b. **Joint swelling**: Inflammation of the synovium leads to swelling and tenderness in the affected joints.

c. **Joint stiffness**: Morning stiffness lasting for more than 30 minutes is a common symptom of RA and may improve with movement.

d. **Joint deformities**: Over time, untreated RA can cause joint deformities, such as swan-neck deformity (hyperextension of the proximal interphalangeal joint and flexion of the distal interphalangeal joint) and boutonniere deformity (flexion of the proximal interphalangeal joint and hyperextension of the distal interphalangeal joint).

2. **Systemic Symptoms:**

   a. **Fatigue**: Chronic inflammation and pain associated with RA can lead to fatigue, weakness, and reduced energy levels.

   b. **Fever**: Some individuals with RA may experience low-grade fever, particularly during disease flares.

   c. **Weight loss**: Unintentional weight loss may occur in individuals with severe RA, particularly if inflammation affects appetite and nutrition.

3. **Extra-articular Manifestations:**

   a. RA can affect other organs and systems in the body, leading to extra-articular manifestations such as:

      i. **Rheumatoid nodules**: Firm, painless nodules that develop under the skin, commonly over bony prominences.

      ii. **Rheumatoid vasculitis**: Inflammation of blood vessels, which can lead to skin ulcers, nerve damage, and organ dysfunction.

      iii. **Cardiopulmonary complications**: RA is associated with an increased risk of cardiovascular disease, interstitial lung disease, and pleural effusion.

iv. **Eye involvement**: RA-related eye complications include dry eyes, scleritis, and uveitis.

4. **Symmetrical Involvement:**
   a. RA typically affects multiple joints symmetrically, meaning that the same joints on both sides of the body are affected.
   b. Commonly affected joints include the small joints of the hands and feet, wrists, elbows, knees, and ankles.

Risk Factors:

1. **Genetic Factors:**
   a. **Family history**: Individuals with a family history of RA are at an increased risk of developing the disease. Certain genetic variations, particularly within the human leukocyte antigen (HLA) gene complex, are associated with a higher risk of RA.
   b. **Ethnicity**: RA is more common in certain ethnic groups, including individuals of European descent.
   c. Specific genetic variants, such as the presence of HLA-DRB1 alleles encoding the "shared epitope," are strongly associated with an increased risk of RA.

2. **Environmental Factors:**
   a. **Smoking**: Cigarette smoking is one of the most significant modifiable risk factors for RA. Smokers, particularly those with a genetic predisposition, have a higher risk of developing RA and experiencing more severe disease.
   b. **Infections**: Certain infections, such as periodontal disease and Epstein-Barr virus infection, have been implicated as potential triggers for RA in genetically susceptible individuals.
   c. **Hormonal factors**: Hormonal changes, such as those occurring during pregnancy and menopause, may influence RA risk. Some

women may experience symptom onset or exacerbation of RA symptoms during these periods.

3. **Lifestyle Factors:**
   a. **Obesity:** Excess body weight, particularly in the abdominal region, is associated with an increased risk of developing RA and experiencing more severe disease manifestations.
   b. **Diet:** Dietary factors, such as high intake of red meat, processed foods, and sugar-sweetened beverages, and low intake of fruits, vegetables, and omega-3 fatty acids, may contribute to RA risk.
4. **Other Medical Conditions:**
   a. **Certain medical conditions, such as periodontal disease, chronic lung diseases** (e.g., chronic obstructive pulmonary disease), and certain autoimmune diseases (e.g., systemic lupus erythematosus), are associated with an increased risk of RA.

Diagnosis:

1. **Clinical Evaluation:**
   a. Diagnosis of RA is based on a combination of clinical findings, medical history, physical examination, and laboratory tests.
   b. Common symptoms include joint pain, swelling, stiffness (particularly in the morning), and decreased joint function. RA typically affects multiple joints symmetrically.
   c. The presence of systemic symptoms such as fatigue, low-grade fever, and weight loss may also suggest RA.
2. **Laboratory Tests:**
   a. **Rheumatoid factor (RF):** RF is an autoantibody commonly found in the blood of individuals with RA. However, RF can also be present in other autoimmune diseases and in some healthy individuals.

b. **Anti-cyclic citrullinated peptide (anti-CCP) antibodies**: Anti-CCP antibodies are more specific for RA and are often detected in the early stages of the disease.

c. **Acute phase reactants**: Blood tests may show elevated levels of acute phase reactants, such as C-reactive protein (CRP) and erythrocyte sedimentation rate (ESR), which are markers of inflammation.

3. **Imaging Studies:**

a. **X-rays:** X-rays of the affected joints may show characteristic changes such as joint erosion, joint space narrowing, and periarticular osteopenia, particularly in later stages of the disease.

b. **Ultrasound and MRI**: These imaging modalities can detect synovitis (inflammation of the synovium) and joint damage at earlier stages than conventional X-rays.

4. **Clinical Criteria:**

The 2010 American College of Rheumatology/European League Against Rheumatism (ACR/EULAR) classification criteria for RA include a combination of clinical and laboratory parameters, such as joint involvement, serological markers (RF and anti-CCP antibodies), acute phase reactants, and symptom duration.

Early diagnosis and treatment of RA are crucial for preventing joint damage, disability, and systemic complications associated with the disease. A multidisciplinary approach involving rheumatologists, primary care physicians, and other healthcare providers is essential for managing RA effectively and optimizing patient outcomes.

Treatment:

1. **Medications:**

a. **Disease-modifying antirheumatic drugs (DMARDs)**: DMARDs are the mainstay of treatment for RA and work by suppressing inflammation and slowing disease progression. Examples include methotrexate, hydroxychloroquine, sulfasalazine, leflunomide, and biologic DMARDs (e.g., tumor necrosis factor inhibitors, interleukin-6 inhibitors, T-cell inhibitors).

b. **Nonsteroidal anti-inflammatory drugs (NSAIDs)**: NSAIDs such as ibuprofen and naproxen can help relieve pain and reduce inflammation in RA. They are often used for short-term symptom relief.

c. **Corticosteroids:** Oral or injectable corticosteroids (e.g., prednisone, methylprednisolone) may be prescribed to rapidly reduce inflammation and alleviate symptoms during RA flares. However, long-term use of corticosteroids is associated with significant side effects and should be minimized if possible.

d. **Analgesics:** Pain relievers such as acetaminophen may be used to manage mild to moderate pain associated with RA, although they do not have anti-inflammatory effects.

2. **Physical Therapy and Exercise:**
   a. Physical therapy and exercise programs can help improve joint flexibility, strength, and function in individuals with RA.
   b. Range-of-motion exercises, strengthening exercises, and low-impact activities such as swimming and cycling are often recommended to maintain joint mobility and muscle strength.
   c. Occupational therapy can provide adaptive techniques and assistive devices to help individuals with RA perform activities of daily living more easily.

3. **Joint Protection:**
   Joint protection techniques, such as using assistive devices (e.g., splints, braces), maintaining proper posture, and avoiding repetitive

or stressful movements, can help reduce joint strain and prevent further damage.

4. **Surgery:**

    a. In severe cases of RA with significant joint damage and disability, surgical intervention may be necessary.

    b. Joint replacement surgery (arthroplasty) may be performed to replace damaged joints, such as the hips or knees, with artificial implants.

    c. Synovectomy, the surgical removal of inflamed synovial tissue, may be considered in select cases to alleviate pain and inflammation.

5. **Lifestyle Modifications:**

    a. **Smoking cessation**: Quitting smoking can improve RA symptoms and reduce the risk of disease progression.

    b. **Weight management**: Maintaining a healthy weight through diet and exercise can help reduce joint strain and improve overall health.

Complications:

1. **Joint Damage and Deformities:**

    a. Untreated or inadequately controlled RA can lead to progressive joint damage, erosion of cartilage and bone, and joint deformities such as swan-neck deformity, boutonniere deformity, and joint subluxation.

2. **Functional Impairment:**

    RA can cause significant functional impairment and disability, limiting the ability to perform daily activities and affecting quality of life.

3. **Systemic Complications:**

a. RA is associated with an increased risk of systemic complications, including cardiovascular disease, osteoporosis, interstitial lung disease, and Sjögren's syndrome.

b. Cardiovascular complications, such as coronary artery disease and heart failure, are leading causes of morbidity and mortality in individuals with RA.

4. Rheumatoid Nodules:

Rheumatoid nodules are firm, painless nodules that may develop under the skin, typically over bony prominences such as the elbows, fingers, or heels.

5. Infections:

Chronic inflammation and immunosuppressive medications used to treat RA can increase the risk of infections, including respiratory infections, urinary tract infections, and opportunistic infections.

6. Mental Health Issues:

Living with a chronic disease like RA can take a toll on mental health, leading to depression, anxiety, and decreased quality of life.

Early diagnosis, aggressive treatment, and regular monitoring are essential for managing RA effectively and minimizing the risk of complications. A multidisciplinary approach involving rheumatologists, primary care physicians, physical therapists, and other healthcare providers is important for providing comprehensive care to individuals with RA.

Osteoporosis

Osteoporosis is a systemic skeletal disorder characterized by low bone mass and microarchitectural deterioration of bone tissue, leading to increased bone fragility and susceptibility to fractures. Here's a detailed overview:

Pathophysiology:

1. Bone Remodeling:

a. Bone is a dynamic tissue that undergoes constant remodeling through a process called bone turnover.

b. Bone remodeling involves the coordinated action of bone-resorbing cells called osteoclasts and bone-forming cells called osteoblasts.

c. Osteoclasts break down old or damaged bone tissue, while osteoblasts produce new bone tissue to replace it.

d. In healthy individuals, bone remodeling maintains a balance between bone resorption and bone formation, ensuring the integrity and strength of the skeleton.

2. Imbalance in Bone Remodeling:

a. Osteoporosis occurs when there is an imbalance in bone remodeling, resulting in excessive bone resorption relative to bone formation.

b. This imbalance leads to a decrease in bone mass, deterioration of bone microarchitecture, and increased susceptibility to fractures.

3. Hormonal Changes:

a. Estrogen plays a crucial role in maintaining bone health by inhibiting bone resorption and promoting bone formation.

b. In women, estrogen levels decline significantly during menopause, leading to accelerated bone loss and an increased risk of osteoporosis.

c. Similarly, in men, age-related declines in testosterone levels can contribute to bone loss and osteoporosis.

4. Age-related Changes:

a. Aging is associated with several changes in bone tissue, including a decrease in bone density, changes in bone microarchitecture, and impaired bone remodeling.

b. As individuals age, the balance between bone resorption and bone formation shifts towards increased bone resorption, leading to a gradual loss of bone mass.

5. **Nutritional Factors:**

   a. Adequate intake of calcium and vitamin D is essential for maintaining bone health.

   b. Calcium is a key component of bone tissue, while vitamin D is necessary for calcium absorption and bone mineralization.

   c. Inadequate dietary intake of calcium and vitamin D can impair bone formation and increase the risk of osteoporosis.

6. **Lifestyle Factors:**

   a. **Sedentary lifestyle**: Lack of weight-bearing exercise and physical activity can contribute to bone loss and decrease bone density.

   b. **Smoking**: Tobacco use has been associated with decreased bone density and increased risk of fractures.

   c. **Excessive alcohol consumption**: Chronic alcohol abuse can interfere with bone remodeling and increase the risk of osteoporosis.

   d. **Low body weight**: Individuals with low body weight or underweight are at increased risk of osteoporosis due to decreased mechanical loading on the bones.

Risk Factors:

1. **Age:**

   Age is one of the most significant risk factors for osteoporosis. Bone mass peaks in early adulthood and gradually declines with age.

2. **Gender:**

   Women are at a higher risk of developing osteoporosis compared to men, especially after menopause due to estrogen deficiency.

3. **Family History:**

   A family history of osteoporosis or fragility fractures increases an individual's risk of developing the condition.

4. **Hormonal Factors:**

   Hormonal changes, such as menopause in women and age-related declines in testosterone levels in men, increase the risk of osteoporosis.

5. **Nutritional Deficiencies:**

   Inadequate intake of calcium and vitamin D, as well as poor nutrition, can contribute to decreased bone density and increased risk of osteoporosis.

6. **Lifestyle Factors:**

   Sedentary lifestyle, smoking, excessive alcohol consumption, and low body weight are all associated with an increased risk of osteoporosis.

7. **Medical Conditions:**

   Certain medical conditions and medications can increase the risk of osteoporosis, including rheumatoid arthritis, celiac disease, hyperthyroidism, hyperparathyroidism, and long-term use of glucocorticoid medications.

Clinical Presentation:

1. **Asymptomatic Stage:**

   a. Osteoporosis is often asymptomatic in its early stages, and individuals may not be aware of the condition until they experience a fracture or undergo bone density testing.

   b. In some cases, osteoporosis may be discovered incidentally during imaging studies performed for other medical reasons.

2. **Fractures:**

a. Fragility fractures are a common complication of osteoporosis and are often the first clinical manifestation of the disease.

b. Fragility fractures occur with minimal trauma or mechanical stress and commonly affect the spine (vertebral compression fractures), hips (hip fractures), wrists, and ribs.

c. Vertebral compression fractures can lead to back pain, height loss, kyphosis (forward curvature of the spine), and decreased mobility.

3. Bone Pain:

a. Some individuals with osteoporosis may experience chronic or intermittent bone pain, particularly in the back, hips, or wrists.

b. Pain may be exacerbated by physical activity or movement and may be associated with vertebral compression fractures or other musculoskeletal conditions.

4. Loss of Height and Posture Changes:

a. Vertebral compression fractures can lead to a loss of height over time, as well as changes in posture such as kyphosis (hunched back) or stooped posture.

b. Postural changes may affect balance and increase the risk of falls and fractures.

5. Decreased Mobility and Function:

a. Osteoporotic fractures can impair mobility and functional independence, leading to limitations in activities of daily living and decreased quality of life.

b. Fractures, particularly hip fractures, can have a significant impact on mobility, resulting in reduced ability to walk, climb stairs, and perform routine tasks.

Diagnosis:

1. Clinical Assessment:

a. A thorough medical history and physical examination are essential for evaluating risk factors, identifying symptoms, and assessing functional status.

b. Special attention should be paid to risk factors for osteoporosis, including age, gender, family history, medical conditions, medications, and lifestyle factors.

2. **Bone Mineral Density (BMD) Testing:**

   a. BMD testing is the gold standard for diagnosing osteoporosis and assessing fracture risk.

   b. Dual-energy X-ray absorptiometry (DXA or DEXA) is the most widely used method for measuring BMD at the hip and spine.

   c. BMD results are reported as T-scores, which compare an individual's BMD to the average BMD of a young, healthy adult of the same gender. A T-score of -2.5 or lower indicates osteoporosis, while a T-score between -1 and -2.5 indicates osteopenia (low bone mass).

3. **Laboratory Tests:**

   a. Blood tests may be performed to evaluate for underlying medical conditions that can affect bone health, such as vitamin D deficiency, hyperparathyroidism, thyroid disorders, and renal dysfunction.

   b. Serum calcium, phosphorus, alkaline phosphatase, parathyroid hormone (PTH), and 25-hydroxyvitamin D levels may be measured to assess bone metabolism and mineral homeostasis.

4. **Fracture Risk Assessment:**

   a. Fracture risk assessment tools, such as the FRAX (Fracture Risk Assessment Tool), may be used to estimate an individual's 10-year probability of major osteoporotic fractures (including hip, spine, wrist, and humerus fractures) and hip fractures.

b. FRAX integrates clinical risk factors (e.g., age, gender, body mass index, prior fracture, parental hip fracture, smoking, alcohol use) with BMD measurements to calculate fracture risk.

5. **Imaging Studies:**

Imaging studies, such as X-rays, may be performed to evaluate for vertebral fractures, assess bone quality, and rule out other skeletal abnormalities.

6. **Secondary Causes Evaluation:**

In cases of suspected secondary osteoporosis (i.e., osteoporosis secondary to underlying medical conditions or medications), additional investigations may be warranted to identify and address the underlying cause.

Early diagnosis and intervention are crucial for preventing fractures, preserving bone health, and improving outcomes in individuals with osteoporosis. A comprehensive approach to diagnosis should include clinical assessment, BMD testing, fracture risk assessment, and evaluation for secondary causes of osteoporosis.

Treatment and Management:

1. **Lifestyle Modifications:**

   a. **Calcium and Vitamin D:** Adequate intake of calcium (1000-1200 mg/day) and vitamin D (800-1000 IU/day) is essential for maintaining bone health. Calcium-rich foods include dairy products, leafy greens, and fortified foods. Vitamin D can be obtained from sunlight exposure and supplements.

   b. **Weight-Bearing Exercise**: Regular weight-bearing and muscle-strengthening exercises, such as walking, jogging, dancing, and resistance training, help improve bone density, strength, and balance, reducing the risk of fractures.

c. **Smoking Cessation and Limiting Alcohol**: Quitting smoking and limiting alcohol consumption can help reduce bone loss and fracture risk in individuals with osteoporosis.

2. **Medications:**

   a. **Bisphosphonates**: Bisphosphonates, such as alendronate, risedronate, ibandronate, and zoledronic acid, are commonly prescribed medications for osteoporosis. They work by inhibiting bone resorption and reducing fracture risk.

   b. **Selective Estrogen Receptor Modulators (SERMs)**: Medications such as raloxifene act as estrogen agonists in some tissues (e.g., bone) and antagonists in others (e.g., breast). SERMs can help prevent bone loss and reduce fracture risk in postmenopausal women.

   c. **Monoclonal Antibodies**: Denosumab is a monoclonal antibody that inhibits bone resorption by targeting RANK ligand, a key regulator of osteoclast activity. It is administered subcutaneously every 6 months.

   d. **Hormone Replacement Therapy (HRT):** Estrogen therapy may be considered in postmenopausal women for the prevention of osteoporosis-related fractures. However, the use of HRT is associated with risks and benefits that should be carefully weighed.

3. **Calcium and Vitamin D Supplements:**

   In individuals with inadequate dietary intake or absorption of calcium and vitamin D, supplements may be recommended to meet daily requirements and optimize bone health.

4. **Monitoring and Follow-up:**

   a. Regular monitoring of bone density and fracture risk, as well as assessment of treatment response, is important for managing osteoporosis effectively.

b. Follow-up visits with healthcare providers, including bone density testing and evaluation of medication efficacy and safety, are essential for optimizing treatment outcomes and preventing complications.

Prevention:

1. **Healthy Lifestyle:**

   a. Maintain a balanced diet rich in calcium and vitamin D, and engage in regular weight-bearing exercise and physical activity to promote bone health.

   b. Avoid smoking and limit alcohol consumption to reduce the risk of bone loss and fractures.

2. **Fall Prevention:**

   Take measures to prevent falls and minimize the risk of fractures, such as removing tripping hazards, improving lighting, using handrails and assistive devices, and wearing appropriate footwear.

3. **Screening and Early Intervention:**

   a. Screen for osteoporosis and assess fracture risk in high-risk individuals, including postmenopausal women, older adults, individuals with a history of fragility fractures, and those with medical conditions or medications that increase fracture risk.

   b. Implement preventive measures and initiate treatment early to prevent bone loss and reduce fracture risk.

4. **Education and Awareness:**

   a. Educate patients and the public about the importance of bone health, risk factors for osteoporosis, and preventive measures to reduce fracture risk.

   b. Raise awareness about osteoporosis screening, diagnosis, and treatment options among healthcare providers and the general population.

By adopting a comprehensive approach to treatment, management, and prevention, individuals with osteoporosis can reduce fracture risk, maintain bone health, and improve overall quality of life. Early diagnosis, lifestyle modifications, appropriate medication therapy, and regular follow-up are key components of effective osteoporosis management.

Gout

Gout is a form of inflammatory arthritis characterized by sudden and severe attacks of pain, redness, swelling, and tenderness in the joints, most commonly the big toe. It occurs due to the buildup of uric acid crystals in the joints and surrounding tissues. Here's a detailed overview:

Gout is a form of inflammatory arthritis characterized by recurrent attacks of severe joint pain, swelling, redness, and warmth, typically affecting the joint at the base of the big toe. The pathophysiology of gout involves the deposition of monosodium urate (MSU) crystals in the joints and surrounding tissues, leading to inflammation and tissue damage. Here's a detailed overview of the pathophysiology and risk factors associated with gout:

Pathophysiology:

1. **Hyperuricemia:**
    a. The primary underlying abnormality in gout is elevated levels of uric acid in the blood, a condition known as hyperuricemia.
    b. Uric acid is a waste product formed from the breakdown of purines, which are naturally occurring compounds found in certain foods and in the body's cells and tissues.
    c. Hyperuricemia can result from increased production of uric acid, decreased excretion of uric acid by the kidneys, or a combination of both factors.

2. **Monosodium Urate (MSU) Crystal Deposition:**

a. In individuals with hyperuricemia, urate crystals can form and accumulate in the joints and surrounding tissues, particularly in cooler areas of the body.

b. The formation of MSU crystals occurs when uric acid levels exceed the saturation point in the blood, leading to the precipitation of urate crystals.

c. MSU crystals are needle-shaped and can trigger an inflammatory response when they come into contact with the joint lining (synovium) or other tissues, leading to the characteristic symptoms of gout.

3. Inflammatory Response:

a. Upon deposition of MSU crystals in the joints, the immune system recognizes these crystals as foreign invaders and initiates an inflammatory response.

b. Inflammatory mediators, such as cytokines (e.g., interleukin-1β), chemokines, and leukotrienes, are released, leading to activation of inflammatory cells and recruitment of neutrophils to the affected joint.

c. Neutrophils engulf and attempt to phagocytose the MSU crystals, releasing enzymes and reactive oxygen species that further contribute to tissue damage and inflammation.

4. Acute Gouty Attack:

a. The inflammatory response triggered by MSU crystals results in the sudden onset of severe joint pain, swelling, redness, and warmth characteristic of an acute gouty attack.

b. Acute attacks typically peak within 24 to 48 hours and can last for several days to weeks, resolving spontaneously without treatment.

5. Chronic Gout:

a. In some individuals, recurrent acute gouty attacks can lead to chronic gout, characterized by persistent joint inflammation, tophus formation (accumulation of urate crystals), and joint damage.

b. Tophi may develop in the soft tissues surrounding the joints, tendons, and cartilage, causing deformity, erosion, and destruction of the affected tissues over time.

Risk Factors:

1. **Hyperuricemia:**

   a. Elevated levels of uric acid in the blood are the primary risk factor for developing gout. Factors contributing to hyperuricemia include:

      i. Dietary intake of purine-rich foods (e.g., red meat, organ meats, seafood, certain vegetables)

      ii. Excessive alcohol consumption, particularly beer and spirits

      iii. Metabolic disorders such as obesity, metabolic syndrome, and insulin resistance

      iv. Renal impairment or decreased kidney function leading to decreased uric acid excretion

2. **Genetic Predisposition:**

   Genetic factors play a significant role in the development of gout. Variants in genes involved in purine metabolism, uric acid transport, and renal urate handling can influence an individual's susceptibility to hyperuricemia and gout.

3. **Age and Gender:**

   Gout is more common in men than in women, particularly in middle-aged and older adults. However, the incidence of gout in women increases after menopause, suggesting a role of hormonal factors in disease pathogenesis.

4. **Medical Conditions:**

Certain medical conditions and comorbidities are associated with an increased risk of gout, including:

    i.   Hypertension

   ii.   Diabetes mellitus

  iii.   Chronic kidney disease

   iv.   Metabolic syndrome

    v.   Cardiovascular disease

5. Medications:

Certain medications can increase the risk of hyperuricemia and gout, including diuretics (especially thiazide diuretics), low-dose aspirin, cyclosporine, and niacin.

6. Lifestyle Factors:

Lifestyle factors such as sedentary lifestyle, poor diet, obesity, and stress can contribute to the development of gout by promoting hyperuricemia and metabolic dysfunction.

GOUT

Gout is a form of inflammatory arthritis characterized by recurrent attacks of severe joint pain, swelling, redness, and warmth, typically affecting the joint at the base of the big toe. The pathophysiology of gout involves the deposition of monosodium urate (MSU) crystals in the joints and surrounding tissues, leading to inflammation and tissue damage. Here's a detailed overview of the pathophysiology and risk factors associated with gout:

Pathophysiology:

1. Hyperuricemia:

   a. The primary underlying abnormality in gout is elevated levels of uric acid in the blood, a condition known as hyperuricemia.

b. Uric acid is a waste product formed from the breakdown of purines, which are naturally occurring compounds found in certain foods and in the body's cells and tissues.

c. Hyperuricemia can result from increased production of uric acid, decreased excretion of uric acid by the kidneys, or a combination of both factors.

2. **Monosodium Urate (MSU) Crystal Deposition:**

a. In individuals with hyperuricemia, urate crystals can form and accumulate in the joints and surrounding tissues, particularly in cooler areas of the body.

b. The formation of MSU crystals occurs when uric acid levels exceed the saturation point in the blood, leading to the precipitation of urate crystals.

c. MSU crystals are needle-shaped and can trigger an inflammatory response when they come into contact with the joint lining (synovium) or other tissues, leading to the characteristic symptoms of gout.

3. **Inflammatory Response:**

a. Upon deposition of MSU crystals in the joints, the immune system recognizes these crystals as foreign invaders and initiates an inflammatory response.

b. Inflammatory mediators, such as cytokines (e.g., interleukin-1β), chemokines, and leukotrienes, are released, leading to activation of inflammatory cells and recruitment of neutrophils to the affected joint.

c. Neutrophils engulf and attempt to phagocytose the MSU crystals, releasing enzymes and reactive oxygen species that further contribute to tissue damage and inflammation.

4. **Acute Gouty Attack:**

a. The inflammatory response triggered by MSU crystals results in the sudden onset of severe joint pain, swelling, redness, and warmth characteristic of an acute gouty attack.

b. Acute attacks typically peak within 24 to 48 hours and can last for several days to weeks, resolving spontaneously without treatment.

5. Chronic Gout:

a. In some individuals, recurrent acute gouty attacks can lead to chronic gout, characterized by persistent joint inflammation, tophus formation (accumulation of urate crystals), and joint damage.

b. Tophi may develop in the soft tissues surrounding the joints, tendons, and cartilage, causing deformity, erosion, and destruction of the affected tissues over time.

Risk Factors:

1. Hyperuricemia:

a. Elevated levels of uric acid in the blood are the primary risk factor for developing gout. Factors contributing to hyperuricemia include:

    i. Dietary intake of purine-rich foods (e.g., red meat, organ meats, seafood, certain vegetables)

    ii. Excessive alcohol consumption, particularly beer and spirits

    iii. Metabolic disorders such as obesity, metabolic syndrome, and insulin resistance

    iv. Renal impairment or decreased kidney function leading to decreased uric acid excretion

2. Genetic Predisposition:

Genetic factors play a significant role in the development of gout. Variants in genes involved in purine metabolism, uric acid transport, and renal urate handling can influence an individual's susceptibility to hyperuricemia and gout.

3. Age and Gender:

Gout is more common in men than in women, particularly in middle-aged and older adults. However, the incidence of gout in women increases after menopause, suggesting a role of hormonal factors in disease pathogenesis.

4. **Medical Conditions:**

    a. Certain medical conditions and comorbidities are associated with an increased risk of gout, including:

        i.   Hypertension
        ii. Diabetes mellitus
        iii. Chronic kidney disease
        iv. Metabolic syndrome
        v.   Cardiovascular disease

5. **Medications:**

    Certain medications can increase the risk of hyperuricemia and gout, including diuretics (especially thiazide diuretics), low-dose aspirin, cyclosporine, and niacin.

6. **Lifestyle Factors:**

    Lifestyle factors such as sedentary lifestyle, poor diet, obesity, and stress can contribute to the development of gout by promoting hyperuricemia and metabolic dysfunction.

Clinical Presentation:

1. **Acute Gouty Arthritis:**

    a. The hallmark feature of gout is the sudden onset of severe joint pain, swelling, redness, and warmth, typically affecting the joint at the base of the big toe (first metatarsophalangeal joint).

    b. Acute gouty arthritis often presents as an abrupt attack of intense pain, commonly described as excruciating, throbbing, or crushing in nature.

c. The affected joint may become tender to touch, and even the weight of a bedsheet can cause severe pain (allodynia).

d. Symptoms typically peak within 24 to 48 hours and can last for several days to weeks if left untreated.

2. Other Affected Joints:

a. While the first metatarsophalangeal joint is the most commonly affected site, gout can also involve other joints, including the ankles, knees, heels, wrists, fingers, and elbows.

b. The presentation of gout in these joints may be similar to that of acute gouty arthritis, with severe pain, swelling, redness, and warmth.

3. Tophaceous Gout:

a. In chronic or untreated cases of gout, tophi may develop in the soft tissues surrounding the joints, tendons, and cartilage.

b. Tophi are chalky deposits of monosodium urate crystals and can vary in size from small nodules to large, disfiguring masses.

c. Tophi are typically painless but can cause deformity, erosion, and destruction of the affected tissues over time.

4. Systemic Symptoms:

a. Acute gouty attacks may be associated with systemic symptoms such as fever, chills, malaise, and fatigue.

b. These systemic symptoms are thought to be related to the inflammatory response triggered by the deposition of monosodium urate crystals in the joints.

5. Triggers:

a. Acute gouty attacks can be triggered by various factors, including:

   i. **Dietary triggers**: Consumption of purine-rich foods (e.g., red meat, organ meats, seafood, certain vegetables), alcohol (especially beer and spirits), and sugary beverages.

ii. **Medication**s: Certain medications, such as diuretics (especially thiazide diuretics), low-dose aspirin, cyclosporine, and niacin, can precipitate gout attacks.

iii. **Trauma or surgery:** Physical trauma, surgery, or medical procedures can sometimes trigger acute gouty attacks in susceptible individuals.

Diagnosis:

1. **Clinical Assessment:**

   a. A detailed medical history and physical examination are essential for evaluating symptoms, identifying risk factors, and assessing joint involvement.

   b. Special attention should be paid to the pattern of joint involvement, severity and duration of symptoms, presence of tophi, and potential triggers of gouty attacks.

2. **Joint Aspiration and Synovial Fluid Analysis:**

   a. Joint aspiration and analysis of synovial fluid are the gold standard for diagnosing gout.

   b. Synovial fluid analysis reveals the presence of negatively birefringent monosodium urate crystals under polarized light microscopy, which confirms the diagnosis of gout.

   c. In acute gouty attacks, synovial fluid is typically inflammatory, with elevated white blood cell count (>2000 cells/mm^3) and neutrophil predominance.

3. **Serum Uric Acid Levels:**

   a. Serum uric acid levels may be measured to assess for hyperuricemia, although elevated levels alone are not diagnostic of gout as many individuals with hyperuricemia do not develop gout, and gout can occur in the absence of hyperuricemia.

b. Serum uric acid levels may be normal or even low during acute gouty attacks due to the precipitation of urate crystals in the joints.

4. **Imaging Studies:**

   a. Imaging studies such as X-rays, ultrasound, or dual-energy computed tomography (DECT) may be performed to evaluate for joint damage, tophi, or urate crystal deposition.

   b. X-rays may show characteristic findings of gout, including soft tissue swelling, joint space narrowing, subcortical cysts, and overhanging margins (Martel's sign) in chronic cases.

5. **Differential Diagnosis:**

   a. Gout should be differentiated from other causes of acute arthritis, including septic arthritis, pseudogout (calcium pyrophosphate deposition disease), rheumatoid arthritis, osteoarthritis, and reactive arthritis.

Accurate diagnosis of gout is essential for initiating appropriate treatment and management strategies to alleviate symptoms, prevent acute attacks, and reduce the risk of long-term complications. A comprehensive approach to diagnosis includes clinical assessment, joint aspiration, synovial fluid analysis, serum uric acid measurement, and imaging studies as needed.

Treatment and Management:

1. **Acute Gouty Attacks:**

   a. **Nonsteroidal anti-inflammatory drugs (NSAIDs):** NSAIDs such as indomethacin, naproxen, or ibuprofen are commonly used to relieve pain and reduce inflammation during acute gouty attacks.

   b. **Colchicine:** Colchicine is an anti-inflammatory medication that can be used to relieve pain and inflammation in acute gout. It is most effective when started early during an attack.

c. **Corticosteroids:** Oral or intra-articular corticosteroids may be prescribed for individuals who cannot tolerate NSAIDs or colchicine, or in cases of severe gouty arthritis.

2. **Chronic Gout Management:**
   a. **Lifestyle Modifications:**
      i. **Dietary changes:** Limit intake of purine-rich foods (e.g., red meat, organ meats, seafood, certain vegetables), alcohol (especially beer and spirits), and sugary beverages.
      ii. **Weight management:** Achieve and maintain a healthy weight through diet and exercise to reduce the risk of gout attacks.
      iii. **Hydration:** Maintain adequate hydration by drinking plenty of fluids, particularly water, to help prevent urate crystal formation.

3. **Medications to Lower Uric Acid Levels:**
   a. **Urate-lowering therapy (ULT):** ULT is recommended for individuals with recurrent gout attacks, tophi, or complications of gout such as kidney stones or urate nephropathy.
   b. **Allopurinol:** Allopurinol is the most commonly used urate-lowering medication and works by inhibiting the enzyme xanthine oxidase, reducing uric acid production.
   c. **Febuxostat:** Febuxostat is another xanthine oxidase inhibitor that may be used as an alternative to allopurinol in individuals with intolerance or inadequate response to allopurinol.
   d. **Uricosuric agents:** Uricosuric agents such as probenecid and lesinurad increase renal excretion of uric acid and may be used in individuals with underexcretion of uric acid.
   e. **Pegloticase:** Pegloticase is a recombinant uricase enzyme that converts uric acid into a more soluble form, allowing for rapid

elimination of uric acid from the body. It is reserved for individuals with severe, refractory gout who have failed other treatments.

4. Management of Tophaceous Gout:

    a. In cases of chronic gout with tophi, treatment may include combination therapy with ULT and anti-inflammatory medications to reduce tophi size and prevent new tophi formation.

    b. Surgical excision of tophi may be considered for large or symptomatic tophi that do not respond to medical therapy.

Complications:

1. Recurrent Gout Attacks:

Untreated or inadequately managed gout can lead to recurrent acute gouty attacks, resulting in progressive joint damage, disability, and decreased quality of life.

2. Tophi Formation:

    a. Chronic gout can lead to the formation of tophi, which are deposits of urate crystals in the soft tissues surrounding the joints, tendons, and cartilage.

    b. Tophi may cause pain, swelling, deformity, and erosion of the affected tissues, leading to functional impairment and joint damage.

3. Joint Damage:

    a. Chronic inflammation and repeated gout attacks can result in joint damage, deformity, and destruction, particularly in untreated or poorly controlled cases of gout.

    b. Joint damage may lead to decreased mobility, stiffness, and loss of joint function.

4. Renal Complications:

a. Long-standing hyperuricemia and gout can lead to the development of urate nephropathy, characterized by the deposition of urate crystals in the kidneys and renal impairment.

b. Urate nephropathy may progress to chronic kidney disease, kidney stones, and eventually end-stage renal disease in severe cases.

Prevention:

1. Lifestyle Modifications:

a. Adopt a healthy diet low in purine-rich foods, alcohol, and sugary beverages, and high in fruits, vegetables, whole grains, and lean proteins.

b. Maintain a healthy weight through diet and regular physical activity to reduce the risk of hyperuricemia and gout attacks.

2. Medication Adherence:

a. Adhere to prescribed medications for lowering uric acid levels (e.g., allopurinol, febuxostat) as directed by a healthcare provider to prevent gout attacks and complications.

3. Regular Follow-up:

a. Schedule regular follow-up visits with a healthcare provider for monitoring of uric acid levels, assessment of gout activity, and adjustment of treatment as needed.

b. Monitor for signs and symptoms of gout flares and seek prompt medical attention if symptoms worsen or new symptoms develop.

4. Hydration:

a. Maintain adequate hydration by drinking plenty of fluids, particularly water, to help prevent urate crystal formation and reduce the risk of gout attacks.

By implementing a comprehensive approach to treatment, management, and prevention, individuals with gout can effectively control symptoms, reduce the frequency of acute attacks, prevent complications, and improve overall quality of life. Close collaboration with a healthcare provider, adherence to prescribed medications, and lifestyle modifications are key components of successful gout management.

CANCER

1. **Definition of Cancer:**

   Cancer is a group of diseases characterized by the uncontrolled growth and spread of abnormal cells. These cells have the ability to invade and destroy normal tissues and organs, leading to the formation of tumors and the disruption of normal bodily functions.

2. **Multifactorial Nature:**

   a. Cancer is a multifactorial disease, meaning it arises from a complex interplay of genetic, environmental, and lifestyle factors.

   b. Genetic mutations play a crucial role in the development of cancer by disrupting the normal regulation of cell growth and division.

   c. Environmental factors such as exposure to carcinogens (e.g., tobacco smoke, ultraviolet radiation, certain chemicals), infectious agents (e.g., viruses, bacteria), and dietary factors (e.g., high-fat diet, lack of fruits and vegetables) can increase the risk of cancer.

3. **Hallmarks of Cancer:**

   a. Cancer cells acquire several characteristic features, often referred to as the "hallmarks of cancer," that distinguish them from normal cells:

      i. **Sustained proliferative signaling**: Cancer cells exhibit uncontrolled proliferation, driven by genetic mutations that activate growth-promoting pathways.

      ii. **Evasion of growth suppressors**: Cancer cells bypass mechanisms that normally inhibit cell growth and division, allowing them to proliferate unchecked.

iii. **Resistance to cell death (apoptosis)**: Cancer cells evade programmed cell death, allowing them to survive and accumulate genetic mutations.

iv. **Replicative immortality**: Cancer cells acquire the ability to divide indefinitely, bypassing the normal limits on cell replication.

v. **Induction of angiogenesis**: Cancer cells stimulate the formation of new blood vessels to supply oxygen and nutrients, promoting tumor growth and metastasis.

vi. **Activation of invasion and metastasis**: Cancer cells acquire the ability to invade surrounding tissues and spread to distant sites in the body, forming secondary tumors (metastases).

vii. **Reprogramming of energy metabolism**: Cancer cells undergo metabolic changes to support their rapid growth and proliferation.

viii. **Evasion of immune destruction**: Cancer cells evade detection and destruction by the immune system, allowing them to proliferate and spread.

4. **Tumor Classification:**

   a. Tumors are classified based on their tissue of origin, histological features, and molecular characteristics.

   b. Carcinomas arise from epithelial tissues and account for the majority of cancers, including breast, lung, prostate, and colon cancers.

   c. Sarcomas originate from mesenchymal tissues such as bone, muscle, and connective tissue.

   d. Lymphomas and leukemias arise from blood-forming cells and lymphoid tissues.

e. Central nervous system tumors develop in the brain and spinal cord.

5. Diagnosis and Staging:

a. Diagnosis of cancer involves a combination of clinical evaluation, imaging studies (e.g., X-rays, CT scans, MRI scans), laboratory tests (e.g., blood tests, tumor markers), and tissue biopsy for histological examination.

b. Staging of cancer is based on the extent of tumor growth, invasion into surrounding tissues, involvement of lymph nodes, and presence of metastases. Staging helps determine prognosis and guide treatment decisions.

6. Treatment:

a. Cancer treatment aims to eradicate or control the growth of cancer cells, relieve symptoms, and improve quality of life.

b. Treatment modalities may include surgery, chemotherapy, radiation therapy, targeted therapy, immunotherapy, hormone therapy, and stem cell transplantation.

c. Treatment plans are tailored to individual patients based on factors such as tumor type, stage, location, and molecular characteristics, as well as the patient's overall health and preferences.

7. Prevention and Screening:

a. Cancer prevention strategies focus on reducing modifiable risk factors such as tobacco use, unhealthy diet, physical inactivity, and exposure to carcinogens.

b. Screening programs aim to detect cancer at an early stage when it is more treatable. Common screening tests include mammography for breast cancer, colonoscopy for colorectal cancer, Pap smear for cervical cancer, and PSA test for prostate cancer.

Types of cancer:

Cancer is a complex group of diseases characterized by the uncontrolled growth and spread of abnormal cells. There are more than 100 different types of cancer, each with its own set of characteristics, risk factors, and treatment options. Here are some of the most common types:

1. Breast Cancer: A cancer that forms in the cells of the breast, most commonly in the ducts (ductal carcinoma) or lobules (lobular carcinoma). It is the most common cancer in women worldwide.
2. Lung Cancer: Occurs when abnormal cells grow uncontrollably in one or both lungs, often linked to smoking but can also occur in non-smokers.
3. Colorectal Cancer: A cancer that starts in the colon or rectum, typically developing from polyps, abnormal growths in the colon or rectum lining.
4. Prostate Cancer: A cancer that develops in the prostate gland, which is part of the male reproductive system.
5. Skin Cancer: Includes several types such as melanoma (the most serious form), basal cell carcinoma, and squamous cell carcinoma, which develop in the skin's cells.
6. Bladder Cancer: Occurs when abnormal cells in the bladder grow uncontrollably, often causing blood in the urine and urinary changes.
7. Kidney (Renal) Cancer: A cancer that forms in the kidneys, typically in the lining of small tubes (renal cell carcinoma).
8. Thyroid Cancer: Arises from the cells of the thyroid gland, which produces hormones that regulate metabolism.
9. Leukemia: A cancer of the blood or bone marrow, characterized by the rapid production of abnormal white blood cells.
10. Lymphoma: A cancer of the lymphatic system, which includes lymph nodes, lymphatic vessels, and lymphocytes (a type of white blood cell). Types include Hodgkin lymphoma and non-Hodgkin lymphoma.

11. Liver Cancer: Most often begins in the cells of the liver (hepatocellular carcinoma) but can also start in the bile ducts (cholangiocarcinoma).

12. Pancreatic Cancer: A cancer that forms in the tissues of the pancreas, an organ in the abdomen that produces enzymes to aid digestion and hormones to regulate blood sugar levels.

13. Ovarian Cancer: Develops in the ovaries, part of the female reproductive system, and is often detected at a later stage due to few early symptoms.

14. Endometrial Cancer: Arises from the lining of the uterus (endometrium), most commonly in postmenopausal women.

15. Cervical Cancer: Occurs in the cells of the cervix, the lower part of the uterus, often linked to human papillomavirus (HPV) infection.

Classification of cancer

Cancer classification is a complex process that involves categorizing tumors based on various factors, including their tissue of origin, histological features, molecular characteristics, and clinical behavior. Here's a detailed overview of the classification of cancer:

1. **Tissue of Origin:**

    a. Tumors are classified based on the type of tissue from which they originate. The main categories include:

        i. **Carcinomas**: These cancers arise from epithelial tissues, which line the surfaces and cavities of organs. Examples include breast carcinoma, lung carcinoma, prostate carcinoma, and colon carcinoma.

        ii. **Sarcomas**: Sarcomas develop from mesenchymal tissues, such as bone, muscle, fat, and connective tissue. Examples include osteosarcoma (bone), leiomyosarcoma (smooth muscle), and liposarcoma (fat).

iii. **Lymphomas and leukemias:** These cancers originate from blood-forming cells and lymphoid tissues. Lymphomas affect the lymphatic system, while leukemias primarily involve the bone marrow and blood. Examples include Hodgkin lymphoma, non-Hodgkin lymphoma, and acute lymphoblastic leukemia.

iv. **Central nervous system tumors**: These tumors arise in the brain and spinal cord and include gliomas, meningiomas, and medulloblastomas.

2. Histological Features:

a. Histological classification involves examining tumor tissue under a microscope to assess its cellular characteristics and organization.

b. Histological subtypes provide additional information about tumor behavior, prognosis, and response to treatment.

c. For example, breast carcinomas may be classified into subtypes such as ductal carcinoma, lobular carcinoma, and inflammatory carcinoma based on the appearance of tumor cells and their growth patterns.

3. Molecular Characteristics:

a. Advances in molecular biology and genomics have led to the identification of specific genetic mutations, gene expression patterns, and molecular pathways associated with different types of cancer.

b. Molecular classification allows for more precise diagnosis, prognosis, and targeted treatment strategies.

c. Examples of molecular subtypes include HER2-positive breast cancer, BRAF-mutant melanoma, and EGFR-mutant non-small cell lung cancer.

4. Clinical Behavior:

a. Tumors may be classified based on their clinical behavior, including their growth rate, invasiveness, metastatic potential, and response to treatment.

b. Clinical classification helps guide treatment decisions and predict patient outcomes.

c. For example, cancers may be classified as localized (confined to the primary site), locally advanced (invading nearby tissues or structures), or metastatic (spread to distant sites).

5. **Staging:**

a. Staging is a standardized system used to classify the extent of cancer spread based on factors such as tumor size, lymph node involvement, and presence of metastases.

b. Staging helps determine prognosis and guide treatment decisions.

c. The most commonly used staging system for solid tumors is the TNM system, which categorizes tumors based on Tumor size, lymph Node involvement, and Metastasis.

6. **Specialized Classifications:**

a. Certain types of cancer have specialized classification systems based on unique features or clinical characteristics.

b. For example, the Gleason score is used to grade prostate cancer based on the architecture of tumor cells observed under a microscope.

c. The International Classification of Diseases for Oncology (ICD-O) provides a standardized system for coding and classifying cancer diagnoses for epidemiological and research purposes.

Etiology of cancer

The etiology of cancer, or the causes of cancer, is multifactorial and involves a complex interplay of genetic, environmental, lifestyle, and other risk factors. Here's a detailed overview of the etiology of cancer:

1. **Genetic Factors:**
   a. Genetic mutations play a crucial role in the development of cancer by disrupting normal cellular processes that regulate cell growth, division, and death.
   b. Some individuals inherit genetic mutations that increase their susceptibility to certain types of cancer. These inherited mutations may be present in genes such as BRCA1 and BRCA2 (associated with breast and ovarian cancer), TP53 (associated with various cancers), and APC (associated with colorectal cancer).
   c. Additionally, acquired (somatic) mutations can occur spontaneously or as a result of exposure to carcinogens, radiation, or other environmental factors.

2. **Environmental Factors:**
   a. Environmental exposures to carcinogens, substances or agents that promote cancer development, can increase the risk of cancer.
   b. Carcinogens may include:
      i. **Chemical carcinogens**: Found in tobacco smoke, air pollution, industrial chemicals, pesticides, and certain food additives.
      ii. **Physical carcinogens:** Such as ultraviolet (UV) radiation from sunlight (associated with skin cancer), ionizing radiation from medical imaging or nuclear fallout, and asbestos fibers (associated with lung cancer and mesothelioma).
      iii. **Biological carcinogens**: Including certain viruses (e.g., human papillomavirus [HPV] associated with cervical

cancer, hepatitis B and C viruses associated with liver cancer) and bacteria (e.g., Helicobacter pylori associated with stomach cancer).

3. **Lifestyle Factors:**

   a. Lifestyle choices and behaviors can significantly impact cancer risk:

      i. **Tobacco use**: Smoking is the leading cause of preventable cancer deaths worldwide and is associated with various cancers, including lung, throat, mouth, esophageal, and bladder cancer.

      ii. **Diet:** Consumption of a diet high in processed meats, red meats, saturated fats, and low in fruits, vegetables, and fiber is associated with an increased risk of certain cancers, particularly colorectal cancer.

      iii. **Physical inactivity**: Lack of regular physical activity is linked to an increased risk of obesity and several cancers, including breast, colon, and endometrial cancer.

      iv. **Alcohol consumption**: Heavy alcohol consumption is a known risk factor for cancers of the mouth, throat, esophagus, liver, colon, and breast.

4. **Hormonal Factors:**

   a. Hormonal imbalances or exposures can influence cancer risk:

      i. **Hormone replacement therapy (HRT)**: Long-term use of estrogen-progestin hormone replacement therapy in postmenopausal women is associated with an increased risk of breast cancer.

      ii. **Reproductive factors**: Early age at menarche, late age at menopause, nulliparity (never having given birth), and late age at first full-term pregnancy are associated with an increased risk of breast cancer.

   iii. **Androgen**s: High levels of androgens (male hormones) are associated with an increased risk of prostate cancer.

5. **Infectious Agents:**

   a. Certain infectious agents, including viruses, bacteria, and parasites, can cause chronic infections that increase the risk of cancer:

      i. **Viruse**s: Examples include HPV (associated with cervical, anal, and oropharyngeal cancers), hepatitis B and C viruses (associated with liver cancer), and Epstein-Barr virus (associated with lymphomas and nasopharyngeal cancer).

      ii. **Bacteria**: Helicobacter pylori infection is a major risk factor for stomach cancer.

      iii. **Parasite**s: Infection with the parasite Schistosoma haematobium is associated with bladder cancer.

6. **Age, Gender, and Genetics:**

   a. **Age:** Cancer risk increases with age, with most cancers occurring in individuals over 65 years old.

   b. **Gender:** Certain cancers are more common in one gender than the other (e.g., breast cancer in females, prostate cancer in males).

   c. **Genetics:** Family history of cancer, inherited genetic mutations, and specific genetic syndromes (e.g., Lynch syndrome, hereditary breast and ovarian cancer syndrome) can increase cancer risk.

Pathogenesis of cancer

The pathogenesis of cancer refers to the process by which normal cells undergo transformation into cancerous cells and the subsequent progression of the disease. It involves a series of complex molecular and cellular events that disrupt the normal regulation of cell growth, division, and death. Here's a detailed overview of the pathogenesis of cancer:

1. **Initiation:**
   a. The process of cancer initiation involves the initial genetic alterations that transform a normal cell into a cancerous cell.
   b. Genetic mutations, either inherited or acquired, can occur in critical genes that regulate cell growth, division, and apoptosis (programmed cell death).
   c. Carcinogens, such as chemicals, radiation, and viruses, can induce DNA damage and genetic mutations that initiate the development of cancer.

2. **Promotion:**
   a. Following initiation, cancer-promoting factors stimulate the growth and proliferation of initiated cells, promoting the expansion of pre-cancerous lesions.
   b. Tumor promoters may include growth factors, hormones, inflammatory mediators, and other signaling molecules that activate cellular pathways involved in cell proliferation and survival.
   c. Chronic inflammation, oxidative stress, and hormonal imbalances can contribute to the promotion of cancer by creating a tumor-promoting microenvironment that supports the growth and survival of cancer cells.

3. **Progression:**
   a. Cancer progression is characterized by the accumulation of additional genetic alterations and the evolution of pre-cancerous lesions into invasive and metastatic tumors.

b. Genetic instability and clonal evolution drive the acquisition of new mutations and the selection of more aggressive cancer cell phenotypes.

c. Key pathways involved in cancer progression include those regulating cell cycle control, DNA repair, apoptosis, angiogenesis, invasion, and metastasis.

d. Cancer cells acquire the ability to invade surrounding tissues, enter the bloodstream or lymphatic system, and establish secondary tumors (metastases) at distant sites in the body.

4. Tumor Microenvironment:

a. The tumor microenvironment plays a critical role in cancer pathogenesis by influencing tumor growth, invasion, angiogenesis, and immune evasion.

b. Tumor-associated stromal cells, including fibroblasts, immune cells, endothelial cells, and pericytes, interact with cancer cells and contribute to tumor progression.

c. Extracellular matrix (ECM) components, such as collagen, fibronectin, and hyaluronic acid, provide structural support for tumor growth and facilitate cell-cell and cell-ECM interactions.

d. Hypoxia, nutrient deprivation, and acidic pH within the tumor microenvironment promote the selection of more aggressive cancer cell phenotypes and contribute to treatment resistance.

5. Metastasis:

a. Metastasis is the spread of cancer cells from the primary tumor to distant sites in the body, leading to the formation of secondary tumors.

b. The metastatic cascade involves a series of sequential steps, including local invasion, intravasation into blood or lymphatic vessels, survival in the circulation, extravasation at distant sites, and colonization of secondary organs.

   c. Cancer cells may undergo epithelial-to-mesenchymal transition (EMT), a process that enhances their migratory and invasive properties, facilitating metastatic dissemination.

6. Tumor Heterogeneity:

   a. Tumor heterogeneity refers to the presence of distinct subpopulations of cancer cells within a tumor, characterized by differences in genetic, epigenetic, and phenotypic features.

   b. Intratumoral heterogeneity arises from genetic mutations, clonal evolution, microenvironmental factors, and therapeutic selection pressures.

   c. Tumor heterogeneity poses challenges for cancer diagnosis, treatment, and prognosis, as different subclones may exhibit variable responses to therapy and contribute to disease recurrence and progression.

Multiple Choice Questions (MCQs):

1. What is the most common type of cancer arising from epithelial tissues?

   a) Sarcoma

   b) Lymphoma

   c) Carcinoma

   d) Leukemia

2. Which vitamin is essential for calcium absorption and bone mineralization?

   a) Vitamin A

   b) Vitamin B12

   c) Vitamin D

   d) Vitamin E

3. What is the gold standard for measuring bone mineral density?

a) MRI

b) Ultrasound

c) X-ray

d) Dual-energy X-ray absorptiometry (DXA)

4. Which factor is considered a major risk factor for developing gout?

a) Low purine diet

b) Excessive water intake

c) High alcohol consumption

d) High calcium intake

5. Rheumatoid arthritis is primarily classified as which type of disorder?

a) Degenerative joint disease

b) Metabolic bone disease

c) Autoimmune disorder

d) Infectious joint disease

6. What is the primary effect of osteoporosis on bones?

a) Increased bone density

b) Decreased bone density

c) Increased bone flexibility

d) Decreased bone marrow production

7. Which hormone's level decline is a significant risk factor for osteoporosis in women?

a) Testosterone

b) Insulin

c) Estrogen

d) Adrenaline

8. Paget's disease of bone primarily affects:

a) Children

b) Teenagers

c) Adults

d) Elderly

9. Which type of arthritis involves uric acid crystal buildup in the joints?

   a) Osteoarthritis

   b) Rheumatoid arthritis

   c) Gout

   d) Ankylosing spondylitis

10. What is the typical site for gout to first present?

   a) Elbow

   b) Knee

   c) Big toe

   d) Wrist

11. Which dietary component can exacerbate gout symptoms?

   a) Purines

   b) Vitamin C

   c) Omega-3 fatty acids

   d) Fiber

12. What type of cancer is commonly associated with asbestos exposure?

   a) Skin cancer

   b) Brain cancer

   c) Lung cancer

   d) Bone cancer

13. The formation of new blood vessels in cancer is known as:

   a) Necrosis

   b) Metastasis

   c) Angiogenesis

   d) Apoptosis

14. Which test is commonly used to screen for prostate cancer?

   a) Pap smear

   b) Colonoscopy

c) PSA test

d) Mammography

15. What does the presence of rheumatoid factor (RF) indicate?

a) Infectious arthritis

b) Gout

c) Osteoarthritis

d) Rheumatoid arthritis

16. Which cell type is predominantly involved in osteoporosis?

a) Osteoclasts

b) Osteoblasts

c) Chondrocytes

d) Fibroblasts

17. Ankylosing spondylitis primarily affects which part of the body?

a) Hands and feet

b) Spine

c) Skull

d) Pelvis

18. What is a common symptom of a fracture?

a) Color blindness

b) Severe itchiness

c) Crack or break in a bone

d) High blood pressure

19. Which lifestyle factor is a known risk factor for multiple cancer types?

a) High sugar intake

b) Tobacco use

c) Low protein diet

d) High fiber intake

20. What is "morning stiffness" a common symptom of?

a) Osteoporosis

b) Gout

c) Rheumatoid arthritis

d) Paget's disease

Short Answer Type Questions (Subjective)

1. What is osteoarthritis and what are its main symptoms?

2. Describe the role of the immune system in rheumatoid arthritis.

3. What are the risk factors associated with osteoporosis?

4. Explain how fractures are treated depending on their severity and location.

5. What causes gout and which joint is most commonly affected?

6. Describe the symptoms and treatment options for Ankylosing Spondylitis.

7. What is Paget's Disease and how can it affect the bones?

8. How is osteoporosis diagnosed?

9. What dietary factors can exacerbate symptoms of gout?

10. Discuss the process of bone remodeling in the context of osteoporosis.

11. What are the clinical features of rheumatoid arthritis?

12. Explain the importance of vitamin D in bone health.

13. How does smoking influence the risk of osteoporosis?

14. What are the genetic and environmental factors that can lead to rheumatoid arthritis?

15. What lifestyle modifications can help manage rheumatoid arthritis?

16. How do bisphosphonates work in the treatment of osteoporosis?

17. Describe the role of synovial fluid analysis in diagnosing gout.

18. What are the implications of hyperuricemia in gout?

19. How do autoimmune reactions contribute to the pathogenesis of rheumatoid arthritis?

20. Explain the function of anti-CCP antibodies in the diagnosis of rheumatoid arthritis.

Long Answer Type Questions (Subjective)

1. Discuss the pathophysiology of gout and the role of monosodium urate crystals in its development.
2. Explain the multifactorial nature of cancer and the role of genetic mutations in its development.
3. Describe the different types of cancer classifications based on tissue of origin and provide examples of each.
4. Explain the process of bone density testing and how it helps in diagnosing osteoporosis.
5. Discuss the stages of cancer progression and the role of the tumor microenvironment in advancing cancer pathogenesis.
6. Describe the treatment strategies for managing osteoporosis and the role of lifestyle changes in its prevention.
7. Explain the relationship between diet and gout, particularly focusing on the role of purine-rich foods and alcohol.
8. Discuss the hallmarks of cancer, focusing on sustained proliferative signaling and resistance to cell death.
9. Explain how chronic inflammation contributes to the pathogenesis of rheumatoid arthritis and the long-term effects on joint health.
10. Describe the diagnostic criteria for rheumatoid arthritis and the significance of rheumatoid factor and anti-CCP antibodies in its diagnosis.

Answer Key for MCQs:

1. (c) Carcinoma
2. (c) Vitamin D

3. (d) Dual-energy X-ray absorptiometry (DXA)

4. (c) High alcohol consumption

5. (c) Autoimmune disorder

6. (b) Decreased bone density

7. (c) Estrogen

8. (d) Elderly

9. (c) Gout

10.(c) Big toe

11.(a) Purines

12.(c) Lung cancer

13.(c) Angiogenesis

14.(c) PSA test

15.(d) Rheumatoid arthritis

16.(a) Osteoclasts

17.(b) Spine

18.(c) Crack or break in a bone

19.(b) Tobacco use

20.(c) Rheumatoid arthritis

CHAPTER - 7

INFECTION AND SEXUALLY TRANSMITTED DISEASES

INFECTIOUS DISEASES

Infectious diseases are caused by pathogenic microorganisms such as bacteria, viruses, parasites, or fungi. These pathogens can be transmitted directly or indirectly from one person to another, or from animals to humans, leading to illness or infection. Understanding infectious diseases is crucial for public health, as they can have significant impacts on individuals, communities, and even global populations.

Here's a detailed introduction to various aspects of infectious diseases:

1. **Types of Pathogens:**
   a. **Bacteria**: Single-celled organisms that can cause infections such as strep throat, tuberculosis, and urinary tract infections.
   b. **Viruses:** Tiny infectious agents that replicate inside living cells, causing diseases like influenza, HIV/AIDS, and COVID-19.
   c. **Parasites**: Organisms that live on or inside other organisms and cause diseases such as malaria, schistosomiasis, and toxoplasmosis.
   d. **Fungi:** Microorganisms like yeasts and molds that can cause fungal infections such as athlete's foot, candidiasis, and aspergillosis.

2. **Modes of Transmission:**
   a. **Direct Transmission**: Occurs through physical contact between an infected person and a susceptible individual, such as through respiratory droplets (coughing, sneezing), bodily fluids (blood, saliva), or skin-to-skin contact.
   b. **Indirect Transmission**: Happens through contact with contaminated surfaces, objects, food, or water.

c. **Vector-Borne Transmission**: Involves transmission by vectors such as mosquitoes, ticks, fleas, and flies, which carry and transmit pathogens from one host to another.

3. **Epidemiology and Spread:**

   a. **Outbreaks**: Occurrence of cases of a particular disease in excess of what would normally be expected in a defined community, geographical area, or season.

   b. **Epidemics:** Occurrence of cases of a disease in a community or region that is clearly in excess of normal expectancy.

   c. **Pandemics**: Epidemics that have spread over several countries or continents, affecting a large number of people worldwide.

4. **Symptoms and Clinical Manifestations:**

   a. Symptoms of infectious diseases vary widely depending on the specific pathogen involved. They can include fever, fatigue, cough, diarrhea, rash, muscle aches, and more severe complications in some cases.

5. **Prevention and Control:**

   a. **Vaccination**: Immunization programs are essential for preventing the spread of many infectious diseases by providing immunity against specific pathogens.

   b. **Hygiene Practices**: Simple measures like handwashing, proper sanitation, and food safety can significantly reduce the risk of transmission.

   c. **Vector Control**: Strategies to control vectors, such as mosquito nets, insecticides, and environmental management, can help prevent vector-borne diseases.

   d. **Antibiotics and Antivirals**: Medications can be used to treat bacterial and viral infections, although misuse and overuse can lead to antibiotic resistance.

6. **Public Health Interventions:**
    a. Public health authorities play a crucial role in monitoring, controlling, and preventing infectious diseases through surveillance, outbreak investigation, and response strategies.
    b. Education and communication efforts are essential for raising awareness about infectious diseases, promoting healthy behaviors, and dispelling myths and misinformation.
7. **Global Health Impacts:**
    a. Infectious diseases have significant socioeconomic impacts, affecting productivity, healthcare systems, and economic development, particularly in low- and middle-income countries.
    b. Emerging infectious diseases pose ongoing challenges due to factors such as globalization, urbanization, antimicrobial resistance, and environmental changes.

Meningitis

Meningitis is a serious infectious disease characterized by inflammation of the meninges, the protective membranes that surround the brain and spinal cord. It can be caused by a variety of pathogens, including bacteria, viruses, fungi, and, less commonly, parasites. Meningitis can lead to severe complications, including neurological damage, hearing loss, and death if not promptly diagnosed and treated.

Meningitis:

Meningitis is an inflammation of the meninges, the protective membranes that surround the brain and spinal cord. It can be caused by infectious agents such as bacteria, viruses, fungi, or parasites, as well as non-infectious factors like certain medications, autoimmune diseases, or cancer. Meningitis can be a life-threatening condition and requires prompt medical attention. Here's a detailed overview of the types, transmission, and symptoms of meningitis:

1. **Types of Meningitis:**
   a. **Bacterial Meningitis**: Bacterial meningitis is a severe form of meningitis caused by bacterial pathogens. Common bacterial causes include:
      i. **Neisseria meningitidis**: Also known as meningococcus, this bacterium is a leading cause of bacterial meningitis, particularly in adolescents and young adults. It can also cause meningococcal sepsis, a life-threatening condition.
      ii. **Streptococcus pneumoniae**: This bacterium, also known as pneumococcus, is a leading cause of bacterial meningitis in adults, particularly those with underlying medical conditions or weakened immune systems.
      iii. **Haemophilus influenzae type b (Hib)**: Hib was a significant cause of bacterial meningitis in children before the introduction of the Hib vaccine.
      iv. **Listeria monocytogenes**: Listeria can cause meningitis, particularly in newborns, older adults, pregnant women, and individuals with weakened immune systems.
   b. **Viral Meningitis**: Viral meningitis, also known as aseptic meningitis, is the most common form of meningitis and is typically caused by viruses. Common viral causes include enteroviruses (such as coxsackievirus and echovirus), herpesviruses (such as herpes simplex virus and varicella-zoster virus), and others (such as mumps virus and lymphocytic choriomeningitis virus).
   c. **Fungal Meningitis**: Fungal meningitis is a less common but serious form of meningitis caused by fungal pathogens such as Cryptococcus neoformans, Candida species, and others. It is more

likely to occur in individuals with weakened immune systems, such as those with HIV/AIDS or undergoing immunosuppressive therapy.

d. **Parasitic Meningitis**: Parasitic meningitis is rare and is caused by parasites such as Naegleria fowleri (primary amoebic meningoencephalitis), which is typically acquired through contaminated water, or Angiostrongylus cantonensis (eosinophilic meningitis), which is transmitted through ingestion of infected snails or contaminated food.

e. **Non-Infectious Meningitis**: Meningitis can also be caused by non-infectious factors, including certain medications (such as nonsteroidal anti-inflammatory drugs [NSAIDs] or antibiotics), autoimmune diseases (such as lupus or sarcoidosis), cancer, or chemical irritation.

2. Transmission:

a. The transmission of meningitis depends on the underlying cause:

i. **Bacterial Meningitis**: Bacterial meningitis is typically transmitted through respiratory droplets from an infected person's coughing or sneezing. Close contact with an infected individual or sharing respiratory secretions can also facilitate transmission.

ii. **Viral Meningitis**: Viral meningitis is usually spread through direct contact with respiratory secretions, fecal-oral transmission, or contact with contaminated surfaces or objects.

iii. **Fungal Meningitis**: Fungal meningitis is not transmitted from person to person but is acquired through inhalation of fungal spores, ingestion of contaminated food or water, or direct inoculation into the body (such as during surgery or trauma).

iv. **Parasitic Meningitis**: Parasitic meningitis is acquired through exposure to contaminated water, soil, or food sources, or through contact with infected animals or vectors.

3. **Symptoms:**

a. The symptoms of meningitis can vary depending on the cause, age, and overall health of the individual. Common symptoms may include:

i. Sudden onset of fever

ii. Severe headache

iii. Stiff neck (meningismus)

iv. Photophobia (sensitivity to light)

v. Nausea and vomiting

vi. Confusion or altered mental status

vii. Seizures

viii. Skin rash (particularly in bacterial meningitis caused by Neisseria meningitidis)

ix. Difficulty concentrating

x. Poor appetite

xi. Irritability (particularly in infants and young children)

b. In severe cases, meningitis can progress rapidly and lead to life-threatening complications such as seizures, coma, septic shock, and death. Therefore, prompt medical evaluation and treatment are essential for individuals suspected of having meningitis.

Meningitis is a serious medical condition that requires prompt diagnosis and appropriate treatment. The specific treatment and prognosis depend on the underlying cause of the meningitis, as well as the individual's overall health and any underlying medical conditions. Vaccination against certain bacterial pathogens (such as Neisseria meningitidis, Streptococcus pneumoniae, and Haemophilus influenzae type b) and practicing good hygiene and infection control measures can help prevent some cases of meningitis.

1. **Diagnosis:**

    a. **Clinical Evaluation**: Diagnosis of meningitis begins with a thorough clinical evaluation, including a detailed medical history and physical examination. Key symptoms suggestive of meningitis include fever, headache, neck stiffness (meningismus), altered mental status, photophobia (sensitivity to light), and skin rash.

    b. **Lumbar Puncture (Spinal Tap):** A lumbar puncture is a crucial diagnostic procedure in suspected cases of meningitis. During this procedure, a needle is inserted into the spinal canal in the lower back to collect cerebrospinal fluid (CSF) for analysis. CSF analysis includes examination of cell count, protein, glucose levels, and microbiological cultures (bacterial, viral, or fungal).

    c. **Imaging Studies**: Imaging studies such as computed tomography (CT) or magnetic resonance imaging (MRI) of the brain may be performed to assess for complications of meningitis, such as cerebral edema, hydrocephalus, or abscess formation. These imaging modalities can help guide treatment decisions and assess response to therapy.

    d. **Laboratory Tests**: Blood tests, including complete blood count (CBC), inflammatory markers (such as C-reactive protein [CRP] or erythrocyte sedimentation rate [ESR]), and blood cultures, may be obtained to assess for systemic inflammation and identify the causative organism in cases of bacterial meningitis.

2. **Treatment:**

    a. **Bacterial Meningitis:**

i. **Empirical Antibiotic Therapy**: Empirical antibiotic therapy is initiated immediately upon suspicion of bacterial meningitis, even before the causative organism is identified. Broad-spectrum antibiotics such as third-generation cephalosporins (e.g., ceftriaxone or cefotaxime) are typically used to cover common bacterial pathogens.

ii. **Specific Antibiotic Therapy**: Once the causative organism is identified and susceptibility testing is available, antibiotic therapy may be adjusted accordingly to target the specific pathogen and optimize outcomes. For example, penicillin or ampicillin may be used for meningococcal meningitis, while vancomycin may be added for suspected or confirmed cases of pneumococcal meningitis with resistance concerns.

b. **Viral Meningitis:**

i. **Supportive Care**: Viral meningitis is usually self-limiting, and treatment is primarily supportive. This may include rest, hydration, pain relief (e.g., acetaminophen or nonsteroidal anti-inflammatory drugs [NSAIDs]), and management of symptoms such as nausea and vomiting.

ii. **Antiviral Therapy**: In cases of severe or complicated viral meningitis (e.g., herpes simplex virus [HSV] or varicella-zoster virus [VZV] meningitis), antiviral medications such as acyclovir may be administered empirically until specific viral diagnosis is confirmed.

c. **Fungal Meningitis:**

i. **Antifungal Therapy**: Fungal meningitis requires treatment with antifungal medications, such as amphotericin B or fluconazole, depending on the specific fungal pathogen and susceptibility testing results. Treatment duration and regimen may vary depending on the severity of infection and response to therapy.

d. **Parasitic Meningitis:**

  i. **Antiparasitic Therapy**: Parasitic meningitis, such as that caused by Naegleria fowleri or Angiostrongylus cantonensis, requires specific antiparasitic medications based on the causative organism. Treatment may include medications such as amphotericin B or albendazole, along with supportive care to manage symptoms and complications.

3. **Prevention:**

  a. **Vaccination**: Vaccination is a key preventive measure against certain types of bacterial meningitis. Vaccines are available for pathogens such as Neisseria meningitidis (meningococcus), Streptococcus pneumoniae (pneumococcus), and Haemophilus influenzae type b (Hib). Vaccination schedules and recommendations vary by age, risk factors, and regional epidemiology.

  b. **Hygiene and Infection Control**: Practicing good hygiene and infection control measures can help reduce the risk of meningitis transmission. This includes frequent handwashing, avoiding close contact with individuals who are sick, covering the mouth and nose when coughing or sneezing, and maintaining a clean environment.

  c. **Chemoprophylaxis**: In outbreaks of bacterial meningitis caused by certain pathogens, chemoprophylaxis with antibiotics may be recommended for close contacts of infected individuals to prevent secondary transmission. Examples include rifampin or ciprofloxacin for contacts of meningococcal meningitis cases.

  d. **Avoiding Risk Factors**: Avoiding known risk factors for meningitis, such as unprotected sexual activity, illicit drug use, and exposure to contaminated water or soil, can help reduce the likelihood of acquiring certain types of meningitis, such as sexually transmitted meningitis or parasitic meningitis.

Early recognition, prompt diagnosis, and appropriate treatment of meningitis are crucial for improving outcomes and reducing the risk of complications and long-term sequelae. Additionally, vaccination and preventive measures play a vital role in reducing the burden of meningitis and protecting individuals and communities from this serious infectious disease.

Meningitis can have serious consequences, including neurological damage and death, particularly if not promptly diagnosed and treated. Public health efforts to promote vaccination, improve surveillance, and raise awareness about meningitis are essential for reducing its burden on individuals and communities.

Typhoid

Typhoid fever, also known simply as typhoid, is a systemic infectious disease caused by the bacterium Salmonella enterica serotype Typhi. It is primarily transmitted through the ingestion of food or water contaminated with the feces of an infected person. Typhoid fever is a significant global health concern, particularly in areas with poor sanitation and limited access to clean water. Here's a detailed overview of typhoid fever:

1. **Causative Agent (Pathogen):**
    a. Typhoid fever is caused by the bacterium Salmonella enterica serotype Typhi (S. Typhi). It is a Gram-negative, facultative anaerobic bacterium belonging to the Enterobacteriaceae family.
    b. S. Typhi is primarily transmitted through the fecal-oral route, typically via contaminated food or water. The bacterium can survive for extended periods in water or sewage and can also be transmitted by direct contact with carriers or asymptomatic individuals shedding the bacteria in their feces.

2. **Transmission:**

   a. **Contaminated Food and Water**: The most common mode of transmission is the ingestion of food or water contaminated with S. Typhi bacteria. Contamination can occur during food preparation, storage, or handling by individuals who are carriers of the bacteria or have active typhoid fever.

   b. **Person-to-Person Transmission**: S. Typhi can also be transmitted from person to person through close contact with infected individuals, particularly in settings with poor sanitation and hygiene practices. This can occur through the fecal-oral route, such as when an infected person contaminates food, water, or shared objects with their feces.

3. **Symptoms:**

   a. The symptoms of typhoid fever can vary in severity and typically develop gradually over several days to weeks after exposure to the bacterium. Common symptoms include:

      i. **Fever:** Persistent and gradually increasing fever, often reaching high temperatures (up to 104°F or 40°C).

      ii. **Headache**: Intense headache, often described as throbbing or constant.

      iii. **Malaise and Weakness**: Generalized feelings of fatigue, weakness, and lethargy.

      iv. **Gastrointestinal Symptoms:** Gastrointestinal manifestations are common and may include abdominal pain, nausea, vomiting, diarrhea, or constipation. Diarrhea is more common in the early stages, while constipation may occur later in the illness.

v. **Loss of Appetite**: Decreased appetite and weight loss are common due to gastrointestinal symptoms and systemic illness.

vi. **Rash**: A rose-colored skin rash, known as "rose spots," may appear on the trunk or abdomen in some individuals, particularly during the second week of illness.

vii. **Enlarged Spleen and Liver**: Hepatomegaly (enlarged liver) and splenomegaly (enlarged spleen) may be palpable on physical examination due to systemic involvement.

viii. **Other Symptoms**: Other symptoms may include a dry cough, relative bradycardia (slower than expected heart rate), and altered mental status (in severe cases).

b. If left untreated, typhoid fever can progress to severe complications, including intestinal perforation, gastrointestinal bleeding, encephalopathy, septic shock, and death. Prompt diagnosis and treatment are essential for preventing these complications.

Typhoid fever:

Typhoid fever is a serious infectious disease that can lead to significant morbidity and mortality, particularly in regions with inadequate access to clean water, sanitation facilities, and healthcare services. Prevention efforts focus on improving sanitation and hygiene practices, ensuring access to safe drinking water, vaccination in high-risk populations, and early detection and treatment of cases to prevent transmission and reduce the burden of typhoid fever on affected individuals and communities.

1. **Diagnosis:**

a. **Clinical Presentation**: Diagnosis of typhoid fever often begins with a clinical assessment based on the characteristic symptoms, including prolonged fever, headache, abdominal pain, and gastrointestinal symptoms such as diarrhea or constipation. However, the clinical presentation of typhoid fever can overlap with other febrile illnesses, making it challenging to diagnose based on symptoms alone.

b. Laboratory Tests:

i. **Blood Culture**: Blood culture is the gold standard for diagnosing typhoid fever. It involves obtaining a blood sample from the patient and culturing it in a microbiology laboratory to isolate the causative bacterium, Salmonella enterica serotype Typhi (S. Typhi). Blood cultures are most sensitive during the first week of illness when bacteremia is most likely.

ii. **Bone Marrow Culture**: In cases where blood cultures are negative but clinical suspicion remains high, bone marrow culture may be performed. Bone marrow aspiration allows for a higher yield of S. Typhi organisms, particularly during the second week of illness when bacteremia may be less prominent.

iii. **Serological Tests**: Serological tests, such as the Widal test, are available for detecting antibodies to S. Typhi antigens in the patient's blood. However, these tests have limitations in terms of sensitivity, specificity, and cross-reactivity with other Salmonella species. They are not routinely recommended for diagnosis and may be used as adjunctive tests in certain situations.

iv. **Stool Culture**: Stool culture may be performed to identify carriers of S. Typhi, particularly in outbreak investigations or surveillance efforts. However, stool cultures are less sensitive than blood cultures and may not reliably detect asymptomatic carriers.

2. Treatment:

a. **Antibiotic Therapy:** Treatment of typhoid fever typically involves antibiotic therapy to eradicate the infection and alleviate symptoms. The choice of antibiotic depends on local antimicrobial resistance patterns, patient factors (such as age, pregnancy status, and allergy history), and severity of illness. Commonly used antibiotics include:

   i. **Fluoroquinolones:** Ciprofloxacin and levofloxacin are effective first-line agents for treating uncomplicated typhoid fever in regions with low rates of fluoroquinolone resistance.

   ii. **Third-Generation Cephalosporins:** Ceftriaxone and cefixime are alternative options for empirical therapy or in areas with higher rates of fluoroquinolone resistance.

   iii. **Azithromycin:** Azithromycin may be used as an alternative for patients with fluoroquinolone-resistant strains or those who cannot tolerate fluoroquinolones.

   iv. **Trimethoprim-Sulfamethoxazole (TMP-SMX):** TMP-SMX is an alternative agent for treating uncomplicated typhoid fever, particularly in resource-limited settings where other antibiotics may not be readily available.

b. **Supportive Care:** In addition to antibiotic therapy, supportive care measures are essential to manage symptoms and prevent complications. This may include adequate hydration, rest, fever-reducing medications (such as acetaminophen), and nutritional support.

c. **Hospitalization:** Hospitalization may be necessary for patients with severe or complicated typhoid fever, such as those with intestinal perforation, encephalopathy, or septic shock. Inpatient management allows for close monitoring, intravenous fluid resuscitation, and appropriate antibiotic therapy.

3. **Prevention:**

    a. **Vaccination**: Vaccination is a key preventive measure against typhoid fever, particularly for individuals at high risk of exposure, such as travelers to endemic regions, laboratory personnel handling S. Typhi, and individuals living in areas with a high burden of typhoid fever. Two types of vaccines are available:

        i. **Typhoid Vi Polysaccharide Vaccine**: This injectable vaccine provides protection against typhoid fever caused by S. Typhi. It is recommended for travelers aged two years and older who are traveling to endemic regions or engaging in high-risk activities.

        ii. **Typhoid Conjugate Vaccine**: This newer vaccine offers longer-lasting protection and can be administered to children as young as six months of age. It is recommended for routine immunization in endemic areas and can also be used for travelers.

    b. **Improved Sanitation and Hygiene**: Promoting access to clean water, sanitation facilities, and hygienic practices is essential for preventing the transmission of typhoid fever. This includes efforts to improve water quality, sewage disposal, food hygiene, and personal hygiene practices such as handwashing.

    c. **Food and Water Safety**: Individuals should be advised to consume safe food and water sources to reduce the risk of typhoid fever transmission. This may involve avoiding raw or undercooked foods, consuming bottled or boiled water, and practicing proper food handling and preparation techniques.

d. **Health Education**: Providing education and raising awareness about the signs and symptoms of typhoid fever, as well as preventive measures, can empower individuals and communities to take proactive steps to protect themselves from infection. Health education efforts should target both healthcare providers and the general public.

Early diagnosis, appropriate treatment, and preventive measures are crucial for controlling the spread of typhoid fever and reducing its impact on affected individuals and communities. By implementing a comprehensive approach that combines vaccination, improved sanitation, and hygiene practices, and health education, it is possible to mitigate the burden of typhoid fever and work towards its eventual elimination.

Typhoid fever remains a significant public health challenge in many parts of the world, particularly in low- and middle-income countries with inadequate sanitation and healthcare systems. Comprehensive efforts to improve sanitation, promote vaccination, and enhance public health infrastructure are essential for controlling the spread of typhoid fever and reducing its burden on affected communities.

Leprosy

Leprosy, also known as Hansen's disease, is a chronic infectious disease caused by the bacterium Mycobacterium leprae. Leprosy primarily affects the skin, peripheral nerves, mucosa of the upper respiratory tract, and eyes, leading to a range of clinical manifestations. Despite being curable and non-fatal, leprosy can cause significant disabilities and social stigma if not diagnosed and treated promptly. Here's a detailed overview of leprosy:

1. **Causative Agent (Pathogen):**

a. Leprosy, also known as Hansen's disease, is caused by the bacterium Mycobacterium leprae. It is an acid-fast, intracellular bacterium that primarily affects the skin and peripheral nerves.

b. M. leprae has a slow growth rate and a predilection for cooler regions of the body, such as the skin, superficial nerves, and mucous membranes of the upper respiratory tract.

2. Transmission:

a. The exact mode of transmission of M. leprae is not fully understood, but it is believed to occur through prolonged and close contact with respiratory droplets from untreated individuals with lepromatous or multibacillary leprosy.

b. Transmission is thought to be relatively inefficient, and only a small proportion of individuals exposed to M. leprae develop clinical disease. Additionally, leprosy is not highly contagious and does not spread easily in the general population.

3. Clinical Manifestations:

a. Leprosy presents as a spectrum of clinical manifestations, ranging from paucibacillary (tuberculoid) leprosy to multibacillary (lepromatous) leprosy, with intermediate forms in between. The clinical manifestations are influenced by the individual's immune response to the bacterium.

b. Tuberculoid Leprosy:

   i. Tuberculoid leprosy is characterized by a strong cell-mediated immune response against M. leprae, leading to localized and well-defined skin lesions with few bacilli.

   ii. Clinical features may include:

      1. Hypopigmented or erythematous skin patches with well-defined borders.

2. Loss of sensation (anesthesia) in affected areas due to nerve damage.

3. Thickened peripheral nerves, particularly in the affected regions.

4. Limited involvement of skin and nerves, with relatively few bacteria detected on biopsy.

c. Lepromatous Leprosy:

i. Lepromatous leprosy is characterized by a weak cell-mediated immune response and high bacterial load, resulting in widespread skin lesions and systemic involvement.

ii. Clinical features may include:

1. Diffuse, infiltrative skin lesions with a "leonine facies" appearance, characterized by thickened, nodular, and disfiguring skin folds, particularly on the face.

2. Peripheral nerve involvement leading to sensory loss, muscle weakness, and trophic changes, such as ulceration and deformity of hands and feet.

3. Involvement of mucous membranes, eyes, and internal organs in advanced cases.

4. Presence of numerous acid-fast bacilli on skin biopsy or slit-skin smear examination.

d. Borderline Leprosy:

i. Borderline leprosy represents intermediate forms between tuberculoid and lepromatous leprosy, with variable clinical features and immune responses.

ii. Borderline tuberculoid leprosy exhibits features of both tuberculoid and lepromatous leprosy, with less pronounced nerve involvement and milder skin lesions.

iii. Borderline lepromatous leprosy presents with more diffuse skin lesions and nerve involvement compared to borderline tuberculoid leprosy, but less severe than lepromatous leprosy.

e. **Other Forms:**

i. In addition to tuberculoid, lepromatous, and borderline leprosy, there are rare and atypical forms of leprosy, including indeterminate leprosy, pure neuritic leprosy (involvement of nerves without skin lesions), and reversal reaction (immune-mediated exacerbation of leprosy symptoms).

f. The clinical course and prognosis of leprosy depend on the type of disease, extent of skin and nerve involvement, immune response, and promptness of treatment. Early diagnosis and multidrug therapy can prevent progression, disability, and deformity associated with leprosy.

Leprosy is a chronic infectious disease that affects the skin, peripheral nerves, and mucous membranes, leading to a spectrum of clinical manifestations ranging from localized skin lesions to widespread systemic involvement. While effective treatment with multidrug therapy has significantly reduced the burden of leprosy worldwide, early diagnosis, timely treatment, and ongoing surveillance efforts remain essential for achieving sustained control and eventual elimination of leprosy as a public health problem.

1. **Diagnosis:**

a. **Clinical Evaluation**: Diagnosis of leprosy begins with a thorough clinical evaluation by a healthcare provider, including a detailed medical history and physical examination. Key features suggestive of leprosy include skin lesions, peripheral nerve involvement, and sensory or motor deficits.

b. **Skin Biopsy**: Skin biopsy is a cornerstone of leprosy diagnosis, particularly for cases with atypical or ambiguous clinical presentations. A biopsy of an active skin lesion is obtained and examined under a microscope for the presence of acid-fast bacilli (AFB) using Ziehl-Neelsen staining or fluorescent microscopy.

c. **Slit-Skin Smear Examination**: Slit-skin smear examination involves obtaining samples from skin lesions, nasal mucosa, or ear lobes and staining them to detect acid-fast bacilli. This test is useful for confirming the diagnosis and assessing the bacillary load, which helps classify leprosy into paucibacillary or multibacillary forms.

d. **Nerve Biopsy**: Nerve biopsy may be performed in cases with suspected peripheral nerve involvement or neuropathy. Biopsy samples are examined microscopically for the presence of AFB and histopathological changes characteristic of leprosy neuropathy.

e. **Immunological Tests**: Immunological tests, such as serology or molecular assays (e.g., polymerase chain reaction [PCR]), are under investigation for their potential utility in leprosy diagnosis, particularly in cases with indeterminate or paucibacillary disease.

2. Treatment:

a. **Multidrug Therapy (MDT)**: Multidrug therapy is the cornerstone of leprosy treatment and is based on the World Health Organization (WHO) guidelines. MDT consists of a combination of antibiotics administered over a fixed duration, tailored to the type and severity of leprosy:

   i. **Paucibacillary Leprosy**: Paucibacillary leprosy, characterized by limited skin lesions and low bacterial load, is treated with a six-month course of rifampicin and dapsone, supplemented with clofazimine for the first three months.

ii. **Multibacillary Leprosy**: Multibacillary leprosy, characterized by extensive skin lesions and high bacterial load, is treated with a 12-month course of rifampicin, dapsone, and clofazimine, administered monthly under supervision.

b. **Monitoring and Follow-up**: Patients undergoing MDT require regular monitoring and follow-up to assess treatment response, monitor for adverse effects, and ensure treatment completion. Clinical evaluation, slit-skin smear examination, and other relevant investigations may be performed at specified intervals during and after treatment.

3. **Prevention:**

a. **Early Detection and Treatment**: Early detection and prompt initiation of treatment are crucial for preventing transmission, reducing the risk of complications, and preventing disability associated with leprosy. Healthcare providers should maintain a high index of suspicion for leprosy in endemic areas and promptly refer suspected cases for diagnosis and treatment.

b. **Contact Tracing and Screening**: Contact tracing and screening of close contacts of individuals diagnosed with leprosy can help identify additional cases and prevent transmission within households and communities. Household members, particularly children and other vulnerable individuals, should be screened for signs and symptoms of leprosy and offered preventive therapy if indicated.

c. **Health Education and Community Engagement**: Health education and community engagement initiatives play a vital role in raising awareness about leprosy, reducing stigma and discrimination, promoting early detection, and encouraging treatment adherence. Education campaigns should target both affected individuals and the general population to dispel myths and misconceptions about leprosy.

    d. **Vaccination**: While no effective vaccine against leprosy is currently available for widespread use, research into leprosy vaccines continues, with several candidates under investigation in clinical trials. Vaccination strategies may play a role in future efforts to control leprosy transmission and reduce the burden of the disease in endemic areas.

Leprosy is a curable infectious disease, and with early diagnosis and appropriate treatment, the majority of cases can be effectively cured and disability prevented. However, sustained efforts are needed to ensure equitable access to diagnostic and treatment services, address social and economic barriers, and implement comprehensive prevention strategies to achieve the goal of leprosy elimination as a public health problem.

Tuberculosis

Tuberculosis (TB) is a contagious infectious disease caused by the bacterium Mycobacterium tuberculosis. It primarily affects the lungs (pulmonary TB), but it can also affect other parts of the body (extrapulmonary TB). TB is a major global health concern, with millions of new cases and deaths reported each year. Here's a detailed overview of tuberculosis:

1. **Causative Agent:**

    a. Tuberculosis is caused by Mycobacterium tuberculosis, a slow-growing, aerobic bacterium with a waxy cell wall composed of mycolic acids. Other mycobacterial species, such as M. bovis and M. africanum, can also cause tuberculosis in humans, albeit less commonly.

2. **Transmission:**

a. TB is primarily transmitted through the inhalation of respiratory droplets containing M. tuberculosis bacteria expelled by individuals with active TB disease, especially during coughing, sneezing, or speaking. Close and prolonged contact with an infectious individual is typically required for transmission.

b. Factors such as overcrowded living conditions, poor ventilation, and compromised immune systems increase the risk of TB transmission.

3. **Clinical Manifestations:**

a. TB can manifest in various forms, depending on the site of infection and the immune response of the host.

b. **Pulmonary TB:** Common symptoms include persistent cough (often with sputum production), chest pain, hemoptysis (coughing up blood), fatigue, weight loss, fever, and night sweats. Chest X-rays may show infiltrates, cavities, or other abnormalities in the lungs.

c. **Extrapulmonary TB:** TB can affect other organs and tissues, leading to symptoms specific to the affected site. Examples include lymphadenitis (enlarged lymph nodes), pleuritis (inflammation of the pleura), meningitis (inflammation of the meninges), bone and joint involvement, and abdominal TB (e.g., peritoneal TB).

4. **Diagnosis:**

a. Diagnosis of TB involves a combination of clinical evaluation, imaging studies, and laboratory tests.

b. Tuberculin skin tests (TST) and interferon-gamma release assays (IGRAs) can help detect latent TB infection (LTBI) by assessing immune responses to M. tuberculosis antigens.

c. Microbiological confirmation of active TB disease is typically achieved through sputum smear microscopy, culture, and molecular tests (e.g., GeneXpert MTB/RIF assay).

d. Chest X-rays, computed tomography (CT) scans, and other imaging modalities may aid in the diagnosis and assessment of pulmonary and extrapulmonary TB.

5. Treatment:

a. TB is treated with combination antimicrobial therapy, typically involving multiple antibiotics to prevent the development of drug resistance.

b. The standard treatment regimen for drug-susceptible TB consists of an intensive phase (2 months) followed by a continuation phase (4–6 months) of therapy with isoniazid, rifampicin, pyrazinamide, and ethambutol.

c. Drug-resistant TB (e.g., multidrug-resistant TB, extensively drug-resistant TB) requires specialized treatment regimens based on drug susceptibility testing results and may involve second-line antibiotics with potentially greater toxicity and reduced efficacy.

6. Prevention:

a. TB prevention strategies include early detection and treatment of active cases, contact tracing and screening of close contacts, treatment of latent TB infection (especially in high-risk individuals), and vaccination.

b. Bacille Calmette-Guérin (BCG) vaccine is a live attenuated vaccine used in many countries to prevent severe forms of TB, particularly in children. While BCG vaccine offers some protection against severe forms of TB in children, its effectiveness against pulmonary TB varies widely and is limited in adults.

7. Global Health Impact:

a. TB remains one of the top infectious disease killers worldwide, causing significant morbidity and mortality, particularly in low- and middle-income countries.

b. Socioeconomic factors, including poverty, malnutrition, overcrowding, and limited access to healthcare, contribute to the burden of TB in many regions.

c. The emergence of drug-resistant TB strains poses additional challenges to TB control efforts, highlighting the importance of effective surveillance, treatment, and prevention strategies.

Efforts to combat tuberculosis require a multifaceted approach, including improved diagnostics, expanded access to treatment and care, research into new drugs and vaccines, and addressing social determinants of health. Global collaboration and investment in TB control are essential for achieving the goal of ending the TB epidemic by 2030, as outlined by the World Health Organization's End TB Strategy.

URINARY TRACT INFECTIONS

Urinary tract infections (UTIs) are common bacterial infections that affect the urinary system, which includes the kidneys, ureters, bladder, and urethra. UTIs can range from mild, uncomplicated infections to more severe and recurrent cases that require medical intervention. Here's a detailed overview of urinary tract infections:

1. **Types of UTIs:**

   a. **Lower UTI (Cystitis)**: Infections of the bladder are the most common type of UTI. Symptoms include frequent urination, urgency, dysuria (painful urination), hematuria (blood in the urine), and lower abdominal discomfort.

   b. **Upper UTI (Pyelonephritis)**: Infections of the kidneys are less common but can be more severe. Symptoms may include fever, chills, flank pain, nausea, vomiting, and systemic symptoms of infection.

c. **Recurrent UTIs**: Some individuals experience recurrent UTIs, defined as three or more infections within one year or two or more within six months. Recurrent UTIs may be associated with underlying risk factors such as anatomical abnormalities, urinary tract obstruction, urinary retention, or immunodeficiency.

2. **Causative Agents:**

a. The majority of UTIs are caused by bacteria, with Escherichia coli (E. coli) being the most common pathogen responsible for both uncomplicated and complicated UTIs. Other bacteria such as Klebsiella, Proteus, Enterococcus, and Staphylococcus saprophyticus may also cause UTIs.

b. Fungal (yeast) infections, such as those caused by Candida species, can occur in individuals with risk factors such as diabetes, immunosuppression, or prolonged antibiotic use.

3. **Risk Factors:**

a. Various factors increase the risk of developing UTIs, including female gender (due to shorter urethra), sexual activity, urinary catheterization, anatomical abnormalities (e.g., vesicoureteral reflux), urinary tract obstructions (e.g., kidney stones), pregnancy, diabetes, immunosuppression, and recent antibiotic use.

4. **Diagnosis:**

a. Diagnosis of UTIs typically involves a combination of clinical assessment, urinalysis, and urine culture.

b. Urinalysis can detect the presence of white blood cells, red blood cells, and bacteria in the urine, as well as assess for signs of urinary tract inflammation or infection.

c. Urine culture is used to identify the causative organism and determine its susceptibility to antibiotics. It is particularly important for confirming the diagnosis of UTIs and guiding appropriate antibiotic therapy, especially in cases of recurrent or complicated infections.

5. **Treatment:**

a. Antibiotic therapy is the mainstay of treatment for UTIs, with the choice of antibiotic depending on factors such as the severity of infection, the suspected or identified pathogen, and antibiotic susceptibility testing results.

b. Commonly used antibiotics for uncomplicated UTIs include trimethoprim-sulfamethoxazole (TMP-SMX), nitrofurantoin, fosfomycin, and fluoroquinolones (such as ciprofloxacin).

c. Complicated or recurrent UTIs may require longer courses of antibiotics or different antibiotic agents based on culture and sensitivity results.

6. **Prevention:**

a. Strategies to prevent UTIs include promoting good hygiene practices (such as wiping from front to back after urination or bowel movements), staying hydrated, urinating frequently, avoiding prolonged urinary catheterization, practicing safe sex, and promptly treating underlying conditions that increase the risk of UTIs.

b. For individuals with recurrent UTIs, preventive measures such as prophylactic antibiotics, cranberry products, or vaginal estrogen therapy may be considered based on individual risk factors and preferences.

UTIs are common infections that can cause significant discomfort and complications if left untreated. Early recognition, appropriate treatment, and preventive measures are essential for managing UTIs effectively and reducing the risk of recurrence or complications. If you suspect you have a UTI, it's important to seek medical attention for proper diagnosis and treatment.

SEXUALLY TRANSMITTED DISEASES

Sexually transmitted diseases (STDs), also referred to as sexually transmitted infections (STIs), are infections that are spread through sexual contact, including vaginal, anal, and oral sex. These infections can be caused by bacteria, viruses, parasites, or fungi and can lead to a range of symptoms, from mild discomfort to severe health complications. Understanding STDs is crucial for prevention, diagnosis, and treatment. Here's a detailed introduction to sexually transmitted diseases:

1. **Types of STDs:**
    a. **Bacterial Infections**: Examples include chlamydia, gonorrhea, and syphilis. These infections are caused by bacteria and can usually be treated with antibiotics.
    b. **Viral Infections: Examples include human immunodeficiency virus (HIV), herpes simplex** virus (HSV), human papillomavirus (HPV), and hepatitis B and C viruses. Viral STDs are typically managed rather than cured, although antiviral medications and other treatments may help manage symptoms and reduce transmission.
    c. **Parasitic Infections**: Examples include trichomoniasis, caused by the parasite Trichomonas vaginalis. Parasitic STDs can be treated with antiparasitic medications.
    d. **Fungal Infections**: While less common, fungal infections such as candidiasis (yeast infection) can also be sexually transmitted.
2. **Modes of Transmission:**

a. STDs are primarily transmitted through sexual contact, including vaginal, anal, and oral sex. Transmission can occur through contact with infected genital fluids, mucous membranes, or skin.

b. Some STDs can also be transmitted through non-sexual means, such as from mother to child during childbirth (vertical transmission), blood transfusions, or sharing contaminated needles or injection equipment.

3. **Symptoms and Complications:**

a. Symptoms of STDs vary depending on the type of infection but may include genital discharge, pain or burning during urination, genital itching or sores, pelvic pain, and abnormal vaginal bleeding.

b. Some STDs, particularly in their early stages, may not cause noticeable symptoms, leading to silent transmission and potential long-term complications if left untreated.

c. Complications of untreated STDs can include infertility, chronic pelvic pain, ectopic pregnancy, pregnancy complications, increased risk of certain cancers (e.g., cervical cancer with HPV infection), neurological damage (e.g., neurosyphilis), and increased susceptibility to other infections (e.g., HIV transmission with untreated STIs).

4. **Diagnosis and Testing:**

a. Diagnosis of STDs typically involves a combination of medical history, physical examination, laboratory testing (such as blood tests, urine tests, swabs of genital or oral lesions, and molecular tests), and partner notification.

b. Some STDs, like HIV and syphilis, can be detected through routine screening tests, while others may require specific symptoms or risk factors to trigger testing.

5. **Prevention:**

   a. Prevention of STDs relies on a combination of strategies, including safer sexual practices (such as consistent and correct condom use, reducing the number of sexual partners, and mutual monogamy with an uninfected partner), vaccination (e.g., HPV vaccine), regular screening and testing, and prompt treatment of infections.

   b. Education, communication, and access to sexual health services are crucial for promoting awareness, reducing stigma, and empowering individuals to make informed decisions about their sexual health.

6. **Treatment and Management:**

   a. Treatment of STDs varies depending on the type of infection but may involve antibiotics, antiviral medications, antiparasitic drugs, or antifungal agents.

   b. Early diagnosis and prompt treatment are essential for managing STDs effectively, preventing complications, and reducing the risk of transmission to sexual partners.

AIDS

Acquired Immunodeficiency Syndrome (AIDS) is a severe, late-stage manifestation of infection with the Human Immunodeficiency Virus (HIV). HIV attacks the body's immune system, specifically targeting CD4+ T cells, which are crucial for the body's defense against infections and diseases. Without treatment, HIV infection can progress to AIDS, which is characterized by a severely weakened immune system and increased susceptibility to opportunistic infections and certain cancers. Here's a detailed overview of AIDS:

1. **Causative Agent:**

   a. AIDS is caused by the Human Immunodeficiency Virus (HIV), which belongs to the family of retroviruses. HIV primarily targets CD4+ T cells, macrophages, and dendritic cells, gradually weakening the immune system and impairing its ability to fight off infections.

2. **Modes of Transmission:**

   a. HIV is primarily transmitted through specific bodily fluids, including blood, semen, vaginal fluids, and breast milk. The main modes of HIV transmission include unprotected sexual intercourse (vaginal, anal, or oral), sharing contaminated needles or injection equipment, and from mother to child during pregnancy, childbirth, or breastfeeding.

   b. Other less common modes of transmission include occupational exposure (such as needlestick injuries in healthcare settings) and blood transfusions or organ transplants from HIV-infected donors (though this is rare in regions with strict screening protocols).

3. **Clinical Stages of HIV Infection:**

   a. HIV infection progresses through several clinical stages:

      i. **Acute HIV Infection**: The initial stage of infection, characterized by a flu-like illness (acute retroviral syndrome) occurring 2-4 weeks after exposure to the virus.

      ii. **Chronic HIV Infection (Asymptomatic HIV)**: In this stage, the virus replicates at lower levels, and individuals may remain asymptomatic for many years. However, HIV is still active and continues to damage the immune system.

      iii. **AIDS**: AIDS is the most advanced stage of HIV infection, diagnosed when the CD4+ T cell count falls below a certain threshold (usually < 200 cells/mm^3) or when certain opportunistic infections or cancers occur.

4. **Symptoms and Complications:**

   a. Symptoms of AIDS are primarily due to the body's inability to fight off infections and may include recurrent fever, night sweats, chronic diarrhea, unexplained weight loss, oral thrush (Candida infection of the mouth), and opportunistic infections such as Pneumocystis jirovecii pneumonia (PCP), tuberculosis (TB), cytomegalovirus (CMV) infection, and certain cancers like Kaposi's sarcoma and non-Hodgkin lymphoma.

b. AIDS-related complications can lead to significant morbidity and mortality if not promptly diagnosed and treated. The most common cause of death in people with AIDS is opportunistic infections.

5. Diagnosis:

a. Diagnosis of HIV infection is typically made through blood tests that detect HIV antibodies, antigens, or viral RNA. Tests may include enzyme-linked immunosorbent assay (ELISA), Western blot, rapid tests, and nucleic acid tests (NAT).

b. Diagnosis of AIDS is based on clinical criteria, including the presence of specific opportunistic infections, cancers, or a CD4+ T cell count below 200 cells/mm^3.

6. Treatment and Management:

a. Antiretroviral therapy (ART) is the cornerstone of HIV/AIDS management. ART consists of combinations of antiretroviral drugs that suppress viral replication, reduce HIV-related morbidity and mortality, and improve the immune function of individuals living with HIV.

b. Treatment with ART can also prevent HIV transmission to sexual partners (treatment as prevention) and from mother to child during childbirth and breastfeeding (prevention of mother-to-child transmission).

c. Adherence to ART is crucial for achieving and maintaining viral suppression and preventing the development of drug resistance.

7. Prevention:

a. Prevention of HIV/AIDS involves a combination of behavioral, biomedical, and structural interventions. Strategies include promoting safer sexual practices (e.g., condom use, reducing the number of sexual partners), harm reduction programs for people who inject drugs (e.g., needle exchange programs), pre-exposure prophylaxis (PrEP) for high-risk individuals, early diagnosis and treatment of HIV infection, and reducing stigma and discrimination associated with HIV/AIDS.

AIDS continues to be a significant global health challenge, particularly in regions with high HIV prevalence and limited access to healthcare resources. Comprehensive approaches that address social determinants of health, promote equitable access to HIV testing and treatment services, and empower individuals and communities to engage in HIV prevention and care are essential for achieving the goal of ending the HIV/AIDS epidemic.

Syphilis

Syphilis is a sexually transmitted infection (STI) caused by the bacterium Treponema pallidum. It is a chronic, systemic disease that progresses through several stages if left untreated. Syphilis can affect multiple organ systems and lead to serious health complications, including neurological, cardiovascular, and ocular manifestations. Here's a detailed overview of syphilis:

1. **Causative Agent:**

   Syphilis is caused by the bacterium Treponema pallidum, a spiral-shaped, motile bacterium that can penetrate intact mucous membranes or microscopic abrasions in the skin during sexual contact. T. pallidum cannot survive outside the human body for long periods, making sexual transmission the primary mode of infection.

2. **Transmission:**

Syphilis is primarily transmitted through sexual contact, including vaginal, anal, and oral sex, with an infected individual. Transmission can occur through direct contact with syphilitic sores (chancres), which are highly infectious, as well as through contact with mucous membranes or skin lesions during sexual activity.

3. **Clinical Stages:**
   a. Syphilis progresses through several distinct stages, each characterized by specific clinical manifestations:
      i. **Primary Syphilis**: The initial stage begins with the appearance of a painless, firm, round ulcer called a chancre at the site of infection (genital, anal, or oral). Chancres typically heal spontaneously within a few weeks, even without treatment.
      ii. **Secondary Syphilis**: If left untreated, syphilis progresses to the secondary stage, characterized by a widespread rash that may involve the trunk, palms, and soles, as well as flu-like symptoms such as fever, sore throat, fatigue, and swollen lymph nodes. Mucous membrane lesions, hair loss, and systemic manifestations may also occur.
      iii. **Latent Syphilis**: After the secondary stage, syphilis enters a latent phase, during which there are no visible symptoms, but the infection persists without treatment. Latent syphilis is divided into early latent (within one year of primary infection) and late latent (more than one year after primary infection) stages.
      iv. **Tertiary Syphilis**: In some cases, untreated syphilis can progress to the tertiary stage, which may occur years or decades after the initial infection. Tertiary syphilis can lead to severe complications, including neurosyphilis (affecting

the central nervous system), cardiovascular syphilis (affecting the heart and blood vessels), and gummatous syphilis (formation of destructive granulomas in various tissues).

4. **Diagnosis:**

   a. Diagnosis of syphilis typically involves a combination of clinical evaluation, serological tests, and, if necessary, direct visualization of lesions or laboratory testing of tissue samples.

   b. Serological tests include nontreponemal tests (such as the Venereal Disease Research Laboratory [VDRL] test and the rapid plasma reagin [RPR] test) and treponemal tests (such as the Treponema pallidum particle agglutination [TP-PA] assay and enzyme immunoassays [EIAs]). Positive nontreponemal tests are usually confirmed with treponemal tests.

5. **Treatment:**

   a. Syphilis is treatable with antibiotics, typically penicillin G administered by injection. For individuals with penicillin allergy, alternative antibiotics such as doxycycline or azithromycin may be used.

   b. The choice of antibiotic and treatment regimen depends on the stage and severity of the disease, as well as individual factors such as allergy status and pregnancy.

6. **Prevention:**

   a. Prevention of syphilis involves promoting safer sexual practices, including consistent and correct condom use, reducing the number of sexual partners, and mutual monogamy with an uninfected partner.

   b. Screening and early detection of syphilis in high-risk populations, including sexually active individuals, men who have sex with men, pregnant women, and individuals with HIV infection, are important for timely treatment and prevention of transmission.

   c. Partner notification and testing are crucial for identifying and treating sexual contacts of individuals diagnosed with syphilis to interrupt transmission chains.

Syphilis remains a significant public health concern globally, particularly in populations with high rates of STIs, inadequate access to healthcare services, and barriers to syphilis testing and treatment. Comprehensive approaches that combine education, screening, diagnosis, treatment, and prevention efforts are essential for controlling the spread of syphilis and reducing its impact on affected individuals and communities.

Gonorrhea

Gonorrhea is a common sexually transmitted infection (STI) caused by the bacterium Neisseria gonorrhoeae. It primarily affects the mucous membranes of the genital tract, but it can also infect the throat, rectum, and eyes. Gonorrhea can lead to serious health complications if left untreated, including pelvic inflammatory disease (PID), infertility, and increased risk of HIV transmission. Here's a detailed overview of gonorrhea:

1. **Causative Agent:**
   a. Gonorrhea is caused by the bacterium Neisseria gonorrhoeae, a Gram-negative diplococcus. N. gonorrhoeae primarily infects the mucous membranes of the genital tract, but it can also colonize the throat, rectum, and eyes.

2. **Transmission:**
   a. Gonorrhea is primarily transmitted through sexual contact, including vaginal, anal, and oral sex, with an infected individual. Transmission can occur through contact with infected genital secretions or mucous membranes.

b. The bacterium can also be transmitted from an infected mother to her newborn during childbirth, leading to neonatal conjunctivitis or, rarely, systemic infection.

3. Clinical Manifestations:

a. Symptoms of gonorrhea vary depending on the site of infection and gender but may include:

　　i. **Genital Gonorrhea**: Symptoms in men may include urethral discharge, dysuria (painful urination), and urethral itching or irritation. In women, symptoms may include vaginal discharge, dysuria, pelvic pain, and abnormal vaginal bleeding.

　　ii. **Rectal Gonorrhea:** Symptoms may include anal discharge, itching, pain, bleeding, and discomfort during bowel movements.

　　iii. **Pharyngeal Gonorrhea**: Most cases are asymptomatic, but symptoms may include sore throat, difficulty swallowing, and swollen lymph nodes in the neck.

b. Asymptomatic gonorrhea is common, particularly in women and individuals with rectal or pharyngeal infections, leading to underdiagnosis and silent transmission.

4. Complications:

a. Untreated gonorrhea can lead to serious health complications, including:

　　i. **Pelvic Inflammatory Disease (PID)**: In women, untreated gonorrhea can ascend from the cervix to the upper reproductive organs, causing inflammation and scarring of the fallopian tubes, ovaries, and surrounding tissues. PID can lead to chronic pelvic pain, infertility, and ectopic pregnancy.

ii. **Disseminated Gonococcal Infection (DGI)**: In rare cases, N. gonorrhoeae can spread to the bloodstream, causing systemic infection and potentially affecting multiple organs, including the joints, skin, and heart valves.

iii. **Increased Risk of HIV Transmission**: Gonorrhea infection can increase the risk of HIV acquisition and transmission due to inflammation and disruption of mucosal barriers.

5. **Diagnosis:**

a. Diagnosis of gonorrhea typically involves laboratory testing of clinical specimens, including urethral, cervical, rectal, or pharyngeal swabs, as well as urine samples.

b. Common diagnostic tests include nucleic acid amplification tests (NAATs), which detect N. gonorrhoeae DNA or RNA, and culture-based methods.

6. **Treatment:**

a. Gonorrhea is treated with antibiotics, typically a single dose or short course of antibiotics to ensure complete eradication of the infection.

b. Due to increasing antimicrobial resistance, the choice of antibiotic may vary depending on local resistance patterns and individual factors such as allergy status and concurrent infections.

7. **Prevention:**

a. Prevention of gonorrhea involves promoting safer sexual practices, including consistent and correct condom use, reducing the number of sexual partners, and mutual monogamy with an uninfected partner.

b. Screening and early detection of gonorrhea in high-risk populations, including sexually active individuals, men who have sex with men, and individuals with multiple partners, are important for timely treatment and prevention of complications.

Gonorrhea remains a significant public health concern globally, with high rates of transmission and increasing antimicrobial resistance. Comprehensive approaches that combine education, screening, diagnosis, treatment, partner notification, and prevention efforts are essential for controlling the spread of gonorrhea and reducing its impact on affected individuals and communities.

MCQs:

1) Which of the following is a bacterial pathogen that can cause meningitis?
   a) Neisseria meningitidis
   b) HIV
   c) Naegleria fowleri
   d) Candida

2) What is the primary mode of transmission for tuberculosis (TB)?
   a) Blood transfusions
   b) Sexual contact
   c) Inhalation of respiratory droplets
   d) Contaminated water

3) Which infection is known as Hansen's disease?
   a) Leprosy
   b) Gonorrhea
   c) Syphilis
   d) Typhoid

4) Which of the following is a fungal pathogen that can cause infections?
   a) Escherichia coli
   b) Candida
   c) Mycobacterium tuberculosis
   d) Salmonella Typhi

5) What is the primary method for diagnosing syphilis?

   a) Physical examination

   b) Blood culture

   c) Serological tests

   d) Urine analysis

6) Which of the following STDs is characterized by the development of a painless ulcer known as a chancre?

   a) Gonorrhea

   b) Chlamydia

   c) HIV

   d) Syphilis

7) Which vaccine is used to prevent certain types of bacterial meningitis?

   a) BCG

   b) MMR

   c) HPV

   d) Meningococcal vaccine

8) What type of infectious agent causes AIDS?

   a) Bacteria

   b) Virus

   c) Fungus

   d) Parasite

9) Which of the following is NOT a complication of untreated gonorrhea?

   a) Pelvic inflammatory disease

   b) Chronic pelvic pain

   c) Opportunistic infections

   d) Disseminated gonococcal infection

10)   Which diagnostic test is considered the gold standard for diagnosing typhoid fever?

   a) Widal test

b) Blood culture

c) PCR

d) Stool culture

11) What is the main treatment for fungal meningitis?

a) Antibiotic therapy

b) Antiviral therapy

c) Antifungal therapy

d) Supportive care

12) Which pathogen is responsible for causing typhoid fever?

a) Mycobacterium tuberculosis

b) Salmonella enterica serotype Typhi

c) Neisseria gonorrhoeae

d) Treponema pallidum

13) Which method is used to prevent the spread of tuberculosis?

a) Antifungal medications

b) Vaccination with BCG

c) Antiparasitic drugs

d) None of the above

14) What symptom is common to many viral infectious diseases, including influenza and COVID-19?

a) Rash

b) Cough

c) Diarrhea

d) Urinary retention

15) Which STD can lead to cervical cancer if left untreated?

a) Gonorrhea

b) Human papillomavirus (HPV)

c) Syphilis

d) HIV

16) Which condition is a severe form of tuberculosis affecting the lungs?

   a) Meningitis

   b) Hepatitis

   c) Pulmonary tuberculosis

   d) Leprosy

17) How is leprosy primarily transmitted?

   a) Sexual contact

   b) Respiratory droplets

   c) Blood transfusions

   d) Contaminated food

18) What is the first-line treatment for uncomplicated urinary tract infections?

   a) Antifungal medications

   b) Antibiotics

   c) Antivirals

   d) Antiparasitics

19) What type of vaccine is used to prevent human immunodeficiency virus (HIV) infection?

   a) Live attenuated vaccine

   b) Inactivated vaccine

   c) Subunit vaccine

   d) There is currently no effective vaccine for HIV

20) Which of the following is a preventive measure for sexually transmitted diseases?

   a) Regular exercise

   b) Blood transfusions

   c) Use of antibiotics

   d) Consistent use of condoms

Short Answer Type Questions (Subjective):

1. What is the primary cause of infectious diseases?
2. Name two bacteria responsible for causing bacterial meningitis.
3. Describe the primary mode of transmission for tuberculosis.
4. What are the clinical manifestations of lepromatous leprosy?
5. What is the gold standard for diagnosing typhoid fever?
6. List two preventive measures against urinary tract infections (UTIs).
7. What are the common symptoms of primary syphilis?
8. How is HIV primarily transmitted?
9. What is the function of the Bacille Calmette-Guérin (BCG) vaccine?
10. Explain the difference between pulmonary TB and extrapulmonary TB.
11. What are "rose spots" and which disease are they associated with?
12. How can gonorrhea lead to increased risk of HIV transmission?
13. What type of pathogen causes AIDS?
14. Name a common fungal pathogen that can cause infections in humans.
15. What are the main symptoms of viral meningitis?
16. Describe the role of antibiotics in the treatment of infectious diseases.
17. What is the significance of the CD4+ T cell count in HIV infection?
18. How is syphilis transmitted?
19. What are the primary complications associated with untreated gonorrhea?
20. Describe how typhoid fever is transmitted.

Long Answer Type Questions (Subjective):

1. Discuss the role of public health interventions in controlling the spread of infectious diseases, including examples of specific diseases and strategies.
2. Explain the diagnosis, treatment, and prevention of meningitis, highlighting the differences between bacterial and viral forms.

3. Describe the global health impacts of tuberculosis, including the challenges of drug-resistant strains and the strategies for its control.

4. Outline the transmission dynamics, symptoms, and treatment options for HIV/AIDS, and discuss the importance of early diagnosis and antiretroviral therapy.

5. Analyze the factors contributing to the spread of typhoid fever in low- and middle-income countries and discuss measures to prevent it.

6. Provide a detailed overview of the clinical manifestations, diagnosis, and treatment of leprosy, emphasizing the importance of early detection.

7. Discuss the complications of untreated sexually transmitted diseases (STDs), focusing on the long-term health impacts and the importance of prevention and timely treatment.

8. Explain the principles behind the vaccination strategies used for preventing diseases like meningitis and tuberculosis, including the types of vaccines and their effectiveness.

9. Describe the mechanisms by which gonorrhea can lead to complications such as pelvic inflammatory disease (PID) and disseminated gonococcal infection (DGI).

10. Evaluate the challenges in managing urinary tract infections (UTIs), including issues related to antibiotic resistance and recurrent infections.

Answer Key:

1. (a) Neisseria meningitidis
2. (c) Inhalation of respiratory droplets
3. (a) Leprosy
4. (b) Candida
5. (c) Serological tests
6. (d) Syphilis
7. (d) Meningococcal vaccine

8. (b) Virus

9. (c) Opportunistic infections

10.(b) Blood culture

11.(c) Antifungal therapy

12.(b) Salmonella enterica serotype Typhi

13.(b) Vaccination with BCG

14.(b) Cough

15.(b) Human papillomavirus (HPV)

16.(c) Pulmonary tuberculosis

17.(b) Respiratory droplets

18.(b) Antibiotics

19.(d) There is currently no effective vaccine for HIV

20.(d) Consistent use of condoms